ALSO BY ANNE SHEFFIELD

How You Can Survive When They're Depressed

Sorrow's Web

Overcoming the Legacy of Maternal Depression

ANNE SHEFFIELD

THE FREE PRESS

NEW YORK   LONDON   TORONTO
SYDNEY   SINGAPORE

THE FREE PRESS
A Division of Simon & Schuster Inc.
1230 Avenue of the Americas
New York, NY 10020

THE FREE PRESS and colophon are trademarks
of Simon & Schuster Inc.

Designed by Kyoko Watanabe

Manufactured in the United States of America

10   9   8   7   6   5   4   3   2   1

Library of Congress Cataloging-in-Publication Data

Sheffield, Anne.
Sorrow's web : overcoming the legacy of maternal depression /
Anne Sheffield.
        p.   cm.
Includes bibliographical references and index.
1. Mothers—Mental health.   2. Women—Mental health.
3. Depressed persons—Family relationships.   4. Mother and child.
I. Title.
RC451.4.W6 S53 2000
616.85'082—dc21   00-034146
ISBN 0-684-87085-1

To my daughter,
Pandora

Contents

Preface   xi

1. Shedding New Light on an Old Problem   1

2. The Legacy of a Mother's Depression: 12
   Survivor's Syndrome

3. What Have I Got? Why Me? Why Women?   34

4. The Dyadic Dance of Mother and Child   54

5. When Depression Cuts In After   78
   Childbirth

6. Taking a Mother's Depression to School   100

7. Enter Depression, Exit Marital Harmony   133

8. All About Treatment   160

9. A Father's Role in a Mother's Depression   201

10. When Older Mothers Are Depressed   216

Contents

11. Maternal Depression: Past, Present,   239
    and Future

    Appendix: Resources   255

    Notes   259

    Index   275

There are writers who write because they are writers by trade, turning out book after excellent book on a wide variety of unrelated subjects. I am not such a writer. I began putting words on the page four years ago because I had come to understand the power of someone else's depression—in my case, my mother's—to create a negative environment for all who live within its purview, and because I wished to share that insight with all the others who, trapped in such a situation, are unaware of the true cause of their distress.

The contemplated magazine article became a book, *How You Can Survive When They're Depressed,* in which I describe the five overlapping stages of depression fallout: confusion, self-doubt, demoralization, resentment and anger, and, finally, the desire to distance oneself from the depressed person. Although I drew on my personal experience, I also benefited from a weekly support group for spouses and partners, parents and children of a depression sufferer, and from countless interviews with friends, acquaintances, and even strangers who were embroiled in similar circumstances. Whatever their relationship to the depressed person, depression fallout sufferers conformed to that pattern, often using the selfsame words and phrases to express their distress, a pattern that has held true in the interviews I have subsequently conducted with offspring of a depressed mother.

When Linda Kahn, the editor who shepherded that work through the writing process, suggested I tackle the topic of maternal depression and its effects on children, I naively thought it would be an easy book to write. Whenever the subject came up in casual conversation, it evoked a chorus of encouragement from people whose mother had been or was depressed, indicating that there would be an ample supply of interviewees. I then discovered that a veritable army of psychiatrists, psychologists, and experts in child development had been investigating my "new" topic for over twenty years, and that they had built a voluminous body of scientific literature supporting the thesis that a mother's depression has deleterious effects on her children. But what began as an exercise in research and reporting became a disturbing journey of self-discovery. Gradually I became uneasily aware that my mother's unrecognized depression had profoundly affected my psyche and that, unbeknownst to me, it had in one way or another shaped and fueled virtually every aspect of my life, both personally and professionally.

Sorrow's Web is the product of that journey. Completing it has set me free from burdensome memories and habits formed during childhood and adolescence and carried, untouched by understanding or reason, into adulthood. The research, the self-searching, and the interviews have all combined to ignite in me a passionate conviction that maternal depression, a common and eminently treatable illness, deserves a wide audience, not only among mothers of every age and their grown children, but also among health professionals and policymakers. It is a problem I know intimately both as the daughter of a depressed mother and as a depressed mother myself.

The aim of this book is to accurately convey to lay readers in nontechnical language the conclusions the experts have drawn. In writing it, I have also relied heavily on the insights and experiences offered by many interviewees, using them to humanize the unnamed, faceless mothers and children who compose the patient populations studied. Although some of the personal stories related in these pages come from friends, many others found their way to me through the website for my first book (www.depressionfallout.com); an invitation posted there to e-mail comments provoked hundreds of replies.

The first four chapters of the book approach the problem of maternal depression from different vantage points. Chapter 1 is my own story of growing up with a depressed mother. Chapter 2 recounts an evening spent at a support group for grown children of a mother suffering from depression or a related disorder, during which I recognized in the members a mind-set remarkably similar to my own. The next chapter answers three basic questions: What is this illness called depression, why do some mothers suffer from it while others do not, and why are women seemingly more susceptible to depression than men? Chapter 4 explores the mother-child relationship from its evolutionary underpinnings to the role a mother plays in setting her child on the path of psychological, social, and cognitive development, and how her depression can disturb that process.

The next two chapters present the research on the effects of maternal depression at specific ages: infancy, toddlerhood, school age, and adolescence. They set the stage for a better understanding of an as-yet-uninvestigated issue: How do such offspring fare when they reach adulthood?

Keeping a relationship intact when one partner suffers from depression is extremely difficult. Understanding the depression-driven dynamic at work between partners and knowing how to counter it can reduce parental tensions and protect children from the ravages of marital disharmony. These are the principal points covered in Chapter 7.

While every chapter offers suggestions about how negative effects on children can be avoided, minimized, or corrected, the only surefire way to short-circuit depression's impact on both its sufferers and those who live with them is through treatment. This is the topic of Chapter 8, which includes numerous "insider tips" solicited from expert practitioners.

Chapter 9 is addressed to fathers, who are often unaware both of the source of their partner's behavior and of the critical role they can play in ameliorating the impact of maternal depression on children. Here, too, specific strategies are suggested.

Older women with depression often find themselves alienated from their grown children. Chapter 10 presents the stories of two such women whose own mothers were also depressed, as well as my own experience as a depressed mother and the problems it caused for my relationship with my child. Since we older folk suffering from this illness often receive short shrift from doctors, the chapters also addresses the close connection between depression and many major health problems. The final chapter is both a summary and a rallying cry to everyone who has been touched by depression, whether as parent, child, partner, or spouse, to help move this critical issue from academic journals and private sorrows to the public agenda.

Writing this book would not have been possible without the help of many people. Dr. Donald F. Klein, an acknowledged dean of psychiatric research and research director of the New York State Psychiatric Institute, has made innumerable contributions that inform and illuminate every page. Among the many others whose work and wisdom underlie and inform both the research and the personal interviews, I would like to offer special thanks to Myrna M. Weissman, professor of epidemiology at the Columbia College of Physicians and Surgeons; Constance Hammen, professor of psychology at UCLA; Kay Redfield Jamison, professor of psychiatry at Johns Hopkins; and Dr. Harold S. Koplewicz, director of the Child Study Center at New York University. Their work embodies excellence. I also wish to thank Dr. T. Berry Brazelton, who in the early stages of this book offered heartening encouragement by confirming the importance of the topic.

All but two of my interviewees have chosen to remain anonymous. I have honored that wish by altering details of their life circumstances, but the feelings and thoughts they express breathe life into what might otherwise be a rather dry and academic work. I reiterate here my everlasting gratitude for their generosity and honesty, and their willingness to share their stories not only with me but also with my readers. My special thanks go to the courageous duo who granted permission to use their real names: psychologist Martha Manning, who endured a crippling depression and the concomitant awareness that it might prove emotionally damaging to her child, and her daughter, Keara Manning Depenbrock, who has words of wisdom for other children whose mothers are depressed.

My editor, Philip Rappaport, gave me excellent and much-needed advice and patiently listened to the usual roster of authorly complaints, grievances, and general carping about the editing process, during which we have become good friends. As always, Linda Kahn provided additional help and guidance. My agent, Anne Edelstein, is everything a writer could hope for.

But more than anyone else I thank my remarkable daughter, Pandora, for continuing to love me despite my depression-driven behavior, behavior that might have caused a less wise and devoted child to turn away from me. I dedicate this book to her with everlasting love.

Sorrow's Web

1

Shedding New Light on an Old Problem

An eminent child psychologist once observed that all children need at least one adult who is irrationally enthusiastic about them. I lacked such a parent because my mother suffered from a chronic depression that prevented her from feeling enthusiastic about anything, including me. Neither she nor I is alone in the brand of lasting grief her depression caused us both. One in every four women will suffer from this illness at some time during her life, often during her childbearing years. Although depression is not contagious in the sense that measles and tuberculosis are, its presence virtually ensures that those closest to the depressed person will in their turn suffer from the depression's fallout. Even the most selfless, caring moms cannot, when they are depressed, avoid causing pain and problems for those they love.

Searching my childhood memories for images of my mother, I find I am a poor navigator, unable to hold a true course. I am buffeted by the ill winds of our later relationship, which was an unhappy one. Those recollections are clear, unlike the few remaining from a more distant past. I thought that I had a happy childhood. But the only psychotherapist I ever consulted insisted this was not so, that in fact I was an unhappy child, not on the basis of my memories but because of my lack of them. "You're screening them out," she told me, shaking her head at my stubbornness as though I were being deliberately uncooperative. I would dutifully sift once again through the handful of early recollections about my mother; finding nothing new, I would tell her more about my grandmother, my teachers, my friends, my games and achievements at school. If my therapist was correct in her assertion, I can only congratulate myself on the effective barrier to the truth that I appear to have erected. It served me well for many years, obliterating earlier memories and softening the impact of later ones. When I was twenty-three, that protection crumbled abruptly with my mother's attempted suicide, the only spectacularly overt evidence of her depression. The sympathy this should have engendered in me was dissipated by her statement, issued on recovering from the effects of stomach pumping, that she had done it because I didn't love her.

Before that event, I had spent my life engaged in the business of growing up as the only child of a divorced mother. Perhaps her depression was in those years less enveloping than it subsequently became, or perhaps the bright pleasures of school and the friends and rewards it afforded me were sufficient nourishment for my psyche. My father had left when I was an infant; during my childhood I saw him only once, when at the age of seven my mother allowed me to visit him in Florida where he lived with his second wife and my two young half-sisters. When I returned home, my tales of delighted discovery were ill-received, and I understood that my father did not belong in my thoughts.

When I was nine, my first stepfather arrived and stayed for several years, bringing me two stepsisters and a stepbrother, and the semblance of a normal houseful of parents and kids. My mother's growing negativity and critical outlook now had multiple targets, and I had in my stepsiblings sympathetic allies, but by early high school I was once again the reigning bull's-eye for her dissatisfaction. Nothing I did was right; nothing I did was enough; and everything wrong in her life was, she inferred, my fault. She eschewed the big guns of outright warfare, preferring instead furtive guerilla sallies, disguised as the urgings of a concerned mother: "Why can't you . . . How is it possible that . . . You could at least have . . . But you always . . ." I became more than ever a striver for excellence, propelled by the rewards I believed it would win me, among them her love and support. My mother wanted the same from me, but not in return for hers. The unspoken pact was to be one-sided.

Once again, a new stepfather arrived, a kind and patient man with whom I shared a deep affection. In public my mother displayed pride and pleasure in us, but in our absence she confided to friends the hurt our failings as husband and daughter caused her. Occasionally one of her intimates would pull me aside and urge me to be more supportive and demonstrative, hinting that Tony was already a heavy cross for her to bear. Behind the closed doors of our apartment and fortified with alcohol, she complained to each of us about the other, welding us into an unspoken conspiracy of protection. Not long after my mother's suicide attempt, Tony abruptly decamped during one of my mother's hospital stays for the cancer that eventually killed her. Friends heaped abuse upon him for this abandonment in a time of such need, but, although I missed him terribly, I understood and condoned his departure. Had I been able, I would gladly have escaped.

3

By then I had my own apartment. Finding the distance it afforded me an insufficient shield, I elected to marry an Englishman and moved a comfortable three thousand miles away. But in my haste to escape I chose badly, and I returned shortly with an infant daughter. This steep and sudden fall from excellence seemed persuasive evidence that I was indeed the inadequate and undeserving person my mother had long perceived. Dorian Gray–like, the portrait she had so long been painting became my self-image. Overlaying it with broad brushstrokes—impressive jobs, an enchanting child, and a constant supply of suitors and friends—I kept its existence well hidden, but it bound me to my mother, the artist. Longing for the love and approval she continued to withhold, I sought them with a resentment and anger that matched hers. At her death, my relief at the freedom it portended caused me to add shame and guilt to the toxic mix. Despite the staged appearance of confidence, I felt like the consummate loser.

My memories of my mother after her suicide attempt are clear and unpleasant, colored with a resentment and anger that spread beyond their immediate target. Decades later, these emotions still lie just beneath the surface, waiting for any opportunity to cause dissatisfaction with who and what I am. When I feel brave enough to travel down that road, I find them connected to everything I most dislike about myself: an inability to sustain intimacy; the belief, against ample evidence, that I am a failure and a fraud with its concomitant burden of perfectionism; and a bottomless longing for approval and recognition that I try to hide.

The pathways in my brain that lead to these deficits, I assume, did not spring into being at the moment of her postsuicidal pronouncement. They must have been long in the making, the product of innumerable exchanges between us, each infinitesimally deepening the grooves of feelings, thoughts, and behavior until they settled into a pattern that holds me hostage. Together with that part of me of which I am the sole creator, what I think of as the good part, they constitute the essential me. I have come to accept and to live with the flawed whole, but I remain stubbornly angry at my mother.

What brought me a measure of tolerance and understanding was, paradoxically, my own depression that fully blossomed fifteen years ago. You have to live through this illness to have an inkling of what it does to the human psyche, of how much it distorts and mangles not only the interior but the exterior landscape as well. That a tiny fault in the production of this or that neurochemical can cause such havoc is a testimony to the intricate miracle that is the human brain. While many gifted artists and writers have created lasting beauty from their experience of this illness, for most who suffer from it the principal product is negativity and unhappiness, both for ourselves and for those who live with and love us. It's as though our internal compass has gone dead, leaving us to flounder about in a sea of solitary misery. At a time when we most need love and support, we are least able to ask for and receive it. When depression lifts, either through treatment or because it has run its course for the time being, we suspect that someone has flicked a magic switch. We are dazzled by the light that suddenly comes streaming in, and the world seems inviting; once again it is good to be alive.

Emerging from my own darkness, I caught my first glimpse of my mother as depressed rather than mean-spirited, as unable to love rather than unloving, as the victim of her illness rather than a free agent who chose to be hurtful. The professional help I received was unavailable to her: Antidepressants were rarely prescribed in the mid-1950s, and she viewed psychotherapy as strictly for crazy people. After her suicide attempt, the hospital psychiatrist came to offer his services, but she refused to discuss anything other than where he had gone to college and how he and his family spent their summer vacations. Neither Tony, her sister, nor I had any more success in coaxing forth an explanation. We never discussed it among ourselves or in depth with her, and life traipsed on as before.

The only thing that makes my story unusual is that I am fortunate in understanding that it is not just a sad tale about my mother and myself; it is about her depression and how it dominated our entire relationship. Had she been depression-free, both her life and mine, and our respective views of ourselves and each other, might have been quite different. That insight, so many years in coming, has lightened some of the burdens I have needlessly dragged throughout my life, burdens that also weigh on the many others with a similar background. Many mothers suffer from depression and most feel and behave in a manner akin to that of my mother, not because they are bad, aberrant people but because their illness distorts thinking and feeling.

Why I Focus on Mothers, Not Fathers

I focus on maternal depression for several reasons. First, mothers play a unique, intimate, and defining role in a child's development in ways that even the most devoted fathers do not. Second, a huge body of research, amassed over more than two decades, supports the conclusion that a mother's depression is a handicap for her kids, pushing the learning process off track and disturbing their emotional, social, and, many experts believe, cognitive growth. Maternal depression sets in motion a vicious circle that helps explain why kids of a depressed parent are two to three times more likely to develop depression later in life than are those of a non-depressed parent. Dr. T. Berry Brazelton, parenting maven to millions, rates maternal depression as critically germane to today's major issue, the future of our children. "A depressed mother," he told me, "gives kids a difficult start in life. Because of it, they miss out on what they most need—a sense of security, a positive self-image, and the motivation to learn in school and to succeed."

Experts in the domains of psychiatry, psychology, and child development who study the problem are painstakingly cautious and rely on direct observation rather than anecdotal evidence for their conclusions. Some of the effects they note are seen immediately: Infants with depressed mothers are less likely to thrive physically and are less responsive and secure in their attachment to them. Other consequences show up as behavioral and learning problems among preschool and school-age kids. In adolescents, they play out as poor grades and in such social shortcomings as low self-esteem, trouble making friends and handling authority, lack of emotional equilibrium, and drug and alcohol abuse.

The adult children of depressed mothers remain beyond current research parameters, perhaps because the task of linking later psychosocial problems to earlier life experiences of necessity must depend on personal recollections rather than on observation. But surely the origin of our problems, for example, with intimacy and commitment, is rooted in our experience of growing up with a depressed mother. Because we have not been "studied," we are left to puzzle over our emotional handicap, and to unknowingly pass it along to our own vulnerable offspring. The full roster of issues bearing on generational depression is far from complete.

Recently, research attention has turned to depression during pregnancy, far more prevalent than had been suspected.

New technology yields a three-dimensional image of the fetus in utero, allowing researchers to observe and measure fetal reactions to maternal stress and anxiety. Within just twenty-four hours of birth, babies born to depressed women show signs of differences in central nervous system development. They have less motor activity and endurance and are more irritable, fussier, and harder to soothe than newborns of non-depressed mothers. These new discoveries represent a welcome contribution to the knowledge and understanding of scientists and mothers alike.

The causal relationship between these emotional and behavioral deficits and maternal depression is a complex one because so many factors, including genes and temperament, are involved, all playing out within the larger family context. Depressed mothers feel inadequate and incompetent; their spouses feel shut out and underloved, setting the scene for disagreement and friction. Children, short on reason and long on radar, pick up on all of these vibes. While no one can predict precisely any given child's reaction, few will escape unscathed.

Kids are remarkably resilient, and the potentially toxic effects of a mother's depression won't occur overnight. But prolonged exposure to the neglectful or erratic parenting it engenders does damage over time. Self-awareness on the part of the mother and treatment for her depression can substantially mitigate these destructive effects. Unfortunately, depression is a stealthy opponent. Unlike other illnesses, it causes few serious physical symptoms that might send one running to the doctor and so usually goes undetected, causing trouble before a perceptive relative, teacher, or coach realizes what's the matter. And while depression can, in extreme cases, lead to psychosis and profound despair, requiring hospitalization, it usually just digs in and hides out for a long time under the guise of exhaustion, the sense of being overwhelmed and help-less, plus the sinking conviction that life will never be good again. It's this garden variety of depression that sneakily lays low so many mothers.

Knowing that a mother's depression is a harbinger of prob-lems for kids should be viewed as a previously unavailable lux-ury, not as a reason for maternal guilt. Researching and writing this book has led me to the conviction that depression, with its hateful ability to propagate itself in successive generations, is a foe worthy of national attention and action, a widespread afflic-tion that needs airing and solving. Despite growing public recognition and understanding, countless mothers endure it, few doctors are capable diagnosticians, and innumerable kids and their parents suffer needlessly as a result. The real issue lies in the stubborn silence surrounding it.

The single greatest shaper of my sense of self, then and now, is the experience of growing up in the sphere of my mother's undiagnosed illness. In addition, as so often happens, I inherited a vulnerability to depression through her genes and subsequently passed it along to my own daughter, who also suf-fers from depression. But while our family vulnerability to de-pression may continue to thrive, its potential destructive impact will not. In the light of what is known today both par-ents and kids can beat depression's odds, or at the least ensure less harsh outcomes.

Widespread dissemination of information about maternal depression is the key. While the professional journals are chockablock with articles about the newest research, their find-ings rarely if ever escape the confines of academia. Not only do they fail to reach mothers, but most health professionals who minister to women are also unaware of their implications, or are perhaps unwilling to tackle depression's ripple effect. And although depression is no longer automatically stigmatized, delinquent parenting is.

Of all the human roles, motherhood remains a sanctum of supposed perfection and "bad mother" the most damning of accusations. Although mother bashing is in vogue in some quarters, in most it is the epitome of political incorrectness. This may help explain why all those professional journal articles have never made it into the popular press. A number of psychologists have told me that young depressed mothers, in particular, need to be handled with kid gloves lest they feel accused and guilty. But depressed moms of all ages would give anything for an early diagnosis, and for the opportunity to spare both themselves and their kids pain.

When knowing and willful damage is inflicted on children, the accusation of neglect or abuse is justified. Depressed mothers, however, are reacting to the pain, distress, and emotional distortions of an often-unrecognized condition that narrows their perceptions and demands a focus on self rather than others. They are just as devoted to their children as their non-depressed counterparts, just as aware of their pivotal role in the parenting process, and usually desirous of fulfilling it, facts borne out by all the studies. If they are flawed parents it is through no unnatural fault of their own. Pointing out the facts about maternal depression may be disturbing, but it has nothing to do with blaming or demonizing mothers. The demon is depression. Blame is restricted to those who, once made aware of the problem, choose to ignore it.

Simply stated, it's hard to be a good mother when this illness is in the picture. The following chapter looks at what can happen when a mother's depression arrives early and stays late. It offers insights and solutions both for adult children and for depressed mothers of younger offspring. Many of the people whom you will meet in it were brought up during a time when this medical illness went unrecognized, and when treatment for it was largely unavailable. The legacy they received stands as stark testimony to the consequences of turning a blind eye toward this problem.

2

The Legacy of a Mother's Depression: Survivor's Syndrome

Embarking on a journey of self-discovery is risky. My own led me to both positive and negative insights. Those qualities of which I am proud—loyalty, honesty, diligence, empathy—I attributed to my own effort and will. The distressing ones, principal among them a shifting and shaky self-image, I assigned to the influence of my mother's depression. At first this bifurcated explanation of myself was exhilarating, but doubts about its validity soon surfaced. It began to feel like a copout, a refusal to take responsibility for my flaws and weaknesses. So I started haphazardly nosing about to see if perhaps other adults with similar childhoods resembled me. My early explorations were clumsy; desirous of validation, I gave hints about the answers I was hoping for. Later, the similarity of responses made me more confident; when asked what I was writing about, I provided only the book's title and waited to see what, if anything, would follow.

With or without clues, the answers volunteered form a consistent pattern. Survivors of a mother's depression carry a legacy that I term survivor's syndrome. Its symptoms include a mistrust of intimacy, a striving for perfectionism and the control it offers, a tireless search for approval, and the fear that others will see through our façade of self-assurance to the fraudulent person who lurks behind it. So intricately are all these linked that when the handle of one is cranked, all the rest spring into action like some Rube Goldberg contraption. Worst of all, we go on longing for the love our mother's illness obscured.

The first person to whom children look for positive response and validation is their mother, but if she suffers from depression she may be unable to provide it. Children often strive to gain a mother's love and support by attempting to conform to what they perceive as her demands or by withdrawing from the emotional fray. Either tactic fails, but the lesson sticks long after we leave home. As adults we employ a more sophisticated version of the same failed coping strategy. Like actors, we keep a third eye on the performance we are delivering, monitoring and assessing its impact on our audience. Attempting to mold ourselves into a pleasing and lovable image, we feel out of sync with others. While one internal voice says, "Be as you are," another whispers, "Be what *they* will like." Our persistent need for love and approval propels us to seek them, but on receiving them we are suspicious of their validity, a throwback to our earliest experience of intimacy.

Many of my interviews with adult children of depressed mothers have been serendipitous—a conversation with an old friend, chance meetings at cocktail or dinner parties, even phone calls from strangers referred to me by groups that know of my interest in this subject. When I learned of a local support group for grown children of parents suffering from depression or another psychiatric illness and was assured that I would be welcome at one of its meetings, I leaped at the opportunity to see what a planned discussion might bring. The following report, in which names and other personal data have been changed to preserve privacy, indicates that we offspring of depressed mothers have a great deal in common.

Twelve People, One Voice

One evening every month a dozen or so members sit down to exchange experiences. As in any social gathering, they provide updates on their lives—family, dating, work, school. The difference is that they share a unique bond: a parent who is afflicted by depression, manic depression, or schizophrenia. Wondering if they, too, grappled with the emotional spinoffs that still plague me more than twenty years after my mother's death, I listened as, one by one around the table, they shared their latest news.

Katherine, the group's facilitator, opened by reminding everyone about the need for confidentiality, and that this was one place they could speak openly about experiences necessarily kept secret from friends and coworkers. A willowy woman in her thirties who looks like a model but works in a lawyer's office, she had upsetting news that evening. She had just returned, she told us, from an emergency trip back home to cope with her mother's latest depressive episode. There had been doctors to deal with and a shaken father and siblings to calm. Most stressful of all was the realization that her parent had tried to give up on life and needed hospitalization; responsibility for that decision rested with Katherine. Others present who had been through a similar situation assured her she had made the right decision.

A preppie young woman, decked out in sweater set and pearls, was the next to speak. She told us about her recent promotion, then seamlessly flipped twelve years back into the past, when her father had been wandering the streets as an unmedicated schizophrenic. The jump was arresting and attested to a close connection in her mind between past and present experience. One of the members guided her back to the here and now. True, she agreed, the new job was great, but she had doubts about her ability to fill it. "I'll probably screw up," she told us, "I should have said no." Confidence and a sense of self-worth are hard to come by when you've grown up without them.

Dawnell's turn came next. She shared her fears about a new boyfriend of six months. "I know he thinks it's weird I never ask him in when he brings me home. But that's not the worst part. I always get to a point in every relationship when things go bad. I really like this guy," she added, "but I know he's going to dump me for somebody normal." A number of people around the table nodded in understanding agreement. Dawnell is pretty normal, but her mother has been self-treating her relentless depression with alcohol for a long time now. Mom poses a formidable barrier to guests, and to Dawnell's self-confidence and sense of security as well. So her daughter puts on a pretty face, locks her private life away from sight, and tries to pass as just an ordinary nineteen-year-old.

Earl was the last to speak. Katherine and another member had helped him fill out the forms that won him a scholarship to a university, where he has just completed his freshman year with a 3.4 grade average. The university's lack of student housing is a drawback, so when the library closes for the day Earl goes home to the New Jersey two-room apartment he shares with his mother and the latest in a long series of her lovers. His father took off ten years ago, and his mother blames Earl for that. "Sh-sh-she says I-I-I'm the reason for her bad . . . bad . . ." "Take your time, Earl, we're not in any hurry here," said Katherine. "Bad luck and all her pr . . . problems," he finished. A chorus of don't-you-believe-it and congratulations for his scholastic achievements brought a shy smile to his face and he self-consciously hitched up his drooping hiphop jeans. "Well, thanks," he said, temporarily stutter-free, "thanks a lot."

When my turn came I hesitated before providing a brief run-through of my comparatively golden life. Yes, my mother had been depressed, but we lived an otherwise privileged existence: She was unaware of street people, never struck me in anger, and had a doctor, a family friend, who saw to it that her attempt to exit life landed her in a private room in Roosevelt Hospital, not the psychiatric ward at Bellevue. The group brushed these differentiating details aside. What was important, they said, was that her depression left its mark on my life.

At the close of the meeting I took a risk and asked these battle-scarred young men and women if they would venture a guess about the effects of their parents' illness on their psyches. "It's hard to believe in yourself, you sort of feel like damaged goods." "I get people wrong a lot, like I think they're criticizing me or looking at me funny." "You have a tendency to try and do everything perfectly so that people will like you." And so it went, a reiteration of my own doubts and fears.

Interestingly, having a depressed parent was just about all I had in common with the other members. Their stories were full of the high-impact drama that makes for a best-seller; mine was a humdrum tale lacking in shock value. They were young, the eldest barely pushing forty; I could have been grandmother to several of the members. We had grown up in large cities and remote rural communities, in wealth and in poverty, had dropped out of high school and acquired advanced degrees, had skins of different colors. Nevertheless, these differences masked our similarities. We all shared the same emotional baggage.

When I rummaged through mine a few years ago, I wrote that in down times I believe I'm not worth much of anything, that I am something of a fraud, just sufficiently clever to keep others from seeing it, and that I don't deserve love and happiness and success. Each person at the meeting delivered the selfsame message in his or her own way. All but one person and I were old group hands, familiar with the personal histories of the others. So, too, were we newcomers when the meeting wound up three hours later. For all of us, separating past from present and fact from feeling is difficult. They all lie jumbled together on a continuum stretching from childhood into adulthood. The opportunity to share and compare responses grounds us in reality and helps us to realize that we are not inadequate, unloved, and unlovable. We are, rather, the victims of a common parental affliction.

Of all the negative effects of my mother's depression, it was the suspension of love between us that wrought the greatest damage. Lacking that exchange, we fell prey to other, more negative feelings that seeped in to fill the vacuum. As protection, I tried to build a wall between us, but ultimately it caused me more harm than good. The negative effects set up camp on my side of the wall, and it proved a barrier to love subsequently offered to me by others. When, in the interest of self-discovery, I gave it a whack, it tumbled down, leaving me breathless with anger at my parent, at all the years I had wasted, the self-made problems, the opportunities lost, the potential unfulfilled. Many offspring of depressed mothers do the same.

When the Wall Comes Tumbling Down: Marilyn Monroe

A while ago I came across a magazine article that chronicled the life and death of Marilyn Monroe, indisputably the most famous offspring of a parent who suffered from depression. Like all the female members of my generation, I grew up wishing I could be like this utterly gorgeous, sexy creature. We chunky, acne-ridden teenagers longed for her legs, her pouty come-hither lips, and the attentions of the rich and famous men who also coveted them. If Marilyn Monroe were alive today she would be a venerable seventy-three, but she died at thirty-six from an overdose of sleeping pills, leaving the radiance of her flame largely undimmed by the facts. At the time, no mention was made of her depression, in part because few understood that it was the essential cause for what was in fact suicide, not an unintentional overdose of sleeping pills mixed with alcohol.

Even today the stigma associated with mental illness causes public figures, as well as ordinary citizens, to hide it from view. Marilyn was no different, and the Hollywood cast of characters whose fortunes depended on hers joined in the coverup. Only long after her death in 1962 did the truth begin to emerge: two maternal grandparents and a mother plagued with depression and paranoid schizophrenia, a brother who committed suicide, a desperate determination to transform Norma Jean into the Marilyn of our memory, and a lifelong terror that her own depression would push her over the brink. In the light of such truths, the legend is transmuted into a life similar in many ways to those of countless men and women with a similar parentage.

In his autobiography *Timebends,* Marilyn's third husband, Pulitzer prize–winning playwright Arthur Miller, relates Marilyn's conviction that her soon-to-be-institutionalized grandmother tried to suffocate her when she was thirteen months old. Conventional wisdom has it that the brain is incapable of such early memories. Even Marcel Proust, who autobiographically re-created for his readers the minutiae of his earliest recollections, puts the first of them in his third year of life. But memories are what we make of them. Miller's anecdote set my scalp aprickle for I, too, have a pillow incident in my past.

Almost thirty years ago, along with many of my friends, I attended some weekend retreats led by an amiable man called John Cooper, a practitioner of the then-trendy approach to therapy called transactional analysis. Its inventor, psychiatrist Eric Berne, eschewed the Freudian couch for group games with names like "Kick me," "Gotcha, you son of a bitch," and "I'm only trying to help you," all designed to reveal to participants the coexistence in them of a parent, an adult, and a child, each fighting to become dominant. John concocted some games of his own. One of these involved organizing our chairs into a circle, putting a stool in its center, and then encouraging each of us to conjure up a mental picture of our worst fear and place it on the stool. When it was my turn, I instantly perceived a tidy parcel the size of a fat novel, neatly wrapped in butcher's paper and tied with the white string used to truss a filet of beef or veal. My choked attempts to explain what this prosaic object represented were hindered by compulsive sobbing and accompanied by a photographic memory of being suffocated by, you guessed it, my mother. So vivid were my feelings that for years, as I tried to describe this event to my friends during the 1960s and 1970s—decades during which soul-baring was common practice in my set—I was subject to the same inarticulateness and tears that inhibited me then.

Fashions in conversation change, and one day its rendition sounded, even to my ears, like pretentious melodrama, especially given the fact that I was present to tell the tale. I think it highly improbable that my mother actually tried to do away with me. It is far more likely that that now-vanished image was of the suffocating weight her disappointment, dissatisfaction, and despair imposed on me, all products of a depression that nobody recognized, and for which there was little treatment to be had at the time.

The fading of that image coincided with the realization that memory holds the substance of truth but not the whole story, and that the key to its impact lies in the present. As I have belatedly come to understand, we need not be trapped by our version of the past. Escape comes from filling in the gaps with new information that severs us from the emotions previously associated with it. Once I perceived my mother as acting from depression, not from a willful desire to wound, my memories of her became less immediate and thus less painful. I cannot erase my childhood, but I am no longer captive to it.

Depression, sadness, and loss are a natural trio. Whether or not the children of depressed mothers in turn become depressed, they have their own catalogue of losses. One such woman, quoted in a companion article to the one about Marilyn Monroe, lists hers: "I lost a sense of knowing who I am and of what I wanted. I lost the ability to set my own agenda and to control my life. I lost sight of my own needs. I lost self-confidence. I lost the ability to care for myself properly. I feel out of sync with the normal developmental rhythms. I have been saddened in a chronic way."

First as a child and then as an adult, we grieve for such losses as surely as we grieve for the parent stolen away by illness and for the expressions of love we never received. The sadness is not the overt grief expressed at funerals; it has instead the buzzing persistence of pain with undertones of, Why me? Some grown children, like my resilient childhood friend Sissy, do not succumb to this siren song. She escaped from her depressed mother, the martini-drinking best friend of my own, first to boarding school and then to a distant college; she chose a devoted husband with whom she has three kids; and she stayed out of her parent's reach.

In the middle of my voyage of self-discovery, feeling suddenly exposed and vulnerable, I called Sissy to ask how she dealt with her anger at her mother, and she replied that she had none. When her aging parent fell seriously ill, Sissy came home to see that she didn't die alone. "Ma was pathetic and I felt so sorry for her. Officially it was heart disease, but the drinking didn't help," she told me, adding, "She was so terribly lonely and afraid." "But your mother was depressed just like mine," I insisted. "Surely that must have upset you, too?" "It did at the time," she replied, "but now she just seems to have been miserable and cross." And that was that. Impatient with my efforts to pursue the subject, she shut me up with queries about my daughter and a report on her latest grandchild.

That conversation puzzled me. Why could Sissy so easily shuck a burden that weighed so heavily on me? The answer, confirmed by ample research, is that some children are born resilient while others come into the world more vulnerable to stresses and strains. Since talking to Sissy I have sought out other sons and daughters of depressed mothers. If solace is to be found in numbers, I have been amply rewarded for my efforts. The stories generously offered me have been imparted with the relief that comes from recognition of a fellow sufferer, as well as from the certainty that feelings long hidden from others will be met with empathy, not surprise or embarrassment.

The four tales that follow here are variations on a theme. Each is told by the adult child of a depressed mother and each stars a symptom of survivor's syndrome: Christina's fear of intimacy, Evvie's need for perfectionism and control, Rachel's search for approval, and George's dissatisfaction with his achievements. Together they encompass survivor's syndrome.

Christina: "Intimacy Scares Me"

Christina's Polish parentage is stamped on her high cheekbones and broad forehead framed by a halo of blond curls. When we sat down to talk, her manner was friendly but somewhat wary and distant, as if she were sizing me up before deciding what to reveal and what to hide. On the phone she had eagerly agreed to talk about her mother, whom she remembers as "a very cold person, not normal." Face-to-face, our interview proved to be as much a self-administered therapy session as a recital of the facts. At twenty-five, this attractive young woman is tentatively embarking on her first love affair. Asked how she had managed to fend off all the suitors her looks surely attracted, she ducked the question and talked about growing up in a household muted by sadness and loss.

When Christina was six an accident left her father semi-paralyzed and unable to work. Her mother, devastated and ill-equipped to cope, settled into a depression for which she began taking medication only a year ago. Although wealthy grandparents took care of medical and school bills, money did little to leaven the pall. During the occasional family vacations, both parents tried hard to break out of their sadness, but back home, her mother never laughed and rarely spoke. Christina's sole companion in those days was her brother, older by two years. Raking leaves together one day in the backyard the teenage siblings decided, "Other people's parents are married. Ours just live in the same house."

Then as now Christina was a loner, more at home with books than people. She confesses to having little talent for making friends and attributes this to the absence of intimacy while growing up. "How are you supposed to learn how to do something if no one shows you how?" she queried, still puzzled by the business of loving. Having at last encountered love, she is afraid that if she gives in to it she will lose it as her parents did. And she worries that her lover might discover the "real Christina" behind the cool façade.

In a conversation studded with jargon picked up from self-help books, her principal source of wisdom about human relations, Christina talked a lot about her lack of parental role models, always in terms of intimacy and its absence from her childhood. "Intimacy scares me," she admitted, as does the thought of seeing a psychotherapist. "I don't want to tell all that private stuff to a stranger." Denying herself the solace of talking with others, she talked to herself. Following the advice of self-help primers, she sought courage and determination by mailing herself postcards with messages like "You can do it" and "You're getting stronger and stronger. Keep it up!"

Although determination has earned her a master's degree in biology, it has brought Christina few friends. "It's hard to be one when you're not a whole person," she explained. When she told me that next year she would be a teaching assistant at a university not far from her boyfriend's home base, I commented on her good luck. She hesitated to agree. "Well, maybe, but he really doesn't know me. Seeing so much of each other may, you know . . ." The sentence went unfinished but her meaning was clear: Safety lies in distance.

Christina is extremely bright, the single attribute that seems for her a source of pride and pleasure. "Even as a child I knew my brains were my best ticket to a real life," she said, adding that she always believed God had a plan for her. But Christina didn't leave everything to the Almighty. She made a plan of her own: Study hard, get all A's, end up with honors and a good job far from home. The goals she recounted to me, which did not contain marriage, are in sight, but recently something unexpected happened. Her father died, and a few months later her mother underwent surgery for breast cancer. The twin crises have brought an unexpected bonus. Christina took charge, nursed her mom back to health, and then persuaded her to try antidepressant medication. Both mother and daughter now have a brighter view of life and each other. "We are bonded forever!" she told me with tangible delight, the initial wary air replaced for the moment with shining warmth.

This twenty-five-year-old has many hurdles to jump before reaching safety. The belated "bonding forever" has helped, but all those years of turning inward are a formidable obstacle to close relationships. Christina's brains are all she feels sure of, yet some things cannot be learned solely from books. Examples and experimentation are needed as well, and in this respect she is timid and fearful. In the many conversations I have had with other Christinas, the intimacy issue surfaces like a bar of Ivory soap. They scrabble to push it out of sight, and I know why. Admission of its presence seems somehow shameful, like mounting a platform naked and yelling, "I'm not capable of love—I am unworthy of it." This would make a great number in a Broadway musical, but in real life it is public revelation of a loneliness and sense of alienation from the "normal" people around us that we prefer to hide. We are forever putting out feelers and then drawing them back lest the recipients reject our offerings, leaving us dangling and unwanted for all the world to see.

Evvie: "If I'm in Control I Can Make It All Right"

Evvie's method of coping with a childhood dominated by a depressed mother differs from Christina's. Instead of sending herself cheer-up messages and trying to forget the past, she has undertaken an incomplete reconstruction of memories and is still pushing and shoving them about to make her childhood palatable. During a conference on postpartum depression, Evvie, a psychiatric nurse, suggested we talk. Bustling into the coffee shop she chose for our interview and directing me to order the chicken pot pie, she proceeded directly to the business at hand.

"My mother wasn't critical," she said, "she just didn't care. When I brought my report card home from school, she never looked at it. She didn't even come to my graduation, for heaven's sake!" Rearranging the plates put down by the waitress, Evvie marched briskly through her family history: four brothers and sisters, a charming but feckless and often absent dad, and a mother who erupted into frequent outbursts of anger, only to sink back again into lethargy. "She was like a switch," said her daughter. "Something as stupid as a missing pen could set her off. She'd tear up the house looking for it, flinging sofa cushions on the floor and turning out drawers while she yowled like a crazy woman. She scared the hell out of me, but I tell you, I'm still the best finder in the world."

Evvie is not only a finder but a problem solver, organizer, and advice giver who at fifty-four manages the lives of her siblings and her own family, as well as her eternally depressed mother. When the mists of Alzheimer's fell, it was Evvie who found a nursing home for her mother, divided up the furniture and knickknacks, and put the rambling Victorian house on the market. "I held a yard sale of the leftovers," she recounted. "Some people came up and said how much they would miss my dear mother. I thought they had me confused with someone else and told them no, I was *Joanna's* daughter. I was amazed they could think of her as dear anything."

Listening, I realized the magnitude of effort required to remake recollections and salve the pain they cause. As we talked, two variations of Evvie's mother emerged: the uncaring and angry one who accused a child of stealing the lost pen and "sucked the life's blood out of me, took all my energy," and the one who sometimes sang and danced and played the piano. There was the mother who roamed the house all night and spent her days in bed, and the one who loved nature and bright colors. Side by side they stand in this daughter's mind, the "nightmare waiting to happen" and the accomplished gardener and breadmaker.

Once she married and moved far away, Evvie made monthly trips back home to visit. Her mother would be outside when she arrived, pruning the rosebushes in front of the house. "I expected you yesterday," she would observe accusatorily, or, "I suppose you're late because you stopped for lunch." One day, after receiving such a greeting, Evvie says she got back into the car without a word and drove away. "For three hundred miles I cried and shouted, 'I hate you I hate you I hate you,' and then all of a sudden I felt better. A sort of quiet resolve and relief flowed through me and at last I saw her as she really was, a lonely, depressed woman."

Growing up, Evvie spent all her free time out of the house, but her first real escape from the erratic uncertainty of home came after graduation. She left to attend nursing school, but a job at a local hospital returned her to the family fold. After five broken engagements—"Count them, FIVE!" she cheerfully reported, appending the usual exclamation point—Evvie chose a local man whose happy family made an appealing contrast to her own. As the meeting between the two sets of parents approached, her preparatory description of her mother sailed into purest fantasy. She told her prospective mother-in-law how special Mom was, how charming, how perfect in every way, how much they would enjoy and love each other. The meeting went badly. The warm mother-in-law-to-be encountered with surprise a dour woman strikingly different from the daughter's description. "When I came back to Charley's house afterward, his mom took me aside and made me promise never to make up any more stories," this chronic tale spinner informed me.

There are many roads to self-preservation. Evvie has tried to address a loveless, chaotic childhood by recasting it as an entertaining story about lost pens, unread report cards, a missed graduation, and five broken engagements before entrusting herself to a man. I did not have the heart to ask her how she reconciled the nightmare with the dancer. Today the frightened pen-finder of ten is a middle-aged perfectionist upon whom many other people rely. While I accept her assertion that she is a happy woman today, I doubt her claim that she at last sees her mother as no more than a lonely, depressed woman.

Rachel: "I Don't Feel Lovable"

Rachel and I are total strangers. Thrown precariously off-balance by recent events involving her still-depressed mother, she had reached far back into her own and her parent's past and called Postpartum Services International; that organization in turn referred her to me as a possible source of help.

Fifty-one years ago Rachel's mother suffered a postpartum depression after her only child, Rachel, was born. For six months the newborn infant was shuttled back and forth between a loving immigrant father and a clutch of grandparents, aunts, and uncles. Rachel says she knows perfectly well that the untreated illness explained both her mother's early absence from her life and their subsequent combative relationship. But when she phoned me she seemed to be looking for validation of her feelings, not an explanation. "I've often wanted to do away with her," she said, and was grimly delighted to hear that I had once harbored the same sentiments about my mother, although not that I had since moved beyond murderous desires to pity.

Married with kids of her own, Rachel's underlying rage had landed her in a terrible state. "I suddenly can't deal with my resentment. How could a mother do that?" she kept insisting. "How could she never have wanted to hold me in her arms, never even wanted to lay eyes on me during my first six months of life?" Surprised by the immediacy of feelings she thought she had long since come to terms with, she explained that two weeks ago she had at great expense moved her ailing parent into a medically equipped retirement home. "I hoped that would give us both some peace, but somehow everything is worse than ever." Promising to call again in a few days, she hung up on herself, still muttering with indignation. Marveling yet again at memory's ability to preserve a past untrammeled by reason, I wondered what our next conversation would bring.

Life really is stranger than fiction. When I phoned Rachel to say I hoped she had not changed her mind about talking further, I found her transformed from a daughter consumed with murderous rage to one overwhelmed with yearning grief for the relationship she now would never attain. Three days before, her mother had fallen during the night, undergone immediate surgery for a broken hip, and died before regaining consciousness. "Now I'll never know the beautiful, brilliant woman my dad married," she mourned, and then reverted quickly to her rat-a-tat critical mode. "Mom was so domineering when I was a kid that I wanted to get away from her. When I married she didn't like my husband so no rapport was possible. Later on she was so obnoxious I couldn't have a relationship, and when she became permanently depressed there wasn't anyone to have a relationship with." No, she insisted, she didn't feel guilty. "My mother wanted to die. She talked about it all the time. And it's not my fault I couldn't be there."

The explanation for her mother's six-month absence that Rachel received as a child—"It wasn't her fault, dear, she was very ill"—did little to overcome her mistrust and resentment. "My father saved my life," she told me, stringing together his qualities like a magic necklace of pearls. "He was a charming, kind, wonderful, generous, handsome man, never moody or intense." But he missed the vital woman with whom he had fallen in love. "When he felt really rotten," said Rachel, "he would tell me how she had bowled him over, how proud he had been of her. Dad was always afraid she'd never be normal again." By his account, sometimes this "real wife" did return, dressed in emerald green to go out in the evening and full of wit and charm. She was there for Rachel to see as well, but that memory of her mother flickers while the others hold strong.

"I know our problems weren't entirely Mom's fault. I understand that depression made her like she was, that she wasn't just being willfully mean. I suppose she must have been lonely, and maybe guilty, too. But still," she added, "why didn't she even want to hold me when I was tiny? I have three children of my own. That kind of love is very strong." In our first conversation Rachel had told me that she didn't feel lovable, brushing aside my comments about a husband and three kids who are apparently devoted to her as though they didn't count as evidence of her lovability. Reason and objectivity are difficult for us survivors.

George: "Even My Mother Didn't Love Me"

Self-help books tell you it's hard to love others when you don't love yourself. George, like the survivor he is, would probably phrase it otherwise: "It's hard to love yourself when even your own mother doesn't." He is a solidly built man nearing forty, and although he is not handsome, it is easy to understand why women find him attractive. A physicist by training, he has turned his talents to engineering; some clever machine he invented has brought him a sizeable fortune but something in his demeanor suggests he takes little pride in himself.

We had met at a friend's cocktail party and I had taken the opportunity to satisfy my curiosity about the cosmos. Once I had milked him dry on the subject of black holes, he politely asked me what I did. Told the subject matter of my book in progress, he lost the absent manner my amateur questions had induced and went to fetch two glasses of wine, indicating an interest in talking further. Aha, another one, I thought to myself, and waited to hear what would follow.

When he was growing up, his mother, George told me, had been subject to long bouts of depression. "You were asking about black holes. She was one, a sort of Big Bang in reverse," he said, reverting to the vocabulary of his profession. "Instead of expanding, she reduced her universe to a single dense point of matter. Nothing can resist a black hole, you know. Nothing can ever escape from it." Asked if any effects of that had carried over into the present, he raised an eyebrow. "Are you kidding?" Just then another guest inserted herself between us; the chance for more enlightenment lost, I can only speculate about what George might have said. My files are full of interview quotes that might suit him well, two in particular: "I am dissatisfied with what I have achieved" and "I don't like myself very much."

The first person to whom children look for positive response and validation is their mother, but if she suffers from depression she may, through no fault of her own, be unable to provide them. When you get right down to it, poor self-esteem is the same as not liking yourself, and thinking that other people don't much like you either. Many who lack self-esteem take a practical approach by striving to appear likable. This solution turns out to be a poor one. We keep a third eye on the performance we are delivering, monitoring and assessing our ability as actors. Attempting always to please, we feel out of sync, a bit like Martians trying to pass as Earthlings.

The Quintessential Role of Self-Esteem

If asked to locate one particularly toxic item in my emotional baggage, I would choose the poor image that I, like all us vulnerable survivors, hold of myself. The search for self-esteem has become a mass media cliché. Everyone at some point has filled out those women's magazine questionnaires with True or False statements: "I often wish I were someone else," "At times I think I am no good at all," or the one least often ticked off, "I take a positive view of myself." The inference is that a buoyant self-esteem is to be had for the price of a self-help book or a software program. In thousands of classrooms across the country, children chant in unison blackboard slogans like "We applaud ourselves!" and "Make loving yourself a habit."

Psychologist Martin Seligman, in his book *The Optimistic Child,* condemns such self-esteem measurements and enhancers as puffery arising from the sea change that occurred in the social sciences of the 1960s as America moved into a period of unprecedented wealth and power, with individual consumption driving the economy. "Self-direction, rather than outside forces," he writes, "became the primary explanation of why people do what they do, ushering in an era of accomplishment." Many experts, he points out, now acknowledge that the feel-good principle does nothing for a poor self-image; the best antidote is improvement and doing well.

Seligman, who has spent thirty years working with depressed adults and children, believes that feeling bad about the self does not directly cause failure. The depression-related belief that problems will last forever and undermine everything, by contrast, directly causes a child to stop trying. Giving up leads to more failure, which then goes on to undermine feelings of self-esteem. Parents need to know, he says, that if they are to be guided by the "doing-well" rather than the "feeling-good" approach to parenting, they must be ready to intervene to change the child's thinking about failure, to encourage tolerance of frustration, and to reward persistence rather than mere success.

If feeling and doing are the basis of self-esteem, small wonder that its absence is so closely associated with depression, whether one's own or that of a parent. Depression makes its sufferers feel hopeless and worthless, constricted by negativism and changeless horizons within which the self is embattled and beleaguered. While low self-esteem does not necessarily lead to depression, weak self-esteem is a standard concomitant of it.

The Persistent Self-Image

Psychologist Constance Hammen, who is conducting a long-term research project on depressed mothers and their offspring, wrote me that she has observed low self-esteem in the children she is studying. "We [note they have] not only depression and other symptoms, but also social impairment in their relationships with their families and friends, and more conflict and . . . interpersonal stressors. They are more likely to say 'I do not need to be close to others. It is very important for me to take care of myself, and I prefer not to count on others or to have others count on me,' or, alternatively, 'I want to be very close to others, but I often find that [they] do not care for me as much as I care for them.'"

In the stories I have heard, many survivors slip from initially longing for intimacy into "not needing" it. Somewhere along the line our instinct for survival leaps into action and we opt for sole control of our fate. Hiding behind our misleading mask of aloof independence, we may fool the world but not ourselves. Aware of our vulnerability and solicitous of our tender feelings, we do what we must to defend ourselves. If this means distancing ourselves from those who might hurt us, we are up to the task. Our dealings with them often set off warning bells, alerting us to the danger of discovery. Time to lock the gates, we think, and put up STAY OUT signs. If some visitors know the password and manage to slip inside, we touch up our disguise, a persona to please and appease. If it fails to do so, we banish the intruders and comfort ourselves with a reminder: "See? I was right all along. I am better off alone."

These reactions and beliefs are rooted in our childhood and stem from our mothers' depression; once planted, they are hard to uproot. In his book *Vital Lies, Simple Truths,* Daniel Goleman writes that unloving parents can lower self-esteem and that people with low self-esteem "are prone to oversensitivity to failure, are all too ready to feel rejected, and take a long while to get over disappointment. Their view of life is pessimistic, much like a child insecure in his parent's love." That's a pretty good description of survivor's syndrome, and also of someone who is depressed. You already know about the first; the following chapter describes the second.

3

What Have I Got? Why Me? Why Women?

Depression is painful in unexpected ways. Its sufferers endure a numbing, draining heaviness in which emotions play little part. Life isn't sad; it's pointless. Past, present, and future seem interchangeable, all governed by the need to exist, hour by hour, despite the absence of hope and purpose. Washington psychologist Martha Manning kept a diary (later published with the title *Undercurrents*) during the depression that transformed her from a happy, healthy, and successful wife, mother, professor, and psychotherapist to an automaton haunted by thoughts of suicide. Entries from it trace the progression from a woman whose expanding "to do" pile waits passively on her desk, whose long-overdue phone bill and patients' Medicare forms are "screaming for attention" to one filled with an incapacitating dread that her depression will never end.

Seven months into it, she writes that she is preoccupied with thoughts of death. "In some moment of emptiness or pain, an image of dying comes to me: a car accident, a heart attack, a vicious and quick-killing illness. . . . Rather than feeling the revulsion and fear that would have resulted from thinking about these things several months ago, now I find them strangely comforting." Martha knew that although her husband could survive her self-inflicted departure, she could not leave her child. "A bad mother," she writes later, "is better than a dead mother." That realization won out but failed to protect her from guilt. In a sense, that was the worst of it, knowing that she was taking others along for the catastrophic downhill ride, and that she didn't know how to do it differently.

Many depressed women feel similarly, but few are able to express their feelings at all, let alone with such eloquence. Merely locating paper and pencil to make a grocery list requires energy and focus, both in short supply when depression is present. Other people's concerns seem remote, irrelevant, or beyond response. This isolating illness is remarkable for the ease with which it shrinks the horizons of daily life to a single-minded effort to survive each day. And I suspect that among its legions of sufferers, those least likely to recount such thoughts are mothers.

Martha Manning is much more than the sum of her many roles and professional accomplishments. She's also warm, funny, and down to earth and has a knack for connecting directly, without games or subterfuge. On the face of it, she is an unlikely candidate for the severe depression that ground her to dust for a year. Both she and her husband, Brian Depenbrock, are practicing psychologists. They are knowledgeable about depression, both professionally and personally. Martha's grandmother suffered from it, although it was not labeled as such until she reached her seventies. But despite insight, a good marriage, and a twelve-year-old daughter she adored, Martha's depression waxed and deepened until it squeezed out everything else. "Each morning," she wrote, "when I had to face another day on two hours of sleep and no hope, I leaned against the bathroom door waiting for my daughter Keara to sing in the shower and let her voice invite me to try for one more day."

For many bleak months, Martha's intractable depression resisted an array of medications and psychotherapy. Her daughter Keara was the last remaining tether to a once happy life, but even that bond grew tenuous. "At first you're distracted," she told me, "but you end up so consumed by the depression that tuning in to somebody else takes an extraordinary effort—even for those things that used to be effortless. It's like dialing a local radio station and getting one in Iceland by mistake. My daughter was all of a sudden in Iceland."

Since Keara was a baby, Martha had always tucked her into bed every night. It was for them a special time of confidences. But when her depression hit big-time, says Martha, she could no longer stand that comfortable, cherished routine. "I would sit there thinking, 'How long this is taking,' and wonder how I ever did it before. I felt I was trying to speak a language that I had forgotten. I kept thinking to myself, 'I would recapture this if I could, but I no longer remember how.' I tried hard to fake it, but although that was sometimes possible in the outside world, it didn't work at home with Brian and Keara."

Because both Martha and Brian have always gone the fifty-fifty parenting route, their daughter was spared the total dislocation that many children experience when their mothers become seriously ill. Brian took over the mechanics of Keara's daily life. He knew her teachers and her friends; most important of all, he knew his daughter. When Martha, unable to speak the family language anymore, asked to be excused from the dinner table, Keara and her father talked. He explained that the medications made Mom drowsy and less responsive than normal. Often she was in the car when Brian dropped Martha off at the hospital for treatment, so, said Martha, "She met my doctors, had a mental image of them as normal human beings, not something out of a Frankenstein film. She really hated that hospital. I told her I did, too."

Martha affirms that she was always aware of shortchanging Keara. "I was both absent and present at the same time. She had no way to validate herself in me. God knows," she added ruefully, "I was a horrible role model for her, as a mother and as a woman." Every depressed parent assumes in her own fashion a similar burden of guilt for the distance her illness imposes. "Although she was always very solicitous of me," said Martha, "she just couldn't understand and I couldn't express how I felt. That made me feel awful. Later on, when she knew more about what was happening, she'd come and lean her body into mine, put her arm around me or pat my head." But Keara found a way to communicate how she felt: She shortened her name from Keara Manning Depenbrock to just plain Keara Depenbrock, thus temporarily rejecting her out-of-it mom.

Martha's story has a happy ending. She looks back on this most painful period of her life as having produced something positive and solid. "The years since then have been my happiest and most productive," she says, "and they have also been the best years of my relationship with my daughter. There was something in the combination of vulnerability and stability that protected us. She saw me go to hell. But she was there for the return trip as well."

They have regained the closeness previously shared and Keara, now twenty, again uses her full name. But at the time, her mother's depression was definitely an impediment to that closeness because, explains Keara, "She wasn't available to me, and because something so awful was happening inside of her. I think she spent all the time and energy she had on me—but it wasn't enough. I was often really frustrated."

Most personal stories told by those who have suffered from depression have happy endings because the desire and energy to relate them come after a decision to seek treatment, or because the illness has, at least for the time being, run its course. Only in retrospect can one perceive one's experience of depression as having a beginning, a middle, and an end. In one such tale, a thirty-seven-year-old television producer describes a depression so profound that just getting out of bed was like being born. "I would talk to my producer friends and they sounded like mice on speed," he says. "Meanwhile, I was sitting there trying to figure out whether to slash my wrists or suffocate myself with a Hefty CinchSak. It was like having my skin peeled off, I felt so vulnerable."

Psychologist Kay Redfield Jamison recounts a period of "long and lacerating, black, suicidal depression" during which she was "unbearably miserable and seemingly incapable of any kind of joy or enthusiasm. Everything, every thought, word, movement was an effort," she writes. "Everything that once was sparkling now was flat. I seemed to myself to be dull, boring, inadequate, thick brained, unlit, unresponsive, chill skinned, bloodless, and sparrow drab. I doubted, completely, my ability to do anything well." This brilliant, successful, strikingly attractive woman, best-selling author and recipient of numerous scientific awards, was so overwhelmed by her illness that even the simplest tasks seemed Herculean. "Washing my hair took hours to do, and it drained me for hours afterward; filling the ice-cube tray was beyond my capacity," she wrote, "and I occasionally slept in the same clothes I had worn during the day because I was too exhausted to undress."

Novelist William Styron, writing of the depression that took possession of him, says, "I began to conceive that my mind itself was like one of those outmoded small-town telephone exchanges, being gradually inundated by floodwaters: one by one, the normal circuits began to drown, causing some of the functions of the body and nearly all of those of instinct and intellect to slowly disconnect." As have so many recovered depression sufferers, he describes his return to normalcy as emerging into light, then goes on to write, "I felt myself no longer a husk but a body with some of the body's sweet juices stirring again. I had my first dream in many months, confused but to this day imperishable, with a flute in it somewhere, and a wild goose, and a dancing girl."

Deprived of the gift for words displayed by these sufferers, I once, during a deep dip, made a few scrappy notes of how I felt. "Nothing but a fat, unappetizing slob" and "like a butterfly someone has walked on and squashed" represent the heights of my literary talents during downs, but the feelings gripping me were the same as those experienced by Martha Manning, Kay Jamison, William Styron, and the television producer. Only our choice of language differs.

Depression is still something of a puzzle. The lay public, bombarded with information about it, assumes the experts know all its secrets. While that's far from true, the past fifty years have produced major advances in treatment, enabling millions to lead productive lives. For this everyone should sing hallelujah. Missing, however, is a precise understanding of depression's causes, which appear to involve complex interactions between the parallel universes of the brain and its organ, the mind. The recent tidal wave of explanatory books and articles has successfully moved depression from closet status to relatively frank discussion and acceptance of it as an illness. But they have bred in those of us who suffer from it an odd mixture of familiarity and discomfort. Their message is briskly upbeat, emphasizing how common depression is and how amenable to treatment. Yet when encountered personally, either in ourselves or in someone we love, it becomes a singular journey into uncharted territory, shocking in its power to entrap, devitalize, and destroy. From its depths, a cheery prognosis meant to comfort can sound like a message from outer space.

While the answers to the three following questions won't complete the puzzle, they serve as a useful introduction to how depression works and whom it targets.

Question 1: What Have I Got?

Depression is a common, treatable, yet exceedingly odd illness. Emerging from its grasp, sufferers wonder who and where they have been for the months or years of its duration. "I'm back, I'm me again" is how many describe the delicious reawakening of the senses and intellect that herald its passing, often as abruptly as the click of a switch. The descent into gloom, the transition, and the return to light all owe their origin to changes in the brain's chemistry—more specifically, so goes prevailing theory, to the neurotransmitters serotonin, dopamine, and norepinephrine, which hold sway over our emotions, and over which we personally have little control.

As Martha Manning laments in her diary on her thirty-eighth birthday, "Until last year I lived with the innocent arrogance that my life was the simple product of effort, will, and design." What Martha means is that her depression was not of her own making, nor is anyone's mood disorder a product or sign of absence of effort or will. This illness is nobody's fault; it just happens, sometimes precipitated by a stressful life event but never wanted or willed. Although the puzzle is far from resolved, and much of the evidence is inferred rather than proven, depressive illness is considered by most experts as a biological illness for the following reasons.

The human brain contains about 100 billion cells, or "neurons" as scientists call them. The possible interconnections or "synapses" between neurons are estimated to exceed the number of atoms in the universe. Communication between them is made possible by the neurotransmitters, which act as chemical messengers that jump the infinitesimal gap between cells, no larger than about twenty millionths of a millimeter, in less than one five-thousandth of a second. This communication generates behavior. When everything is in good working order, the receiving cell releases the neurotransmitters, which then fall back into the synaptic gap where they are either deactivated or reabsorbed into the sending cell. This latter process is called "reuptake."

Back in the 1960s scientists were convinced that a failure of reuptake function and the resulting excess or deficiency of this or that neurotransmitter was the surefire reason for depression. Yet despite decades of effort, the only concrete piece of evidence for this widely held theory is that the spinal fluid of suicides has been found to be very low in serotonin—but serotonin is also low in people who are impulsive, as many suicide attempters are. However, and it is a very important however, antidepressant drugs work. The newest versions are specifically designed to target the action of serotonin or a combination of these neurotransmitters, and are extremely effective in treating a variety of depressive illnesses, as well as many anxiety disorders closely associated with them. Since these medications regulate neurotransmitters and relieve depression, it is reasonable to assume the two are closely related. This inferential evidence is good enough to keep many a scientific nose to the grindstone, looking for more solid proof.

There are still many gaps to fill, one being the question of why it takes only ten seconds for medication to alter the neuro-transmitter functioning but three weeks or more for that chemical adjustment to manifest itself in the depressed person's state of mind. Current thinking has it that neurotransmitters are probably the first in a cascade of dominos that ripple through all those areas of the brain responsible for how we think, feel, and behave. That includes regulating appetite, thirst, sleep, and sexual desire; handling the fight-or-flight response; and both gauging emotional reactions such as elation, excitement, anxiety, rage, and aggression and modulating our capacity to start and stop behaviors associated with these emotions. These many interconnected areas govern mental abilities and physical functions disrupted during depressive illness.

Should you wonder just what causes the first domino to fall, you are in good company. Some scientists are investigating the possibility that it could even be some as-yet-unidentified virus; more likely, multiple causes may produce varying sorts of depression. Some appear triggered by life events such as the death of someone loved, loss of a job or income, or anything stressful enough to push a vulnerable person over the edge; others come out of the blue. Some are mild and others incapacitating. Some people experience only one episode, some many. Left untreated, an episode will probably persist for seven to nine months and then mysteriously lift. However, should a second episode follow, the likelihood of a third rises to 80 percent and escalates from there with each period of remission shorter and each depression deeper and more difficult to treat. Some people, myself among them, have more or less chronic depression and can periodically feel it stirring even below the protective barrier of medication. Others suffer from what is known as dysthymia, a chronic but less severe state that leaves them gloomily pessimistic but still more functional than what the experts call major depressive disorder (MDD). Many endure a mixture of depression and one or more of the anxiety disorders (more fully described in Chapter 8, which deals with treatment).

Far less common, more complex, and more difficult to treat is manic depression, a combination of grandiose, out-of-control highs and despairing lows that alternate unpredictably. Cyclothymia is the manic-depressive equivalent of dysthymia: The highs are relatively mild and so are the lows, but neither are any fun. A few have the enviable distinction of suffering from the only truly wonderful mood disorder, chronic hypomania. Feeling exquisitely confident, powerful, and lucky at all times and rational enough to stay out of trouble, they often end up in risk-taking professions like real estate and bond trading. Although hypomanics may lose a fortune here or there, they often win them, too. You know who some of them are if you read the financial pages.

Whatever combination of known or unknown factors is responsible for depressive illness, the estimated number of people saddled with it at any given moment is 18 million in this country alone. The lifetime prevalence rate of one in five holds true in Christchurch, New Zealand, and in Shanghai, in the slums of Los Angeles and the rural hamlets of France, shared equally by the poor and the privileged, the Nobelists and the checkout clerks in your local supermarket. Of them all, only one third seek treatment, some because of the deadbeat stigma that stubbornly clings to depression, but most because its telltale signs are often effectively disguised as reactions to everyday stresses.

A few of the symptoms are physical (experts call them somatic), among them changes in eating and sleeping patterns, tears, and lethargy. But others manifest themselves psychologically, including the sense of being overwhelmed, helpless, isolated, irritable, and unable to enjoy much of anything. To most, the notion that brain chemistry gone mysteriously awry can provoke such feelings seems ludicrous, especially when explanations for them seem patently obvious.

Surely, you think, I am short-tempered because I'm so tired, which also explains why sex seems suddenly so unalluring. I'm not enjoying my family because there's too much to worry about at work. I can't concentrate and get on top of things because there's too much to do and other people aren't fulfilling their responsibilities. You're convinced that everything would be just fine if only you had more time, more sleep, more money, more help, a husband or a boyfriend who was more sympathetic, and quiet, perfectly behaved children. These aren't problems to take to a doctor; they are problems you think you should be able to solve yourself. But it is in the nature of depression to inhibit problem-solving, which in turn leads to feelings of incompetence, low self-esteem, frustration, and despair.

Even confronted with that list of depression's symptoms included in all the books and articles about it, you may still fail to make the connection between them and how you feel. That's because you're you, not an amalgam of faceless individuals. But suppose you took a quiz and had to answer true or false to the following statements and questions?

I'm drinking a lot more than I used to, and exercising less. Neither is my fault.

I wish my husband/boyfriend would stop making sexual demands on me. Can't he see I'm exhausted?

Why do I always have to do everything? Why can't anyone else get it right for once?

My life used to be fun but nothing interesting or amusing ever happens anymore.

The kids are driving me crazy. Sometimes I'm tempted to whack them.

My back/head/stomach/chest hurts and I'm constipated. I probably have cancer/a brain tumor/some other fatal disease.

I feel so remote. Sometimes people sound as though they're talking in an echo chamber.

What's the point of going on a vacation? Everything's the same everywhere.

I missed a big-deal meeting in the office, but they probably didn't notice I wasn't there.

Why can't anyone see there's something wrong with me, something different from before?

I look ugly. I should get a haircut and some new clothes but I'm too tired.

I'm a hopeless incompetent, a loser. No wonder nobody loves me.

I'm fine. Just stop nagging and leave me alone.

I should do something but I'm too exhausted.

If you are depressed, there are far more trues than falses, providing you mustered the energy to take the quiz. The trues reveal as much about the presence of depression as positive responses to the kind of questions a doctor would pose: "Do you have low energy, fatigue, or chronic tiredness?" "Do you find your concentration poor, or that you have difficulty making decisions?"

A physician's questions about suicidal thoughts, even if lately you have perceived life as so pointless that it hardly merits the effort and have contemplated death as a welcome alternative, may nevertheless prompt you to say no. It seems a bit melodramatic to admit to the thought of suicide. I never came clean to my doctor, but I played with extinction and often deliberately crossed the street eyes half shut. Remember how Martha Manning, too, was seduced by such thinking. Even flirtation with suicide tempts Providence. Sometimes such thoughts are controllable, but not always. Among people who suffer from serious, prolonged depression, this melodrama often turns to tragedy. The step from image to decision is enticingly short; some totter on its brink but others tumble into the abyss. A full 15 percent of depression sufferers complete suicide. Many more make the attempt.

Anyone suffering from depression knows that "sad" is a pallid way of describing its impact on the human spirit. Hopeless, helpless, misunderstood, trapped, resentful, desperate, and despairing are closer the mark. The world and its inhabitants, including children and family, appear thoughtless and uncaring. Relationships shatter, jobs and income are lost, work and school performance suffer, and joylessness spreads. Every depression has its own unique fingerprint, but all share common characteristics and all, whether mild or severe, inhibit the ability to savor and cope with whatever life has to offer. One sufferer may sit in a bathrobe watching television all day, eating pizza and Twinkies while ticking off the negatives; another may be sleepless, edgy, and irritable, still able to function in the office behind a mask of competence but quick to discard it on returning home. Despite their different modes of expressing it, both these people are clinically depressed. In the absence of treatment, either may sink and stay at bottom for months before emerging into permanent light; alternatively, they may enjoy remission only to go under again, this time deeper and for longer.

Doctors often inaccurately attribute despondency in their older patients to the social, economic, and health problems associated with aging, and in their younger ones to normal adolescent behavior or the stress of contemporary life. Although adverse events can indeed trigger or feed depression, it is no more natural to be depressed at seventy than at thirteen or thirty. The vast majority of depressions give their recipients the impression of appearing out of nowhere, staying as long as they please, and revisiting or not as they choose.

Putting aside the incalculable costs of personal pain and loss, the U.S. economy's annual bill for depression and related mental illnesses is staggering: $67 billion for direct treatment costs, including hospitalization and medication. Low productivity accounts for another $63 billion, with an additional $12 billion lost as a result of premature deaths, including suicide. Incarceration of more than 250,000 persons with severe mental illnesses in prisons and jails costs an additional $6 billion. No one has yet attempted to assign a dollar figure to depression's share of the costs of substance abuse, broken homes, and imperfectly cared for children.

That's depression and its concomitant problems in a nutshell. If you suspect you have it, you will do yourself and your entire family a big favor by seeing a knowledgeable doctor. Treatment (more fully covered in Chapter 8) is readily available, effective, and fast-acting, inexpensive when compared to the cost of broken families and lost jobs, and usually covered by health insurance if you are lucky enough to have it.

Question 2: Why Me?

A big part of the answer to this question probably lurks in your family tree. Although no one as yet has located a specific depression gene or complex of genes, there is plenty of evidence pointing to heredity as the leading cause, not necessarily of the illness itself but of a vulnerability to it. Some of the evidence for this comes from the intriguing research on identical twins who may, even when separated at birth, share a preference for bow ties and walking backward into the sea when they go bathing.

Less whimsical is the fact that if one identical twin suffers from depression, the odds are seventy to one that the other will too, while the incidence in nonidentical twins is only slightly higher than that in the population at large, estimated to be somewhere around 20 percent. Recently, researchers have been studying the offspring of parents diagnosed as depressed ten or fifteen years ago. There's no ducking the data: These children are three times more likely to develop the illness than are children of non-depressed parents. The statistics now coming in tell us that their grandchildren will also suffer from this illness. Hence the term "generational depression," now working its way into common usage.

Searching for clues in the family tree calls for some memory prodding. As recently as fifteen or twenty years ago people were even less likely than now to identify and apply the label depression to themselves or others. Try out some of these "traits" and see if they apply to members of your family tree: listless; self-centered; eccentric; unreliable; always sick with something; painfully shy and retiring; anxious; controlling; critical; dissatisfied; underachieving; helpless; pessimistic; heavy drinker or illegal drug user; lazy; disengaged from life.

No two or three of these adjectives add up to depression, but a constellation of three or four may uncover, in light of what you now know, a depressed parent or grandparent. A closer look at my wildly eccentric and tyrannical paternal grandmother—who in the early part of this century tore through seven husbands, jumped over tennis nets, and refused for no apparent reason to allow a piano in the house after her father died—would probably today have been diagnosed as suffering from manic depression. If I am correct, that makes my daughter generation number four.

Even when the family tree is loaded, it is impossible to predict that any one member will or will not become depressed. Instead, researchers term all the members as being at risk for depression by virtue of their family history. The more illness in the tree's branches, the higher the risk, but some offspring are more vulnerable to the familial affliction than others. Stressful events, usually referred to as triggers, cause their brain chemistry to flip from normal to dysfunctional (or, as previously noted, it happens for no apparent reason). Stress tolerance levels are individualized; what one person succumbs to, another takes in stride. Reactions to life circumstances are guided by temperament, also a genetic product; some people are born wearing rose-tinted glasses. When the crunch comes, the vulnerable are trapped by depression while others escape its grasp.

But some people whose family trees appear free of psychiatric illness do become depressed. If the cause in such cases is not genetic, then why does this illness spring into being? Nobody knows for sure, but experts looking at depression's gender gap think they have a handle on why women are particularly vulnerable.

Question 3: Why Women?

More women than men suffer from depression by a ratio of two to one. Current thinking assigns this discrepancy to both nature and the environment, citing biological, psychological, and social factors.

The biological factors are the easiest to identify and suggest an as yet unproven link between the female sex hormones, reproductive events, and depression. Boys and girls have similar rates of depression until puberty, at which time it doubles in girls, equalizing only after menopause. Women are at greatest risk for depression during their childbearing years. Until just a short while ago, experts thought that pregnancy provided protection against it, but now they know that 10 percent to 15 percent of women become clinically depressed during pregnancy. At least an equal number develop serious postpartum depression and many more suffer symptoms severe enough to cause problems for themselves and their babies. Another tempting but unproven clue lies in premenstrual mood and behavior changes. For about 5 percent of women, PMS is so disabling that it inhibits their performance at work and at home, but it is more like a cousin than a sister of depression. There are as well striking differences in the way men and women metabolize thyroid hormones, closely related to mood disorders. Since changes in estrogen and progesterone levels also influence thyroid activity, these hormones may possibly contribute, but no solid proof of this exists.

Also suggestive are the male/female differences in circadian rhythm patterns. This complex system, which regulates sleep and activity over each twenty-four-hour period, goes out of whack in virtually everyone with depression, but depressed women are more prone than men to hypersomnia, the technical term for excessive sleeping. Estrogen affects this biological clock and so does serotonin, a major mood regulator. Sex differences in the activity of this neurotransmitter and the effects of estrogen on its function are another clue. Both appear to have an impact on seasonal affective disorder (SAD), a condition characterized by onset of depression at specific times of the year, which is four times more common in women than in men.

Women's lives today include a plethora of stressors, some old, some new, that may increase their vulnerability to depression. The list includes dual work and family responsibilities; single parenting and all the responsibilities it entails; sexual discrimination; and a shrinking of traditional support systems. Common sense suggests that all these factors contribute, but evaluating their precise impact on women's depression rates involves more guesses than hard answers. When one researcher took a focused look at spousal absence, social isolation, financial difficulties, and health problems, she found that women were neither more nor less apt to develop depressive symptoms than were men in the same pickle. Every time the experts think they have an answer, they find instead another question.

Conjectures about the existence of a "feminine" or a "depressive" personality, both dear to the hearts of psychoanalysts and in their minds linked, are unpersuasive, but a new twist in current thinking rings true. It postulates that women's willingness to share the pain of others increases our risk for depression. As wife, mother, friend, and neighbor, a woman is expected to respond to the problems and needs of her intimates, whether or not her own are being met. Thus, what many women consider to be one of our greatest strengths may be a liability when it comes to this illness.

Recently some depression epidemiologists (they are the ones who look at depression statistically) have postulated that women do not actually suffer depression twice as often as men, but that the sexes have different styles when it comes to this illness. Women turn inward, becoming less active and more subjective and ruminative about the causes and implications of their depressed mood, while men react to it more physically, turning outward to activities that distract them from how they feel, such as work, alcohol, sports, aggression, and violence.

Women are also more apt than men to seek professional help for what ails them, so they turn up more consistently in the statistics.

Gender differences also show up in studies on depression and marriage, which some believe confer a greater protective advantage on men than on women. Wives appear to be more vulnerable than husbands to persistent marital problems, a vulnerability associated with symptoms of depression and anxiety. An unhappy marriage, concluded one epidemiological study, constitutes a grave risk to a woman's mental health: She is three times more likely to be depressed than is her husband and indeed, almost half of all women in unhappy marriages are depressed. In happy unions the incidence of depression was much lower, but women were nonetheless almost five times as likely as their mates to experience depression.

The number and age of children to care for also bears on women's risk for depressive symptoms and demoralization, especially among stay-at-home mothers. Working moms who had difficulty arranging for child care and whose husbands did not take on a share of parenting duties had extremely high depression levels; absent these factors, their incidence of depression receded to normal levels. By contrast, having children and access to child care had no effect on husbands.

While it is certainly true that many women become depressed, this is not because we are the "weaker" sex. If you are depressed, you are probably laboring under the impression that you are the world's sole klutz and screw-up. But were Eleanor Roosevelt, Emily Dickinson, Marilyn Monroe, Princess Diana, Georgia O'Keefe, Virginia Woolf, and contemporary achievers like Martha Manning, Marie Osmond, and Tipper Gore—not to mention one out of every five people in the world—all klutzes and screw-ups? And what about all the women who tell their stories in this book, including myself? The answer to that question is a big fat no, but there remains another to be addressed: Why has maternal depression received so much attention from the experts while fathers seem to get off scot-free? A big part of the answer lies in the following chapter.

4

The Dyadic Dance of Mother and Child

An extraordinary intimacy, both physiological and psychological, exists between mother and infant. How that intimacy unfolds and what it means for the infant's development is an astonishing story written eons ago by evolution and continually reinterpreted and annotated by those who study it. The story's plot is still in flux, with subplots coming in and out of fashion, contested or supported by new insights into such mother-infant affairs as bonding, attachment, separation, and mutual regulation. The principal protagonists are nature and nurture, together with their costars, mother and child, but there are minor characters as diverse as orphans, monkeys, mice, and strangers who help clarify the plot. Understanding the intricacies of this story is a prerequisite to grasping what happens when depression joins the cast of the dyadic dance.

About two and a half billion years ago, most primeval unisex genes decided that two sexes were better than one to ensure survival. From that momentous decision eventually flowed human male and female physiology: egg, womb, and breasts for her, sperm and penis for him, and a brain wired to improve the odds that each performed his or her task to the genes' satisfaction. Females were hardwired for a selective and conservationist attitude reflected in their heavy nine-month investment in the creative process. Males, on the other hand, were programmed to sow as many seeds as possible since sperm was their principal contribution to multiplication and preservation of the species in a time when paternal investment was minimal. In basic evolutionary terms, not much has happened since then, with the notable exception that fathers today are presumed invested in parenthood. As to women, whether or not we choose to tackle it, we are programmed for motherhood and no cultural or social upheaval is going to change that essential fact. To understand the power of nature's design is to understand why women so often behave like women and men behave like men, and why mothers, not fathers, are almost always the most important beings in an infant's early existence.

If evolutionary biology dominated our destiny, we would still be carrying on like our prehistoric ancestors: men bashing in the heads of every threatening intruder and dragging females by the dozen into the bushes, and women signaling sexual interest to any male who looks healthy and sufficiently aggressive to protect the resulting young. But biology isn't destiny, as witnessed by the vast panorama of human behavior and the social conventions that now govern society. And while our genes may direct us toward the edge of the behavioral cliff by imparting the makings of a "temperament," they lack the power to shove us over the edge. Our "character"—some might call it our moral fiber—also has a say in what will happen there. Whereas the former is inborn and nudges us to choose this or that way of behaving, the latter is acquired, the result of repeated behavior patterns that arise from our choices. Temperament and charac-

ter are joined at the hip; together they define our personality—
that is, our psychological makeup.

Nature and Nurture: Does One Prevail?

The genetic determinists and the environmentalists have been
wrangling for years about what is responsible for human psychology: DNA or experiences and surroundings. For three
decades or more the determinists have held sway, but the pen-
dulum is starting to swing again. Although distinguished hard-
liners remain on both sides, many equally respected scientists
are positioning themselves in the middle, giving credit to both
genes and life events. Their stance, informed by scientific advances, recognizes that genes continue to produce protein—in
the form of neurotransmitters and other behavior-influencing
brain chemicals—throughout the lifespan and that circumstances have the power to alter the brain's workings. Wray Herbert, writing in *U.S. News & World Report,* sums it up this way:
"Genes produce proteins . . . in many different environments,
or they don't produce those proteins, depending on how rich or
harsh or impoverished those environments are. The interaction
is so thoroughly dynamic and enduring that, as psychologist
William Greenough says, 'To ask what's more important, nature or nurture, is like asking what's more important to a rec-
tangle, its length or its width.'"

Viewed thus, the continuing and often raucous debate about
whether nature or nurture makes us what we are is misleading.
Whether adult or child, we are the product of both, with one
notable distinction: While parents have been constructing their
personalities for quite some time, a baby starts life with not
much more than a temperament and endless promise. During

the early months and years of life, the nurturing he or she receives constitutes, barring illness, the totality of the child's environment. Whoever is the principal provider of that nurturing environment—whether mother or substitute—brings to the task not only her genes but also her environment of accumulated and accumulating experiences. They are the coin of her realm, and she will invest them in the mothering role. Her health, wealth, and prosperity, or lack of them, will all come to bear upon her interactions with her child. As the child grows, he or she will store up and use his or her own experience in the same manner.

The complexity of the interplay between mother and child is what makes parenthood so fascinating and challenging. It also explains why maternal depression needs early detection and swift attention. Depression inhibits a mother's ability to accurately register and respond to her child, no matter what his or her age. Sustaining the necessary level of positive interaction demands patience and will, especially when children are young and take their cues from their mother's facial expression and tone of voice. Every mom who becomes a grandmother marvels once again at the tolerance for noise and misbehavior required by caretakers. Babysitting for members of the newest generation is fun for a day or even a week, but more is exhausting and we wonder how we managed to suppress our annoyance, to modulate our voice, to coo over a shrieking infant at three in the morning. When their parents return to take charge of the offspring, we hand them over with smiles and sighs of relief.

Depressed mothers are far more severely handicapped than even the most exhausted and overtaxed babysitting grandparent. For them, the job of twenty-four-hour-a-day parenting is a pressure cooker nightmare. The bleak grimness of depression mandates withdrawal and retreat. They feel hostile and often angry, resentful, and guilty at the same time. Mothers thus afflicted are fully cognizant of their desire to do and to be otherwise, and of their child's needs. To know and yet be unable to perform as they wish is exquisitely miserable. What is so intolerable about depression, and so incomprehensible to those who have never experienced it, is the helplessness its sufferers feel. Knowing is insufficient motivation to do, and doing seems impossible.

Depressed moms aren't unloving moms but are often flawed parents through no fault of their own. That's because the illness behaves like a computer virus. Once it establishes a secret toehold, it leaps from circuit to circuit, pursuing its own agenda, shorting out established connections and producing bizarre and involuntary patterns of disorder. Depressed mothers are just as devoted to their children as non-depressed ones, but they lose their ability to translate instinct and intent into the appropriate action. Their commands aren't executed accurately. Patience turns to irritability; criticism replaces support; the desire for solitude takes the place of play; and expressions of love are blunted. A child's sensitive antennae—even an infant's—pick up on and react to this. That's when the trouble begins.

A Mother's Contribution to Her Baby's Brain

In textbook jargon a mother and her child constitute a dyad, from the Greek word for pair. The dyadic coupling is essential in order for a baby to thrive and become a social, functioning human being. It implies the continuing intimate connection between mother and child initiated in the womb. Although birth separates them physically, they remain two parts that make a developing whole. If the infant's brain and body are to flourish, both partners must work together to achieve this goal.

Until quite recently, scientists thought that interactions between a mother and her child were only relevant to what an already-formed brain learns. Now they know that the quality of the dyadic relationship actually drives the function, structure, and neurochemical architecture of that bundle of tissue responsible for who and what we are. One hallmark of dyadic harmony is cuddling. Cuddling does much more than make an infant happy. When a mother holds her baby close, her body warmth affects the infant's neuroendocrine system by stimulating the adrenal, thyroid, and pituitary glands. Her touch encourages the production of growth hormones and of sets of cells that affect memory formation as well as our ability to gauge and control many of the emotions. As if that weren't sufficient payoff, cuddling may also up an infant's serotonin levels. Recent studies suggest that infants who are held, comforted, and well attended to have higher levels of this brain chemical than do those of more distant mothers. Serotonin's messages give rise to feelings of pleasure and calm us down when we are frightened or angry. The more we have of it the better we feel; lower levels are implicated in depression.

While most new parents know that an infant's skull is unfinished at birth, they may be amazed to learn that its contents are also a work in progress. At birth, the brain is only one quarter of its ultimate size. In the first six months it will double in size and then do it again by the age of three. Much more is going on than a simple increase in dimensions. Behind the placid infant's exterior, a virtual maelstrom of activity is taking place. Within a few short months of life, his 100 billion brain cells (neurons) will forge 1,000 trillion connections, called synapses—more than the number of atoms in the universe.

This represents quite a feat for a two-pound organ the size of a modest grapefruit. This vast synaptic web is a leaderless, self-organizing system whose many parts cooperate to produce coherent behavior in somewhat the same way a chamber music group manages to produce coherent sounds without a conductor—but without practicing. The web lays the groundwork that in later life will support the ability to think: the ability to use abstractions from memory to help form ideas and to solve problems.

Synapses don't last forever, as anyone over the age of forty can attest; these neural pathways need exercise if they are to survive. Babies are interested in everything around them, which explains why their synapses are multiplying, thriving, and being pruned away at a frenetic pace. Synapses are like flagstones that form pathways, inviting exploration. The well-traveled ones stay linked and endure while those with less inviting or rewarding views fall into disuse or are discarded. By the age of two, a baby's brain has more than twice as many synapses as an adult's. They are the foundation of the endless promise with which each child is born.

What We Have Learned from Monkeys, Orphans, and Mice

Looking for an explanation of what fuels this rewiring frenzy, many researchers have concluded that it is experience. For infants, experience for the most part is mother or a solid substitute. That means not just the presence of someone who keeps the infant fed and warm, but of someone who is empathetically aware of the infant's needs and devoted to meeting them. Glimpses of this truth emerged in the 1950s through pioneering studies by Harry Harlow of baby monkeys. Deprived of all but a bottle of formula embedded in a wire framework and a terrycloth mom (after feeding they returned to cling to "her"), they grew up to be caricatures of normal adult monkeys. What they seemed most to lack was a model for relationships with their monkey peers. Either indifferent or overly aggressive, they didn't have a clue about how to interact. (Eventually, when they were allowed to hang out with all the other monkeys, the experience of motherhood shaped up the females; by their second litter they were reasonably good parents.)

Ethics preclude conducting similar experiments with human babies, but recently international politics have provided a chilling simulacrum. With the fall of communism, thousands of babies reared in Eastern European, Russian, and Chinese orphanages have been brought to the attention of Western psychiatrists and psychologists. Not all of these institutions are reminiscent of Dickensian horrors, but the low ratio of staff to children precludes much more than brisk attention to basic needs: adequate food, a clean environment, a few toys, and an occasional pat on the head. As their American adoptive parents can testify, this is not enough. The children who manifest the most problems are those taken from the orphanage after the age of two, when some window of opportunity appears to have closed. Whether it will open again depends on a number of factors. If the children have the good fortune to be born with a resilience gene embedded in their DNA that helps them cope with a deprived environment, and if the new environment is a super-nurturing one, they may develop normally. Others stand the chance of permanent emotional and cognitive damage. As with Harlow's monkeys, it is the business of relating to others that is most troublesome for these children.

The ability to welcome, make, and maintain relationships is

the glue that bonds us together. Babies appear to be born with a predilection for this glue, a practical evolutionary stroke, since their survival depends upon it. Within an hour of birth they show their interest in looking at humans and listening to their voices. Within a day and a half they have already become more selective, preferring their own mother's voice and smell, and will suck on a pacifier that activates a tape recording of her voice. These actions mark the infant's first tentative steps in the dyadic dance.

Many of the complex steps mother and child take together are intuitively performed without conscious thought. No one, for instance, has to teach a new mother to position her baby an exact distance from her face that accommodates the newborn's limited vision, or to speak in a high, cooing voice that helps the infant learn language, or to favor her left arm (fathers use the right) when she cradles her child so that the infant hears the reassuring beat of her heart.

But never underestimate babies for they, too, set the dance rhythm by employing another of evolution's gifts: cuteness, as psychologist Stephen Pinker calls it. Babies look cute and they act cute. From day one, they make seductive eye contact with their mother, gurgle appreciatively, perk up at the sound of her voice. This is the equivalent of a beseeching plea to become inseparable best friends. Babies can't afford to wait. Mothers, on the other hand, says Pinker, are not so quick off the mark, proceeding from a cool assessment to an appreciation of their infant as a uniquely wonderful individual after about a week, to a gradual deepening of love over the next few years. In the meantime, every brand-new mother who observes her newborn with less than wild enthusiasm can take comfort in knowing that this is normal, short-lived, and poses no threat to her child. Full-fledged bonding is just around the corner.

The Business of Bonding and Attachment Theory

While it is stirringly romantic to think of a mother's attachment to her infant as some made-in-heaven trait lurking in her soul and ignited by the final push, this just isn't so. Once again, the explanation lies in evolution's strategy to perpetuate the genes. For eons, the odds were stacked against a baby's survival. That week or so during which mothers withhold from full commitment to their young is a throwback to prehistory, a hardwired protection against possible loss or a genetic defect in the young. In earlier times, infanticide was standard practice in most cultures; delayed bonding made it possible. (A hangover from those days remains in the eight-day waiting period between the birth and the naming and circumcising of Jewish male babies.) The strategy is practical: feeding, yes, unconditional love, no— at least not until there is proof that it's worth the investment. From evolution's point of view, a protracted period of mourning is a waste of time, time that could be better invested in choosing another father and getting on with the all-important business of procreation. Given the vicissitudes of cave life, it's a wonder nature didn't insist on a longer waiting time before the bonding process takes off.

Bonding was a non-issue until in the 1950s British psychiatrist John Bowlby and others noted behavioral problems in children who had been separated from their parents for long periods of time by war or hospitalization. Extrapolating from his observations, he proposed that the mother-child relationship forms a template for all later ones. Thus was attachment theory born. At his death in 1989, he was still railing against women who "go out to work and make some fiddly little bit of gadgetry, which has no particular social value, and children are looked after in indifferent nurseries." Full-blown attachment theory has been a topic for impassioned debate, despite mounting evidence that a happy working mother and empathetic daytime care add up to children who are more contented and more securely attached than are the children of reluctant stay-at-home mothers, quite a few of whom end up suffering from depression.

Although plenty of experts see Bowlby's feet as made of clay, his suspicion that the psychological unavailability of a parent during periods of depression may be experienced by the infant as a recurrent "loss" is sound. Bowlby theorized that such a loss might place the very young at risk for developing an insecure attachment to the mother and also at risk for depression, a position that some researchers working on the developing brain believe is reflected in their findings. Much of depressive symptomatology is related to loss of pleasure, expectation, hope, and a sense of oneself. This throws bonding and attachment in the limelight when depressed mothers are studied.

The Strange Situation

Although attachment theory, as first articulated, has been bloodied from frequently fervent attacks upon it by feminists, many psychologists, and other dissenters, the process does take place, whether with a mother, a substitute, or a combination of both. The phenomenon is well studied by experts, who use an oddly named twenty-minute playlet with three scenes and precise stage directions called the Strange Situation. This is claimed to evaluate the strength of the attachment bond between a mother and her child. Devised in the 1960s by the late psychologist Mary Ainsworth, the Strange Situation is still the prototypical measurement of attachment. While trained observers watch from behind a two-way mirror, a mother and her one-year-old child enter a room in which there is an inviting pile of toys and a stranger (actually a researcher and thus a member of the jury). Mother exits, leaving babe alone with stranger. Stranger plays with baby for two minutes. Mother returns. Then mother and stranger both depart, leaving baby alone with toys. In two minutes, mother returns again. End of playlet, except for the verdict.

The test's proponents claim that it's not the baby's behavior during separations that counts the most; everyone expects babies to be upset in similar circumstances and many are. It's how she behaves at the moment of reunion, they say, that indicates the strength of the glue that bonds them. Does she rush to her mother for comfort, or perhaps throw her a contented smile that acknowledges her return? Or does she ignore her, or, worse, shriek and wail, refusing to be consoled by any number of hugs and kisses? The former are rated as securely attached, the latter as either insecure-ambivalent or insecure-avoidant.

Further, the baby is a prop in an experiment that is really an evaluation of the mother's parenting skills. Has she been a "sensitive" mother, responding deftly and lovingly to the infant's expressions of want and need? Or has she either been distant or overly intrusive in their interactions? Or has she been inconsistent, sometimes responding appropriately to her child's cues and at other times ignoring or misinterpreting them?

Experts who criticize the Strange Situation reasonably argue that it leads to inaccurate assumptions and heaps undeserved guilt upon the parent. Although I'm not an expert, I am a mother, and an experience of my own leaves me with doubts about the virtues of reading so much into such a short one-time experiment. When many years ago I took my bright and people-loving daughter for her kindergarten entrance exam, I fully expected her to exercise the dynamite force of her charm on the interviewers. Instead, she pulled her dress over her head, squatted on the floor, and refused to do much of anything. Cutting short my babbling insistence that this was highly unusual behavior for her, the authorities asked me to leave the room. When, after an agony of waiting, I was invited back in, she demonstrated zero interest in my presence. Luckily for both of us, I was then blissfully unaware of the implications of her behavior and in any event the school accepted her. Perhaps she was cross with me for some reason of her own; perhaps she was just feeling moody or contrary that day and would have preferred to stay home with her toys. Or perhaps my burgeoning depression, unbeknownst to me, had moved from the wings to center stage in that period and Pandora was reacting to distant and inconsistent parenting on my part. It is this ambivalence that attachment theory dissenters question: Is it fair to rate a child as securely or insecurely attached on the basis of twenty minutes in a strange situation?

It took Bowlby three fat volumes to define his separation and attachment thesis. In them, he describes three distinct stages that go far beyond the limits permitted by the Strange Situation. The first of these is one of protest in which the child cries to attract his mother's attention, struggles to rejoin her, and refuses to be comforted by strangers. Strangers might be, for instance, the nurses who take care of a hospitalized child. The second stage is despair, demonstrated by becoming apathetic, listless, and unresponsive. The last stage is misleadingly called detachment: The child becomes responsive to the nurses and functions normally. What demonstrates that something is amiss is that when the mother shows up, the child turns away from her and seeks his new caregivers. Taken home by his mother, he may for a time become intensely clingy. Dr. Donald

Klein, a psychiatric researcher known for his fearless and usually accurate leaps into uncharted territory, suggests that detachment makes good evolutionary sense, as it inhibits past attachments: Should a mother die, her child is able to form an attachment with a new caretaker. Detachment is a necessary emotional precursor for successful adoption.

Separation anxiety, which does not kick in until a child goes exploring on his or her own, also makes evolutionary sense: It keeps children on a leash and close to home where they can be cared for and protected until able to function on their own. Without it they would soon to be annihilated by predators or, in more contemporary parlance, by a passing car or an encounter with an electrical socket. By the age of two or thereabouts, a child's wish to be near his mother will run up against his desire to explore his environment. He'll begin to take more and more short exploratory trips on his own, frequently looking back and occasionally returning to make sure his maternal security blanket is still available should he need it. When alarmed, frightened, hungry, tired, or ill, his attachment will increase and his need for comforting will be greater. Should the mother walk away, turn her back, or otherwise rebuff him, the youngster will cling more strongly to her. He wants not just any physical presence; he wants one tempered by a whole range of positive feelings connoting attention, reliability, and safety. If he doesn't get what he wants, he's upset: Striving without response or award is exhausting and frustrating.

The Model of Mutual Regulation

The Strange Situation aside, one thing is sure: The mother-infant bond does exist. Researchers have spent a lot more than twenty minutes looking closely at mothers and babies interacting in normal situations, sometimes at home and sometimes in homelike laboratories. Their aim is to more accurately determine what's going on between the two by videotaping and then microanalyzing hours spent together. Both mother and child possess hardwired (that's to say, preexisting) inclinations to help them adapt to their respective roles. Much of what experts know about them comes from this kind of meticulous observation. When all goes well, the interplay between the two is harmonious and mutually rewarding. For the mother, the rewards are emotional; for the baby, they also are the beginnings of psychosocial and cognitive development.

The key prefix here is "inter": interaction, interplay, interrelationship, intersubjectivity. What each does influences the other. One way to grasp this is to look at it through the prism of an infant born with a hearing defect. If his mother is unaware of the real reason for his unresponsiveness, she'll try a number of ways to provoke a reaction by offering a breast, changing a diaper, dangling a toy, or putting a "tired" baby down to rest. When none of these ploys work, she becomes distressed and frustrated by her inability to find and fix what's wrong. That distress communicates itself to the infant, who may cry, fidget, or behave anxiously no matter what she does. This mutual misunderstanding of each other's cues can set off a vicious cycle of anxiety and disappointment, leaving both of them even more vulnerable to ensuing communication errors. Misread cues arising from something so dramatic as a hearing defect serve to highlight what in most circumstances is an entirely normal process of errors and repairs. In fact, such misreadings between mother and baby occur and are corrected at breakneck speed: to be precise, about once every three to five seconds. So say a pair of researchers at the Child Development Unit of Harvard

Medical School, E. Z. Tronick and Katherine Weinberg, who have come up with a model to describe this interactive communication process: the Model of Mutual Regulation.

Previous models were one-sided, assigning the leading role solely to the mother. She proposed and the infant responded by matching his intent and mood to hers. This model assumed that the mother-infant dyad was always in sync, carried along on an undulating wave of ups (joint yesses) and downs (joint noes). By showing that there is a time gap between mother's action and infant's reaction, they demonstrated that the baby has a costarring role in the dyadic dance, and that each evaluates and adjusts to the other's input and output. In fact, it appears that most of the time the two are not in sync but working to attain it.

For an infant, whose entire world is pretty much composed of mother or a surrogate parent, "working to attain" is equivalent to learning with and through her how the world works and also that he has a self that can act upon that world. Babies don't live or learn in a vacuum. Like adults, they can only create meaning in collaboration with others—for instance, by encountering a problem and solving it. Nature has given babies a head start in this respect. They "know" to cry when they are hungry, which is lucky, since they might get fed a lot less if they lay about without fretting. Crying is just one signal at an infant's disposal. She can smile or frown; gaze raptly at her mother's face or look away; gurgle happily or scream with rage; ball her fists and thrash or reach out for a cuddle. These are her contributions to a wordless dialogue that translates into "I like what we're doing," "I don't like what's happening and I want to change it now," "I don't like what's happening but I don't know what to do about it," or "Go on waving that rabbit, I like looking at it." Mothers usually hold up their end of the dialogue by responding appropriately.

A lot of meaning in any relationship is communicated through what researchers call "affect." Affect is our nonverbal method of letting people know how we feel about what we're doing. Lovers, for example, indulge in affective behavior when they gaze into each other's eyes and sigh deeply. If one partner's gaze is shifty and the sigh one of boredom, the other partner may adjust by pulling back and looking hurt or puzzled. The Model of Mutual Regulation emphasizes the role that affect plays in helping a baby make sense of her world. Simplistically put, she begins to understand that if she does A, this will happen and that will make her feel good, while if she does B, something else will happen, making her feel uncomfortable. When her mother is her partner, she learns within the context of their relationship. Depression renders a mother a poor teacher because it makes her ambivalent and inconsistent. Her view of herself is distorted and she often reacts in ways that are unexpected and confusing.

Happiness depends on good relationships, which explains why we invest so much time and effort in making and maintaining them. The first sustained crack an infant has at making one is with his mother. Relationships between babies and their mothers are not that much different from those between two adults in the sense that they depend on an accurate reading of each other's affective cues. When his mother responds correctly to his cues, her baby lets her know she's got it right. If she misinterprets what he's trying to tell her, he'll make another stab or two at trying to get his point across. Then, like the deaf baby, he'll either abandon the attempt and withdraw or act out his frustration by becoming harder to handle, even downright obstreperous. Mothers of obstreperous (or colicky) babies love them, but they don't spend as much time gazing raptly at them and cuddling them as do mothers of placid, smiling Buddhas.

That means the opportunities for error repair diminish and the dyadic relationship suffers.

Parents or Peers?

But does that really mean that all the baby's future relationships will be off-base? Does this early mother-child interaction really result, as Bowlby insists, in a permanent template that will guide the child as he or she seeks other relationships, whether in kindergarten, in college, or at the altar? Maybe not, according to a theory recently articulated by Judith Harris in *The Nurture Assumption* that throws cold water on the implacability of the mother-child attachment process. What evolution didn't predict was the extraordinary complexity and variety of human society. Other organisms don't go to school, and although they mate and reproduce, they do it without benefit of the social and cultural pressures to which we are now all subject. Although Harris agrees with other experts that the developing brain "expects" the baby to be taken care of by one person, or a small number of people, who provide food and comfort and are around a lot, she resolutely disagrees with their view of what that implies for the baby's future relationships.

Peers, not parents, she maintains, are responsible for the behavior our genes don't install. This runs counter to nearly everything that psychologists have been telling us about human development for the past century. Where everybody else had assumed that adolescents rebel against the restrictions imposed on them by adults, Harris thinks that in rebelling adolescents are trying to contrast themselves with adults, and that it follows that if adolescents don't want to be like adults, it's because they want to be like other adolescents. They achieve this by emulating the behavior of their peer group, thereby filling in most of the missing 50 percent of what we call personality. Yes, says Harris, it's true that Harry Harlow's mother-deprived monkeys did grow up to be adult incompetents (at least until their second litter), but only because they were reared without others of their age in the same cage. Yes, institution-reared children do lack the ability to form close relationships, but only if they spend their first four years in an institution. Even then, many of them end up with spouses and children and careers like everyone else, because they learn to adapt. And while there's no doubt that both monkeys and human babies are far happier with doting mothers, unhappiness early on does not necessarily have long-term consequences. We primates are adaptable creatures. When Harlow tried putting young monkeys together in a cage, they managed to learn from each other how to get along. Had they been alone in one with an unsocialized, incompetent mother monkey, they would be less successful in this respect.

Many experts have observed, however, that while parentless institutionalized kids do not regularly become depressed, as adults they often have difficulty in relating normally to others. Although they fall upon everyone they meet like their long-lost best friend and appear forthcoming and attentive, they are totally unconcerned when those "best friends" disappear from their lives. Their connection to others is purely superficial, skin deep, and often exploitative. Below their charming surface lies . . . nothing resembling human empathy. It is as though they had not learned how to care about other human beings. This is an extreme example of a child whose relationship "template" has remained unformed and empty of examples. They are what society calls psychopaths.

Harris's thesis, which has received support from some researchers and disbelieving sneers from others, takes some of the pressure off working parents who can afford quality day care. It also illuminates the thorny issue of nature versus nurture. By expanding nurture to embrace not only what parents provide in the home but also what a child's larger environment contributes to his or her mores, she shrinks the scope of parental influence. But this is not to suggest that it rates a zero. Rather, she argues that whatever parents do to us is overshadowed *in the long run* by what our peers do to us. I teeter between agreeing and disagreeing: Happy experiences with my classmates did offer protection from the full ravages of my mother's behavior toward me, but not from those dysfunctional habits of thought and feeling to which I am still subject. The answer may lie in the temperament my genes handed me, since not everyone with the same childhood experiences clings to them so possessively.

While many studies support Harris's thesis, no sane parent abdicates his or her job in the expectation that a child's peers will eventually do it for them. Even if the relationship model a mother jointly constructs with her baby isn't cast in concrete, it's still critical to the infant's early development—an axiom with which Harris concurs.

Learning Language

Remember that synaptic web in an infant's brain and the mother's role in its formation? While her touch is stimulating those critical glands and growth hormones, the sound of her voice is doing something even more important for the web's healthy construction and expansion. Increasingly sophisticated technologies, such as magnetic resonance imaging (MRI) and electroencephalograms (EEGs), allow researchers to actually watch that web reacting and expanding and reveal that language literally sculpts and reorganizes those neuronal connections as a child grows. Thanks to these tools, we now know that when a baby is eight or nine months old, the part of the brain that stores and indexes many kinds of memory becomes fully functional. This is precisely when babies appear to be able to attach meaning to words. These and other exciting advances reveal that spoken language has an astonishing impact on a baby's capacity to think rationally, solve problems, and reason, and that this foundation appears to be largely established by age one.

The path leading to language begins even before birth, when a developing fetus hears the muffled sound of its mother's voice in the womb, which may explain why newborns prefer their mothers' voice to those of their fathers or other women. Babies have linguistic skills long before they can talk. Within just a few months of birth they have already begun memorizing words without knowing their meaning and have a tacit grip on grammar. Once again, hardwiring is what makes this possible. Nature apparently foresaw that human beings would have a lot to say to each other; indeed, they have invented no less than six thousand different languages to do it in. She accordingly prewired the brain with a template that can accommodate all the basic rules of grammar languages share. Infants also come equipped to perceive every possible sound, or phoneme, of every tongue, be it English, Hindi, or Nkthlakampz, a Northwest American Indian language replete with clicks, pings, and dripping-faucet sounds. A mother who hires a Nkthlakampzic nanny will find that her baby will interpret her noises as meaningfully and as easily as he does his mother's words. In the interest of learning more quickly the phonemes and words of what will be their own native tongue, babies by ten or twelve months begin to tune out those their parents or other caregivers don't use.

It all adds up to a feat of virtuosity performed by little creatures too young to tie their shoelaces. By eighteen months, most toddlers have somehow learned the rule requiring that any verb ending in -ing must be preceded by the verb "to be." If a mother tells her eighteen-month-old son that Mommy and Daddy "have going" to the office this morning, he'll stop listening before the ill-constructed sentence comes to an end. Never mind that the best he can do is "More milk" and "Up, Mommy"; he's hardwired for excellence. By age three, 90 percent of the sentences children utter will be grammatically correct.

Many scientists believe that the number of words an infant hears each day is the single most reliable predictor of later intelligence, school success, and social competence. The size of a toddler's vocabulary, they say, depends in large measure on how much his mother chats with him. One study has demonstrated that at twenty months, the children of talkative moms had 131 more words in their vocabulary than children whose mothers were more taciturn; by age two, the gap had widened to 295 words. The window for acquiring one's native language begins to close around the age of six; children who don't learn it by puberty will never be fluent in any tongue. Just hearing words, though, isn't enough. The tone of voice in which they are spoken also makes a difference, because affirmative feedback is very important to the learning process. A child who hears, "What did we do yesterday? What did we see at the zoo?" will listen much more attentively to the parent than will a child who always hears "Stop doing that" or a bored "Uh-huh."

One more ingredient is necessary for learning: eye contact while speaking. Murmuring "kitchy-kitchy-coo" while attempting simultaneously to hold a baby and wield a vacuum cleaner doesn't do much for the synaptic web. The ability to perceive, conceptualize, understand, reason, associate, and judge develops most rapidly in children whose parents are loving and talkative and look them in the eye while they chat. Turning on the radio or television is a poor substitute since neither can provide eye contact or positive feedback. Infants need the whole package. When a mother's depression impedes this kind of interaction, she is failing to give her infant the building blocks he or she needs.

One of the many studies that reveal the prominent part that adult speech plays in children's language development was conducted by Dr. Betty Hart of the University of Kansas and Dr. Todd Ridley of the University of Alaska. They studied forty-two children born to professional, working-class, or welfare parents. During the first two and a half years of the children's lives, Hart and Ridley spent one hour a month recording every single spoken word and every parent-child interaction in every home. All together, the data include thirteen hundred hours of everyday interactions involving millions of ordinary utterances. At age three, the children were given standardized tests and were then followed as they moved through primary school. The results bolster the argument that quality time counts for more than quantity. The kids who scored the highest were those of professional parents; their children heard an average of twenty-one hundred words an hour. Those of working-class parents heard twelve hundred words, while those with parents on welfare heard only six hundred an hour. Professional parents talked three times as much to their infants as did those on welfare and got positive feedback thirty times an hour, twice as often as working-class parents and five times as often as welfare parents.

But even eye contact and infant-geared "motherese," as researchers call it, are at a minimum when a mother is depressed. This illness forces its sufferers to become inner- rather than outer-directed. It does it so efficiently that there is little or no room for the needs of the rest of the world. Even those whose depression might be classified as mild to moderate are distracted and inattentive, even though their love for their infant is strong. Providing him or her with the building blocks that will constitute not only language but also the means to convey and receive meaning is downgraded from a welcomed challenge to an effortful chore.

A mother whose depression goes untreated finds it difficult to express the love she would otherwise demonstrate to her child. The illness stands as a formidable barrier between them. The lethargy, hopelessness, and deadening lack of appetite for pleasure that are its hallmark symptoms stand in the way of the healthy intimacy so necessary to the child's normal development. Psychologically, socially, or cognitively, the negative effects are apt to turn up sooner or later. When the bonds of intimacy are stretched to the snapping point, there is usually a price to pay. Just what that price may be is discussed in the following chapter.

5

When Depression Cuts In
After Childbirth

Maternal depression is always unwelcome. At every stage in a child's early years, whether during infancy, toddlerhood, or grade school, its effects are visible. Even during pregnancy, researchers are beginning to discover, a mother's depression can influence the development of the fetus in ways that translate into newborns who are fussier and slower to thrive than their peers. Study after study confirms that maternal depression thwarts development in observable, measurable ways that can pile up and endure. Mothers miss out on joy. Offspring do, too, but they also miss out on the chance to embark on unfettered self-discovery, to fully experience the thrill of learning, and to greet the world around them with uninhibited enthusiasm.

The Intolerable Weight of Postpartum Depression

Of all these times of onset, depression following childbirth is perhaps the most harrowing for the mother, colliding as it does with high hopes and anticipation. Nature has programmed infants to "expect" attentive nurturing. Locked in their mutual anticipation, both are disappointed and both react accordingly.

About one of every ten new mothers becomes mired for two months or longer in hopelessness, lethargy, and self-blame, doubting their love for and fearful of harming their babies. Some slip immediately from the passing "baby blues," a few transitory days of weepiness and tentative ineptitude experienced by the majority of women, into full-blown depression; others are untroubled for weeks or even months before the descent begins. Whenever it occurs, postpartum depression (PPD) is a journey into unhappy territory shared by mother and infant.

Earlier this year singer Marie Osmond revealed that a few weeks after the birth of her seventh child she became so overwhelmed by feelings of shame and worthlessness that one day she handed her baby to the sitter, left her a couple of checks and her ATM cash card, and took off in her car, driving up the Pacific coast for hours. She had her cell phone with her, but was so disoriented that she "couldn't figure out where the ringing was coming from." Her distraught husband finally found her in a motel many miles away; to this day she can remember neither its name nor location. "This was," she admits, "the darkest place I'd ever been in my life." Although thanks to antidepressants, psychotherapy, and a loving and supportive husband the worst is over, even now she experiences moments "when I'll start to spiral down again."

Remarkably, depression following childbirth often hits just those women who, like Marie Osmond, seem its least likely candidates. British PPD expert Dr. Katarina Dalton has observed that they are often the very ones who "blossom and exude happiness and vitality in pregnancy." Like most other experts, she acknowledges probable hormonal and genetic connections, but the list of possible additional causes is a long one: past experience of physical, emotional, or sexual abuse; stress during pregnancy or at the time of delivery; a temperamental leaning toward anxiousness and an inability to cope with change; a predisposition to self-criticism; the absence of support from family or friends; a sick or colicky infant; a poor relationship with one's own mother; conflicting feelings about becoming a mother, as well as unrealistic expectations of and lack of preparation for motherhood, not to mention collateral events such as moving house, marital strains, and money worries. Lives there a mother who can't lay claim to several of these stressors? Better to look at PPD's symptoms rather than its causes.

Most postpartum depression symptoms are the same as those of any depression, but some are exaggerated versions. PPD sleep disturbances, for instance, often combine tossing and turning all night with a numbing daytime exhaustion that makes just staying upright a challenge. Some mothers have to force themselves to eat but far more give in to binging on high-carb snacks; the attendant weight gain adds to an already diminished self-esteem. PPD moms pick fights. They are excessively irritable, argumentative, snappish, quarrelsome, and abusive to others, sometimes to the point of bursts of sudden angry violence, throwing things about and slamming doors ferociously.

A fourth symptom wedded to PPD is anxiety about everything, particularly about harming the baby, dropping him, or drowning him in the bath, or fears about just plain not loving or caring for him. But this mother also worries about losing her husband, losing her job, wrecking the car, remembering to buy food, being with other people, and being alone. Nothing is right or easy; everything seems threatening. And she can't cope with any of it.

This constellation of negative feelings and behaviors impinges on the happiness and well-being of both mother and child. The guilty misery expressed by one depressed new mother, whose infant had been fussing and screaming all day, is typical: "I was exhausted trying to comfort her. Everything was just totally impossible and I thought I was going out of my mind. I was feeling so depressed and resentful of her. That made me feel horrible about myself and I started crying again." Another was able to hide her depression for two months, but then her thoughts became even darker. "At times, I didn't want to go near my child but I tried to act like everything was fine. Eventually, I broke down and told my husband. He didn't understand."

The unhappiness and frustration of these mothers is unwittingly communicated to their infants. Babies come into the world preadapted to a caring environment, and they are highly sensitive to the people who take care of them. This helps explain why PPD is so damaging to both. The mother-child attachment gets off to an uneasy start and so does the baby's development. The results may show up soon.

The Face-to-Face Still-Face Paradigm

Imagine running into the dreariest person you know. Your excellent mood takes its first hit as you look at the unresponsive visage confronting you, eyes dull, brow furrowed, mouth down-turned. Determined to make the best of a bad beginning, you launch an effort to inject energy and enthusiasm into the situation, chatting on about the great weather, the movie you saw last night, the booming stock market. Not a ray of sunshine passes over that sad face and the only response you get is a downer "Uh-huh." You try to keep the conversation alive but it quickly winds down and dies because there's no pickup on your cues. Five minutes of this is enough to speed you on your way, taking with you a little piece of the gloom and a promise to yourself to stay out of that person's way in the future.

A baby whose mother is depressed has the same reaction, with one big difference: He or she doesn't have a bunch of friends from whom to pick and choose. Mother is pretty much it for him or her, and while one disappointing encounter with her won't cause any harm—infants have extremely short memories—a long series of them will imprint upon the baby's consciousness a dawning awareness that his or her principal source of pleasure is an unreliable one. And just as you grasped the fact that you had no mastery over your sad friend's world, a baby senses that he or she has no mastery over their small environment. When you encountered your friend you already had a strong sense of yourself and your relationships with others; infants need to develop both, and a depressed mother makes that much more problematic.

Harvard researcher E. Z. Tronick demonstrated this by having young mothers pretend for a few minutes that they were depressed by keeping their face still and unresponsive, and observing their infants' reactions. The effect on the babies was dramatic: Almost immediately the babies detected the change in their mother and tried to get her attention. Failing to do so they looked away, then tried again, repeating this cycle several times before giving up and slumping dispiritedly, comforting themselves as best they could. Disengaged mothers too drained by depression to behave otherwise inadvertently practice this form of neglect. Others are intrusive rather than withdrawn, handling their babies roughly and poking at them, talking in an angry voice and constantly interfering with their activities. Their infants spend most of the time looking away from their mother, seldom fixing on objects and crying only infrequently.

Children of withdrawn mothers are far more likely to fuss and cry a lot, suggesting to Tronick and his research partner Katherine Weinberg that maternal withdrawal may be particularly upsetting to young infants.

Babies reacting to both types of maternal depression are forced to use all the skills at their disposal to cope with their distressed state. Babies of withdrawn mothers develop a coping style suited to their particular needs: They avert their gaze and suck their thumb, becoming passive and withdrawn themselves. Eventually, as researcher Tiffany Field has demonstrated, this behavior becomes a habit that extends beyond their reactions to their mothers to include friendly strangers. As failures accumulate over time, what began as a coping style becomes a habit tinged with sadness and anger. Perceiving the central figure in her world as untrustworthy and unresponsive, the baby takes the further step of perceiving herself as ineffective and helpless. Infants of intrusive mothers, on the other hand, act out their anger at being constantly prodded and interfered with by pushing their mother away or screening her out. Occasionally this gains them some peace, but this coping style, too, becomes a habit, even at times when such behavior is unnecessary. They apply it to others and to toys as well, becoming easily frustrated by them.

disengaged vs. intrusive.

"Red Flag" Symptoms

Dr. Morris Green, professor of pediatrics at Indiana University Medical Center, lists the following as some of the "red flags" that should alert a pediatrician to the possibility of an infant with a depressed mother: excessive crying and irritability, apprehensiveness, listlessness and apathy, feeding and sleep problems, and failure to thrive. As the child grows older, he may add to these symptoms severe or frequent temper tantrums, kicking, scratching, slapping and biting his mother, breath-holding spells, and, in the case of toddlers, out-of-control, oppositional behavior. At school age he may manifest hyperactivity, distractibility, aggressive behavior, low self-esteem, and lack of friends.

In an article entitled "Maternal Depression: Bad for Children's Health," Dr. Green notes that depressed mothers usually do not complain of their emotional state when they bring their child to the doctor, and that almost without exception they neither understand the cause of their feelings nor relate their child's symptoms to their personal distress. He recounts a story about one such mother who was worried that her ten-month-old son was retarded because he was much less outgoing, chatty, and lively than his brother had been at the same age. When she took him to the doctor's office the pediatrician was immediately struck by how sad the mother looked. She sighed, didn't interact playfully with her son, and kept her gaze downward. Her baby mirrored her behavior: He was very sober, didn't respond to the doctor's smile, and kept his arms tightly glued to his chest. Offered a bright-colored cube, he needed repeated assurances that it was all right to grasp it and even then would only "gingerly touch the cube as if it were hot."

The mother's depression, triggered by the tragic death of her husband when her baby was only three months old, played itself out in a despairing loneliness that left her without energy to deal with either her own problems or her young son's need for comfort, play, and expressed love. The pediatrician recommended that she seek grief counseling and engage someone, a teenage neighbor, for instance, to play with her son for several hours each afternoon. Several months later the mother called his office to report excitedly that not only did she feel much better, but her son was now jabbering away, seemed happier, and had even picked up a piece of toast and popped it in his mouth, an encouraging sign, because reluctance to feed themselves is one symptom of infants whose mothers are depressed.

In a similar case study, a British family doctor asked a child psychiatrist to take a look at Timmy, a twenty-one-month-old boy he suspected of being autistic because of his bizarre behavior. When the psychiatrist went round to the child's home he found a lively little kid with very little developed speech, who made a lot of odd noises and gesticulated strangely, as though trying to make contact with the visitor. Meanwhile, his mother sat listlessly on the sofa without responding to either her son or the doctor. During the visit it emerged that she had been depressed ever since Timmy's birth and that her husband was away a great deal. Some astute questioning revealed that Timmy got most of his stimulation from watching television, and that his favorite program was a Kung Fu drama. What had appeared to the family doctor bizarre enough to suggest autism proved instead to be the boy's excellent imitation of Kung Fu grunts and gestures. Lacking other vocal inspiration, Timmy did his best with what he had.

Treatment of his mother's depression, encouragement to her husband to get more involved with both his son and wife, and the boy's enrollment in a play group resulted in a happier family and, in just six months, completely normal speech for Timmy without any other special teaching or care.

These two fine tales of problems cut short by an observant doctor are not typical. Their positive outcome depended on the insight and experience of physicians who took the time to explore the environment of their young patients, notably the state of mind and circumstances of their respective mothers. Few doctors today are willing to go the extra mile, despite the prevalence of postpartum and other depressions, nor do obstetricians routinely alert their patients to the possibility of developing PPD. Until many more professionals who treat women wake up to reality, the burden of initial suspicion and the need to check it out lies with the mothers.

As already pointed out, that's hard to do because depressed mothers tend to assign what's wrong with them to a combination of external pressures and their own shortcomings. They take it for granted that those playground mothers who glow with health, whose own and whose babies' clothes are sparkling clean every morning, and whose poise and patience are on constant display are just better, more competent people, in short, "normal" mothers. Depressed mothers inevitably fault themselves, not their unrecognized illness, and hide their guilt and shame.

Jill, a psychologist, is just the sort of person we nonexperts think will be one of those perfect playground moms. When I spoke with her recently, she exuded a quiet self-assurance that seemed totally at odds with her postpartum depression experience five years ago.

Jill: "I Had No Feeling of Love for Him"

Over a meal of egg rolls and dumplings, Jill described the ten-month-long depression that followed the birth of her first child. She has always been an independent introvert who cherished privacy, she told me, and warned her husband-to-be that she didn't want children because they would force her into a different and unwelcome lifestyle. "He felt the same way, but when I changed my mind a few years later he went along with it. I was still ambivalent about my decision," she said, "and was determined to find a way to really love my baby and to let him know he was wanted." That lingering ambivalence made the depression even more terrifying when it came.

Meeting Jill now, it's hard to believe that this serene brunette, the prototypical girl next door, had suffered from anxiety and panic attacks earlier in her life. During her labor, an undiagnosed Group B strep infection arose, putting her unborn child in jeopardy and triggering her anxiety. She and her son were ill for several days, but both rallied and Peter began to thrive. However, three weeks after the birth, Jill's anxiety attacks returned. Within a week, feelings of despair and loss swept away not only her spirit but also her feelings of love for her son. Despite her savvy and the clues in her past history, when the curtain fell she failed to associate her despair with postpartum depression. "Not one course that I took for my psychology degree even mentioned its existence," she said, "so I kept telling myself I was fine and could manage on my own just like I always had."

Jill tried to keep her nightmare private so as not to spoil her husband's happiness. All of her planned helpers coincidentally took their vacations at the same time, so during the long hot summer, she closed all the blinds as soon as her husband left each morning and remained alone in the house with Peter. Her head was filled with anxious, obsessive thoughts: Her change of mind had been a disaster. She had been right in the first place. She should never have had a baby. She was a terrible mother, and now it was too late to do anything about it.

But the worst of it was that she had no feeling of love for Peter. "That's what convinced me that I made an irrevocable mistake. When I looked at him, nothing happened inside," she told me. Jill's training had taught her the importance to babies of touch and eye contact, "So I spent hours stroking and singing to him. I sang my way through all those awful months, making up my own lyrics, crying and smiling at him. I tried to find one thing every day that I liked about him. It was weeks before I managed to tell myself, 'Okay, he's got pretty hair.'" The first time she really liked him he was five weeks old.

Jill was persuaded by a close friend to hire a "doula" to keep solitude at bay and to help around the house. Even then, she would admit only to needing help with the dishes. It was the doula who suggested that she had postpartum depression and pointed her to recovery. Jill decided against antidepressants and instead used natural remedies to treat her anxiety. Her acute symptoms lifted after the first month, and she gradually recovered during the year. Her son Peter is now a healthy and cheerful five-year-old with a two-year-old sister. Jill says she has the perfect profile for a postpartum depression candidate—fiercely independent, resistant to any help from others, and with a history of anxiety—but she added that it is also one rarely identified in advance by women's health professionals.

Her explanation for walking through fire without medication is that she received extraordinary support from her large family, the doula, her naturopath, and her husband, who she admits was the target for her irritability and anger. Not all PPD sufferers are so lucky. Some of them, the unluckiest of all, enter the terrifying realm of postpartum psychosis, during which they may desire or attempt to harm the baby. Hanna, belatedly diagnosed as suffering from manic depression, told me about her experience of postpartum psychosis.

Hanna and the Nightmare of Postpartum Psychosis

For three short weeks, Hanna, a social worker studying for her master's degree, and her husband, Eli, were a typical suburban couple savoring the delights of their first child. The delivery had been difficult, but to everyone's relief, both Sophie and Hanna were soon in top form. About this time, Eli began to keep a diary. Intended as a father's record of joy, it traces a six-month nightmare for the parents and also offers disturbing evidence of failure on the part of many health professionals to correctly identify and treat even textbook cases of postpartum depression and psychosis.

Early entries take note of how loving a mother Hanna was but mention also the obsessive lists she began to make: lists of the reasons why she was having trouble completing an overdue report she was preparing, of the errands her husband must run, of why she found her own parents so lacking, and of why she felt so blue. One night, fuming with anger at her ob-gyn because he had arrived too late to deliver the baby, she called to berate him. His response was to advise her to take more of the Percocet he had prescribed for pain after delivery.

Despite her exhaustion, Hanna was unable to sleep. One night she frenetically cleaned the house, revisiting already pristine corners to give them yet another scrub in an effort to assuage her guilt for neglecting household chores. During the day her thoughts and words became increasingly disorganized, punctuated with the assertion, "Now I know!" She told Eli that she was suffering from PPD, that she wasn't suffering from PPD, and made more lists to prove her points. Eli called her doctor to voice his growing concerns but even this second warning that something was seriously wrong produced only another prescription, this one for Xanax to calm Hanna's anxiety. Although Hanna had previously seen a therapist, the therapist, too, had little to offer when Eli called to report his wife's state of mind.

The diary entries are full of Eli's love for his increasingly troubled wife and also reveal Hanna's devotion to her baby despite her inner chaos. "She is such a wonderful and tender mother, able to sense Sophie's every need and to respond and comfort her," he wrote on day five, but he grew increasingly frightened for his wife. When a knowledgeable friend suggested that perhaps she was suffering from postpartum depression, he took her to see a therapist at the hospital. The woman to whom they were directed, who was trying to build a private practice of her own, failed to identify Hanna's problem and indeed seemed to radically underestimate its severity, recommending only twice-weekly outpatient psychotherapy. Concerned that if Hanna were hospitalized she might be prevented from breast-feeding and so become even more upset, Eli tried to believe what he was told.

On their return home, Hanna's anxiety and distress intensified each day. One night she called a colleague at two in the morning and announced her fear that she would kill herself. The alarmed colleague asked to speak to her sleeping husband, and early the next morning Eli took his wife to the hospital. Hanna stayed there for nine terrible days, heavily medicated with Haldol (an antipsychotic medication), and was at some point treated with lithium, one of the drugs used for manic depression, the illness she was by then suspected of having. If the nurse was observing her closely she swallowed the lithium, but, fearful that the medication would harm her, whenever possible she hid it under her tongue, then flushed it down the drain as soon as she was alone.

Eli's daily diary records Hanna's swinging moods: Sometimes she sat immobile and expressionless; at others she proclaimed herself either an unfit mother or a genius who would write a book about PPD and make millions. Budding social worker that she was, Hanna in her "up" moods devoted herself

to helping her fellow male and female patients in the psychiatric ✓
ward, naively persuaded that her attentive support and comforting hugs could cure them. As she told Eli, "They are so
badly in need of love." Although the hospital personnel appeared to take no interest in her ministrations, her hospital
records, which she later procured, contain references to "the
patient's preoccupation with sexual matters." Nothing could
have been further from the truth, she told me. When Eli was
with her she reiterated over and over again her love for him and
for their child. "I will always, always love you," she proclaimed.
"Promise me we will never be separated."

There were moments when she was playful and touching,
"like a little rebellious kid," wrote Eli, and others when she was
vengeful and accusatory of her parents, but never of Sophie. At
one point she became so upset and agitated that she was put in a
padded cell, in hospital parlance a "protective room." On
emerging she told Eli that unless he took her home she would
kill herself. That same day the hospital discharged her with a
prescription for a low dose of Haldol, but not for lithium.

The couple went to a quiet inn for a week's recuperative vacation, taking the baby with them. Home again, Hanna seemed
fully recovered and her doctor took her off the Haldol, but
within ten days she plummeted into a black void. Thoughts of
harming Sophie began to float across her mind. "It's not at all that
I *wanted* to," she explained to me, "but these awful thoughts
would just appear in my head, not necessarily when she was crying or being difficult, but when she was just sleeping peacefully.
Anyone who's ever taken a college course in psychology," she
added, "learns that there's a way to explain everything, a reason
behind every thought and action." Following Freud's dictum that
the mind is governed by the unconscious, Hanna became convinced that buried deep within her were wickedness and evil,

suppressed horrors that were now surfacing. Convinced they would lead her to harm Sophie, she asked Eli to take her back to the hospital where once again she was given Haldol and lithium.

Hanna says she was a wreck on returning home, and so lethargic from the Haldol that she couldn't get out of bed. Never left alone lest she harm herself or Sophie, this time she did take her lithium. Gradually the depression lifted; with it went the thoughts of harming her child and an unexpected bonus: She decided to form her own hospital-based support group for mothers suffering from postpartum depression.

A significant number of PPD sufferers, even in the rare instances when their illness includes psychosis, will, like Hanna, be misdiagnosed as simply overtired, overanxious mothers laid low by the rigors of caring for a newborn infant. The devotion that led Eli to record the anticipated joys of fatherhood in his diary produced a guide to help all mothers who suffer from this illness and their husbands and families as well. Its message is clear: Pick up on the warning signs of this illness and take action.

While it is normal for a new mother to feel overwhelmed by the challenge of looking after a baby and at times suspect she is not up to it, most are soon briskly changing diapers with the best of them. If instead the negative feelings and fears persist, and if energy and appetite fail to return to their previous norms, be suspicious, recommends Hanna. Should the doctor be unconcerned, "Trust your own instincts," she says, push the issue, and if necessary, get a second opinion. Although the doctor's gender should not be an issue, Hanna warns that male physicians often have a blind spot when it comes to their female patients' ailments. "Men can't seem to figure women out," she told me. "Even health professionals aren't able to grasp how complex we are both anatomically and emotionally, so they tend to discount our hormone-related problems and fail to take them seriously. That's why it's so terribly important," she added, "that we women understand our vulnerability to depression, that we recognize its signs and persevere until we find a better-informed doctor."

If there is a psychotherapist in the picture, do not blindly rely on his or her opinion if they discount the symptoms. Remember that PPD hits as many as one in every ten mothers. Undetected and untreated, it will cause a great deal of unhappiness for the parents, the child, and also for the marriage. Patient, understanding husbands are in the minority; far more link the changed behavior of their wife to a change in her affection for them, not to depression.

For some women, Hanna among them, postpartum depression may signal the onset of manic depression, usually termed bipolar depression by health professionals. Because antidepressants can trigger mania in undetected bipolar sufferers, diagnosis of PPD should be left to experts. Psychiatrists well versed in PPD know this danger, but few obstetricians and gynecologists do. Not all psychoses are indications that it is present; some are just postpartum depression at its very worst.

Plenty of depressed new moms who are neither psychotic nor bipolar are terrified of harming their child. Instead of thinking, "I'm afraid I'll drop him when he's all soapy from his bath," they become obsessed with thoughts like, "What if I don't wake up to feed her and she starves." Mothers understandably are guiltily ashamed of such unreasonable fears, which play into their view of themselves as inadequate and unfit for motherhood, and try to hide them from family members. But attempts to cover up such warning signs are as dangerous in postpartum depression as they are in politics. Far better to fess up, seek help, and through treatment enjoy an unconditional pleasure in your baby.

Cognitive Development: Learning How to Learn

PPD holds many potential dangers for babies, most of which have already been covered in this chapter, but one remains: its potential for inhibiting their early cognitive development. Current thinking has it that intelligence is dependent on genes, which determine an individual's ability to learn less or more easily, and to apply what is learned to solving problems. But genes do not transmit ready-made multiplication tables and the names of colors. Even children blessed with high intelligence will fail to exercise it fully if their environment does not provide stimulation. For an infant, stimulation is an opportunity to learn. Growing up with a parent whose energies are devoted to physical survival, with little left over for intellectual nourishment of offspring, can stunt, or at the least delay, a child's cognitive development, no matter how promising his or her genes may be. Cognitive, emotional, and social development are tightly interwoven processes; all will flourish or languish in interactive fashion.

Most depressed mothers are self-focused, distracted, and preoccupied with their own thoughts and feelings. They communicate with and respond to their infants in a more sluggish, less immediate manner than do non-depressed parents. Because of the dictates of their illness they tend, for instance, to sit about and let their babies go exploring on their own instead of joining in. Growing infants far prefer a mother who is both a leader and an active participant in the process. A lively, responsive mom who says, "Let's go see what that big red thing is! Look how the ball rolls," followed by, "Oh, yes, you're such a clever little girl to push it. Now I'll push it back to you," will be rewarded with a matching excitement in her baby. One who unenthusiastically says, "Go find the ball," while she watches television surely won't get the same reaction. Her unengaged, lethargic manner is a real-life version of the Face-to-Face Still-Face Paradigm mom who pretended to be depressed and uninterested, and her baby, too, will mimic his mother's sad affect. One infant is developing the capacity to learn from others, such as teachers in nursery school, while the other's potential for doing so is gradually inhibited.

In one poignant study, friendly clinic nurses played with three-month- to six-month-old infants whose mothers were depressed, but because the little kids were accustomed to their mothers' negative mood, they didn't brighten up or join in. Even more disturbing, the nurses "caught" their unresponsiveness and negativity, just as you "caught" the mood of your dreary friend. As they spent time with these listless, unresponsive little babies, the nurses' own manner began to flatten and they played with them less enthusiastically and for a shorter time than with the other babies. Professor Dale Hay of Cambridge University calls this result "social contagion."

What it all adds up to is a poor start for these infants, because they miss out on opportunities to learn how to learn. This is what Dr. Brazelton infers when he says that kids of depressed moms lack motivation to learn in school and to succeed. They have a shorter attention span than their peers whose mothers aren't depressed, are more likely to forget what they have learned, and are less adept at solving such problems as where the ball went when it rolled behind the chair.

These deficits become tangled with insecure attachment to the mother, which in turn impacts on the babies' relations with other adults and, as they grow older, with other children. This chain of development underlies Professor Hay's willingness to go out on a limb and propose that a "mother's postpartum de-

pression permanently affects some children's cognitive abilities." However, Hay points out that when depressed moms do
focus their attention on their infants and engage in the pleasures
of mutual discovery, their babies perform well on cognitive
tests. So once again, there is a solution: When depressed mothers begin to interact positively with their infants—a change that
will come with treatment and encouragement—the negative
effects on their kids can be erased.

Watching the Brain at Work

Experts believe that when maternal depression is in force during the six to eighteen months after birth it is particularly damaging to a child's emotional development because this is just the
developmental period during which the ability to make attachments is formed. It is also a period of very rapid growth in the
brain's frontal lobes. Most information about linkages between
maternal depression and infant development has resulted from
observing and comparing the ways that depressed or non-depressed mothers and their babies behave and interact. Now researchers are also using EEGs (electroencephalograms) to
watch which parts of a baby's brain are doing what and when.

The left and right frontal brain regions are specialized for
expressing different emotions. Activity in the left frontal region
increases when we are feeling positive emotion, such as joy and
interest, while activity in the right frontal region increases during emotions associated with withdrawal, such as distress, sadness, and disgust. These patterns appear to be present very
early in life. In people suffering from depression, activity on the
left, positive emotion side decreases while activity on the right,
withdrawn side increases. Further, this abnormal pattern per-

sists even after the depression has abated. In two separate studies, Geraldine Dawson of the University of Washington and Tiffany Field of the University of Miami have demonstrated that infants of depressed mothers display the same atypical brain activity as their parent, and that theirs, too, tends to linger on, especially if the mother has been down for an extended period of time.

It is important to bear in mind that a diagnosis of maternal depression may well involve more than one risk factor for an infant. There is always the possibility that the child has inherited a genetically transmitted vulnerability to the illness. Perhaps he or she has been adversely affected by unidentified biochemical factors related to the prenatal period, by disrupted social attachments, such as being handed from one stand-in caretaker to another, or by other psychosocial factors, including marital conflict or an alcoholic or abusive parent. In general it is reasonable to expect that the more chronic and severe the mother's depression, the more hits the child's development will take.

How Toddlers and Grade-Schoolers Act Out Their Distress

Toddlers and grade-school kids are just as sensitive as babies to a mother's depression, but their continuing development plays out in a larger sphere, one in which mother-child interactions grow more complex. In this more mature version of the "mutual regulation" model, the child becomes increasingly oppositional and defiant, behavior the mother attempts to control ever more harshly and punitively. Lacking patience and tolerance, she resorts to shouting at, denigrating, threatening, and spanking her child. Disruptive behavior is to be expected in toddlers but usually disappears some time between the ages of three and a half and six, but when Susan Spieker of the University of Washington followed 183 high-risk preschool children born to depressed young mothers, she found that by age six their disruptive behavior was much higher than established norms. Her finding helps explain the kicking, scratching, hitting, and biting that constitute one of Dr. Morris Green's red flags.

A study conducted by Marian Radke-Yarrow and her colleagues that followed one hundred families over three years found similar results. Some of the families included a depressed parent and some did not; all had two children, one between eighteen months and three and a half and one aged five to eight. At both age levels, the behavior of kids of depressed mothers ranked as significantly more disruptive than the behavior of kids of non-depressed moms, both at home and in school. Younger offspring, particularly, displayed insecure attachment to their mother as well as generalized anxiety that increased over time.

There are many such studies showing the sustained adverse reaction of maternal depression on children. One funded by the Department of Health and Human Services looked at the young children of more than twelve hundred women, half depressed to a lesser or greater degree and half not. Kids of moms suffering prolonged depression were far and away the worst off. They were less cooperative, had more problem behaviors, and scored lower on tests of school readiness, expressive language, and verbal comprehension than children of less- or never-depressed mothers.

One final study conducted under the auspices of the National Institute of Maternal and Child Health with the participation of researchers from twenty-three universities deserves mention. It looked at what are called in the trade "externalizing" (characterized by lack of control and hyperactive or aggressive symptoms) and "internalizing" behaviors (withdrawal, anxiety, fatigue, sleep disorders). As do many such studies, it included a developmentally challenging play task for four-year-olds: putting a puzzle together. Mothers were told that they could help their child either verbally or manually.

Children who scored higher on externalizing behaviors were significantly less positive in their emotional tone, social interaction, and attention to the task; those who scored higher on internalizing behaviors were less positive in their social interaction. The researchers were able to link both patterns of behavior to the degree to which the depressed mother scolded or denigrated her child, interfered with his or her reactions, and expressed annoyance and hostility.

Assessing the impact of maternal depression on the very young, who have no or limited capacity for expressing themselves, has drawbacks, relying as it must on tears, tantrums, and academic measurements, such as the "object permanence" test (Does the baby understand that the ball is still there even if it has rolled out of sight?). When children enter school, however, they interact with their peers and teachers, and they take tests. The following chapter looks at how they fare when their mother is depressed, with an emphasis on adolescents.

6

Taking a Mother's Depression
to School

When the children of depressed mothers leave the relatively limited environment of their earliest years and go off to school, they tuck their parent's illness into their lunch box or backpack. That extra weight leads to a number of interrelated problems. Some of these problems, behavioral issues and poor grades, for instance, are observable and measurable. Others, among them diminished self-esteem and a negative view of their possibilities and potential, fester below the surface and feed the ways in which they relate to school, to their friends and teachers, and to their depressed parent. Whether in the lower grades or in high school, they will manifest the same kinds of problems, differing only in age-related matters.

Kids whose mothers are longtime sufferers of severe, untreated depression will fare worse than those of mothers whose depression is mild, occasional, or was a one-time event, or who sought and received treatment early. There will also be some lucky offspring born with a temperament that coats them like Teflon, allowing them to shrug off their parental environment and go their merry way. But that's not the whole story. The evidence, and there is a lot of it, indicates that a substantial percentage of offspring of depressed moms will themselves become depressed, most probably during their adolescence. Before looking at that evidential conclusion, there is a lot of ground to cover, because experts disagree about why this is so. Some take a purely genetic view; others credit psychosocial factors as equally compelling contributing factors.

Nailing Down the Contributing Factors

All stories about a mother's depression share common themes but there are countess variations to be wrung from them because every family, every depressed mother, and every child is different. These differences constitute the "contributing factors" that have been cropping up throughout this book. Because of them even the simplest events can have multiple possible endings. A natural inclination is to skip over the ensuing lists as though they were dinky tidbits and go straight for the meat of the issue: Just exactly what do depressed mothers do and how do their offspring react? But that's akin to grilling a steak without thought to the cut of beef, the marinade and seasonings used, the type of fuel and the intensity of the heat, the cooking time, and the skill of the chef. Even the prospective eaters play a role. Are they a bunch of ten- or sixteen-year-olds, or the boss and his or her spouse? And what about the mood and motivation of the chef: anxious, nervous, confident, hung over, enthusiastic, bored, resentful, distracted, relaxed? All these factors mix and muddle together to bring about widely varied outcomes in both the quality of the meal and the reactions of those who sit down to consume it.

Multiply the myriad possible outcomes of the steak story by hundred or so and you will begin to appreciate the difficulties inherent in predicting and explaining with confidence the psychosocial behavior and the cognitive development of children whose mothers are depressed. Sorting out the factors makes for challenging but rewarding reading that covers four essential areas: the genetic blessings and burdens with which a child is born; a further caveat about the timing, duration, and intensity of the mother's depression; the ways in which a depressed mom and her child act and react to each other; and what has recently been discovered about the way depression travels from one generation to another, followed by some prescriptive advice. All are of particular importance in understanding how adolescents fare when their mother is depressed. As you read this chapter, bring to bear your intimate knowledge of your child, of other members of the household, and of the family environment and dynamic, both before and after depression joined it.

Blessings and Burdens: The Role of Temperament

Every parent with more than one child is struck by the chasms of temperament that usually distinguish one from another. The mother of a mercurial, demanding, two-year-old whirling dervish confided to me her horror at finding herself pregnant again. "I simply can't cope with a second," she said, her voice quavering on the edge of hysteria, "I wasn't cut out for motherhood. I have nothing more to give." Seven months later she produced Julie, a laid-back, roly-poly, smiling Buddha of a baby. While her elder sister Megan, now in the second grade, expresses joy in living by changing her clothes five times a day, rushing from her paints to her rock collection to her jump rope, and clamors for attention, Julie chuckles with delight over the books and dolls with which she passes happy hours alone. When her parents are around, Julie is welcoming and shares her treasures with them, but she demands neither their company nor their attention. Seven years after the birth of her first child, their mother, Leslie, remains bewildered by the differences between her two daughters. "I can hardly believe," she recently observed, "that they are both mine."

Megan and Julie are equally loved, but their mother's relationship with each, and their father's, too, is as different as are the two girls. Zipping through the day with frenetic energy, Megan constantly hears "No, not now, that's enough, calm down, Mummy's busy. Please listen to me, for heaven's sake." Julie's ears are filled with yesses: "Mummy's coming right now. Yes, I want to read the book with you. I love this picture, too. Tell me again, isn't that funny?" Both these girls are grounded in parental security, and both will continue to develop as their respective DNA-given temperaments mandate. Those temperaments will nudge the girls toward different likes and dislikes, different ways of manifesting them, a different set of relationships with the people around them, from parents to peers to teachers, and ultimately to different lives.

Golden-haired Megan is the image of her mother, who is subject to bouts of mild and sometimes deeper depression (she is now on an antidepressant, as is Megan's grandmother). Julie, from her big brown eyes to her perpetual happy grin, takes after her calm and steady dad. Like every human being since time immemorial, they are in large measure a product of their genes and of the environment those genes have encouraged them to seek and construct.

For the first five years of Megan's life, her over-the-top

vitality and need for attention must have taxed her mother and garnered her countless admonitions to be quiet and settle down. At nine she continues to receive them from teachers who recognize her gifts but sprinkle her report cards with comments about her lack of attention, sketchy homework, and a tendency toward disputes with both classmates and authority figures. Despite her mother's changing moods, Julie sailed through her portion of those years without a tremor. A solid B student, she still pores over her books, showing nary a sign of the mood disorders in her family tree nor any indication that her mother's periods of remoteness and irritability disturbed her. Without apparent effort, Julie gets what she seems to want: time to enjoy herself alone and company whenever she wants it. Megan, with all her sharp intelligence and mercurial charm, has to work harder to satisfy her need for attention because she throws up obstacles along the way.

What might a seer predict in the way of a future for each of these children? Choosing a problematic one for Megan would be tempting. Although she is a people-oriented person, her genetically installed temperament already shows signs of interfering with her goal of easily connecting with them. While she has a higher-than-average IQ, her short attention span and difficulty in concentrating on one thing at a time may inhibit full expression of her gifts. Because her mother was depressed off and on for her first five years, the exhaustion and irritability she encountered then must have been as frustrating for an attention-needy child as for her mother. Last but not least, she is, by virtue of two first-degree relatives who have had depression, at risk for it herself. However, Megan has a strong will and supportive parents; between them she may well overcome her present problems.

By contrast, Julie appears headed for permanent contentment characterized by easy friendship and acceptance. Both these speculations could prove faulty, given the family history of depressive illness. No one can predict exactly why, or when, or if it will spring into being.

More About Timing and Severity as Developmental Factors

Depressive illness takes many forms and can have varying effects on both its sufferers and those who love and live with them. Some depressed mothers, like my own, suffer from a pervasive, irritable gloom that may or may not erupt periodically into extended periods of angry frustration and despair. Some drift in and out of mild to medium episodes and then crash. Still others experience a postpartum depression that casts them down for several months and holds them, and by extension their child, hostage to misinterpretation and misunderstanding. Had Julie been the firstborn, her easy temperament might have soothed rather than aggravated her mother's moods. With one tranquil offspring under her belt, this parent's attitude toward mothering in general might have had a less shaky start, better preparing her for a harder-to-handle second child. One thing is sure: Every child whose mother is depressed and remains so is a less happy and secure child for the duration, no matter what genetic hand he or she has been dealt, and the effects will probably linger on.

Maternal depression affects the larger environment of the school years just as it surely as does the home-centered one of the infant and toddler. As a child has more opportunities to interact with a more spacious world, the depressed mother remains a central mediator between the two. Take a look at the equation.

On one side of it stands a depressed mother described by researchers as speaking less often and with less intensity, and responding more slowly; as more irritable and antagonistic, especially in intimate relationships; and as acting in ways that are unlikely to foster positive relationships with those they love. The feelings of hopelessness and hostility that burden her interfere with her ability to be warm and consistent. She is negative toward the demands of parenthood, which makes her vulnerable to feelings of resentment and even rejection of her child and leads her to believe she is less competent and less adequate than other mothers. This doesn't augur well for a child's everyday needs: help with homework, comforting after being bullied by a bigger kid, and a well-stocked fridge filled with Pepsi and ice cream to feed hungry and boisterous teammates after the game.

The school-age kids who stand on the other side of the equation find it difficult to make and keep friends and to get along with authority figures, have trouble exercising control over their emotions, are more prone to acting up, and resist discipline. Like their mothers, they suffer from low self-esteem and expect things to turn out badly. And whatever their intellectual capacity, these kids perform academically below their expected level. Unsurprisingly, they pose a far more demanding parenting challenge than kids like Julie; a mother depleted by depression is unlikely to rise to it.

This is a messy equation. Balancing it requires many of the qualities—empathy, balance, patience, and supportive discipline—that depression obliterates. If the problem is left unresolved over time, especially during critical developmental periods, both mother and child will adjust to the mess instead of cleaning it up. For a child, this can be habit-forming. Even when the mother's depression abates or is treated, her son or daughter may continue to use the inappropriate coping styles they have adopted during bad times, not only at home but also in school.

Research on how kids of depressed mothers get on in school has yielded consistent results: behavioral disturbances in the classroom, "bad" attitudes, poor study habits, and a lack of popularity among their peers. All of these bear upon a child's academic record. More than in any other era, today's highly competitive society mandates achievement. The issue of exactly how a mother's depression does or does not affect her child's intelligence and potential for advancement is critical and needs clarification.

Who's Bright, Who Isn't, and What Difference Does It Make?

Perhaps the single most disturbing assertion is that maternal depression can permanently stunt a child's cognitive, or learning, development, as a number of studies have claimed to demonstrate. While "happiness" is a relative and scientifically fuzzy state, cognitive abilities or deficits are subject to more precise measurement by grades on pop tests and exams based on class norms, and on teacher's reports. There is a big difference between innate intelligence, measured by an IQ test, and how it is applied, which tests can measure. While a depressed mother may indeed saddle her child with academic performance problems that might not otherwise be present, the assertion that she has lowered his or her basic intelligence is questionable. Even Professor Dale Hay, perched confidently out on his chosen limb, inserts the word "some" and a question of timing into an otherwise unequivocal statement: "I propose that the mother's postpartum illness permanently affects some children's cognitive abilities."

Commenting on Hay's conclusion, Dr. Michael Rutter of London University's Institute of Psychiatry, generally acknowledged as the dean of child psychiatry, points out that Hay equivocates. He acknowledges, says Rutter, that the effects sometimes apply only to perceptual-motor skills and sometimes also to verbal skills, sometimes show up in boys only and sometimes in both sexes, and sometimes persist to age five and sometimes do not. Hay builds his conclusion on the possible ability of early, severe maternal depression to alter the infant's brain circuitry in ways that Geraldine Dawson and others are investigating. This thesis, while fascinating, may or may not be true.

Current mainstream thinking has it that IQ, like temperament, is inborn, and that aside from horrible deprivation—like being locked in a closet and denied affection and care for a couple of years—there is little a parent can do to alter it. No matter how depressed, irritable, and remote a mother may be, her offspring will probably hang on to his or her IQ for life. IQ tests, which measure the ability to comprehend, reason, and solve problems compared to other kids of their age, are usually divided into two parts. One focuses on verbal performance, which includes such skills as vocabulary, spelling, and the ability to draw meaning from information; the other assesses performance skills, for instance, drawing a triangle or assembling a complicated structure out of Lego components. Interpreting them rests on the assumption that all four-year-olds or all fourteen-year-olds, for instance, should have attained a certain level of competence. Kids who do better or worse than the average are judged to have higher or lower IQs that will remain constant. In short, it's not so much a matter of how much information a brain receives but the brain's ability to use it that counts. Despite issues of fairness, IQ is a pretty reliable benchmark of what a child, or adult, is capable of in the realm of absorbing and making sense of information and applying it appropriately.

Most of those studying maternal depression's effect on children's cognitive problems do not conclude that their actual IQ has been damaged. What they do believe is that a mother's depression creates an environment within which the child's learning abilities are inhibited. Timmy, the twenty-one-month-old Kung Fu master, offers a good example of this. Timmy was not of below-average intelligence; he did have a cognitive delay brought on by his mother's depression-driven inattention and lack of response to him. When his mother's depression was treated and she began to interact responsively with her son, and when he began playing with other little kids his age, his learning impairment disappeared and his verbal skills rose to the level of his twenty-one-month-old peers. Timmy's lively, friendly manner also played a role in his rapid improvement.

A mother's depression imposes a heavy burden on children because it forces them to focus on and cope with emotional issues that inhibit their cognitive development. At school as elsewhere, an unfocused mind crammed with distressing thoughts is a hindrance. In this respect, kids of depressed mothers are no different from the corporate executive who can't concentrate because she's in the middle of an acrimonious divorce. For unhappy young people, usually appealing subjects seem dull and impenetrable; homework is an agony. Reading and writing are difficult because so many extraneous thoughts and feelings keep getting in the way. For unprepared and apprehensive children like these, tests loom as trials by fire, not simple indicators of comprehension.

If parents and teachers are unaware of the source of a child's emotional turmoil, poor marks will bring admonishments reinforced by punishment instead of patience and encouragement. These kids aren't having conscious thoughts like, "I could do better in school if only everyone understood how I feel," or, "How does anyone expect me to work hard when my life is in turmoil," as an adult might. But the feelings behind such thoughts are there, destroying concentration and the joy of learning, adding up to kids who perform less well than their innate intelligence warrants.

What Goes into the Backpack Comes Out as School Behavior

Ideally, a mother is a good listener, communicator, and problem-solver. None of these desirable attributes are easy for someone suffering from depression, no matter how much she loves her child. Kids who lack support, reasonable disciplinary boundaries, positive reinforcement, and overt affection at home are going to display the lack of them in school. One of the many manifestations of such inadequate parenting is a lack of self-control. When studies report Will or Rebecca show "disruptive behavior," they aren't referring to irrepressible high spirits, clowning, and pushing the envelope. Disruptive behavior means picking fights and other signs of aggression, skipping school or dropping out, vandalism, shouting at teachers, an inability to handle or respond to discipline, and drug and alcohol abuse.

The internal checks and balances that prevent other kids from this kind of behavior aren't functioning properly. Their depressed mothers may themselves be subject to sudden bursts of anger, frustration, or tears. Instead of laying down boundaries and sticking to them, they tend instead to throw up their hands and shout, "You're just impossible. Do as you please and see how far it gets you." Marital discord, which goes hand in hand with a parent's depression and is the subject of a later chapter, is another reliable predictor of problems at school and surely adds to a child's insecurity. Additionally, making scenes and causing trouble will win the child attention; sometimes being noticed for any reason is better than being ignored.

Boys are more apt than girls to act out their unhappiness through aggression, even when they are only a few months old. Girls become more passive and, some experts have reported, solicit the attention they crave by acting very affectionate and well-behaved. Girls perhaps reason that if they are extra good everyone will reward them with love. Either way, these children are shaping images of themselves that will outlast many a mother's depression. How persistent and negative their self-image is depends on the oft-cited list of contributing factors. Kids blessed with a loving, insightful, and reliable father, attentive grandparents or teachers, a high IQ, and a sturdy temperament will fare better than those bereft of them.

Self-Portraits Have More Than One Artist

Issues such as these bear heavily on the poor self-image already in the making at home where positive feedback is at a minimum. Few adults would choose to revisit their adolescence, but recently I came across a memento of my teenage years that carried me straight there. In an era when kids still said golly and kissing was considered daring, I turned thirteen and moved with my family to Chicago. During our year there I kept a diary full of giveaway comments that testify not only to my mother's depression but also to its lasting imprint upon my self-image.

On January first I write that my mother and stepfather "fell into their scotch like always and said nasty things about each other. Everyone scolded me for not being nice." Entries noting that "Mummy, of course, is furious as usual" abound, as do frequent references to arguments, door-slamming, and tears, with asides like "Bad business" and "Horrors!" One entry recounts a long-forgotten scene that ended in her accusatory assertion that I had never loved her—the predecessor, I was surprised to learn, of the pronouncement following her suicide attempt many years later. That battle culminated in my throwing a temper tantrum and my mother hurling (unspecified) insults at my stepfather as well.

More interested in simply recording events than in introspection, I devoted most of the diary's pages to whether a boy had asked me to dance, or even noticed my presence. Other than scattered references to our arguments, my mother rarely enters these pages, with the exception of shopping expeditions to find something into which my overweight body could squeeze. My toes still curl in remembrance of my elegantly slim parent's impatience and disdain for the excessive poundage that began to plague me then and continued to do so until the year following her death. A terror of confrontation and the loss of self-control it engenders in me proved more durable; so, too, my preoccupation with the opinion of others and my longing for attention and approval. Many whose stories appear in these pages confess to similar lasting emotional deficits, the seeds of which were planted during the tender years of early adolescence.

I have a French friend whose mother's depression, she has told me, made her teens a terrible time. A freelance fashion editor, Ginette also writes wonderful short stories in English that she has allowed only a handful of close friends to read. Because they are polished and perceptively touching, we have urged her to show them to a literary agent. Her answer is not just a simple no, but a maddeningly self-deprecatory description of the slightness of her talent, the banality of what she has to say, and her conviction—"I am French, you know, and we are very rational about such matters"—that no one could possibly be interested in their publication. Besides, she adds, her (excellent) English isn't good enough. Asked why she chose to compose them in a language not her own, she answers that it is because they are about the years she spent in this country.

Familiar with every author's anxiety about displaying work to authoritative professionals, I reminded her that she could do so without risking the embarrassment of a face-to-face turndown, and offered to tell my agent to expect a package in the mail. "Oh, no," she said, "I really only write them for myself," thus effectively closing the negative circle she has drawn around herself and her talent.

On the occasions that Ginette and I have shared remembrances of our respective parents, those of her adolescent years are sharper than mine. With a novelist's knack for choosing the detail that sets an overall tone, she recounts her longing for a violin after attending at age twelve her first chamber music concert, and her mother's response: "What for, you'll never be Yehudi Menuhin." Later came the expensive Parisian dressmaker she was taken to because only a genius, she was assured, could do something for her bony frame. Ginette learned her lessons well. Graceful, gorgeous, and talented, she adheres to her mother's vision of her as awkward, skinny, and undeserving.

But that's not the whole story. Like so many children of depressed moms, she anticipates rejection; when it does come, she pounces on it with ironic satisfaction. "It won't work out" and "Of course, I'm not surprised such and such a person doesn't like me" are phrases favored by the Ginettes of this world, no matter what their age. According to my diary, when the most popular girl in my class informed me I wasn't invited to her party, then changed her mind because her mother insisted she also include the most unattractive boy in our circle, I accepted my belated summons stoically. "As Genie says," I wrote, "beggars can't be choosers." Never expect the best to happen is our motto; that way we won't be so disappointed.

Although I have never seen mention of it in the research, I suspect that depressed mothers are particularly prone to competing with their daughters. Depression sufferers are often resentful when others shine. They criticize and belittle, thus stifling signs of bloom and promise and depriving kids of their place in the sun. Teenagers are also self-focused; while this makes them unbearably insular at times, their egos are in need of massaging, not trashing. Low self-esteem feeds on feelings of inadequacy. While it's true that a poor opinion of oneself does not preclude excellence and success, lack of a positive self-image will never rank as a bonus. Many of the reasons children of a depressed mother view themselves poorly have already been covered, but maternal criticism deserves special mention. The reason is illuminated by the following research study.

Criticism and Self-Esteem

In the early 1980s psychologist Constance Hammen of the University of Southern California began a long-term research project to determine how a mother's depression affects her offspring's psychosocial development. Many researchers at that time assumed that depression was primarily genetic in nature. Hammen suspected that the cognitive problems, stressful life events, and dysfunctional relationships so typical of adult depression probably had a childhood origin. Studying both mothers and children over time, she believed, would cast light on why so many females from adolescence on develop depression, and why the prevalence of the illness appears to be rising in young people.

To test her thesis, Professor Hammen recruited sixty-eight mother-child pairs with the mothers divided into four groups: those whose depression was unipolar (experiencing only downs); those whose depression was bipolar (deep downs plus irrational highs); those suffering from insulin-dependent diabetes or severe arthritis (which often require hospitalization and cause family disruption); and those free of any of these problems. The unipolar mothers had to have had a severe episode before giving birth or during the child's early years, and at least one child in each family had to be between the ages of eight and sixteen at the start of the study. All participants were tracked for three years and then followed up every six months to see what, if anything, had changed in the interim.

To get a comparative baseline, mothers were interviewed at the start about their illness and their opinion of their child, and, because stress is a mediator between depression and interpersonal relationships, they also answered questions about their marital relations and those with other family members, as well as about finances, work, and general health. Children were also interviewed; their own and their mothers' comments were supplemented by those of their teachers, and by school report cards. An integral part of the study was direct observation of all four groups of mother-child pairs as they attempted, for just five minutes, to tackle and resolve a problem such as chores, curfew, or allowance.

The findings of Professor Hammen and her coworkers were clear and unequivocal: The children of unipolar moms (even more so than those of bipolar mothers) were impaired across a variety of domains, including social functioning and school and academic performance, and had much more negative opinions of themselves than all the other kids. Not surprisingly, they also had poorer relations with their mothers, who were significantly more negative, disconfirming, and critical in interactions with their offspring.

Many experts have noted a correlation between maternal depression and a child's self-blame, but they had speculated that the kids might unconsciously be mimicking their parent's negative style. Professor Hammen's study revealed otherwise: Sooner or later, these kids came to accept their mother's view of them as the truth. Low self-esteem finds a permanent place in their backpack. Feeling ineffective and worthless, their social life and academic performance suffered.

What Hammen characterizes as "the enormous amount of conflict," including major fights, that marks depressed mother-and-child relationships creates incessant strain for both. In the solve-a-problem test, depressed mothers were variously uninvolved in the effort, tried to avoid the discussion, and made more off-track, irrelevant, and unproductive comments than the other mothers. When she quizzed the kids about what they understood about their mothers' condition, specifically those who were unipolar, most of them "readily perceived her depression but were especially likely to regard irritability as the most salient change in her."

Moreover, when their mother became irritable they often reported that they, too, felt depressed; older children, in particular, said they got angry. One doesn't have to be a depressed parent to appreciate how quickly a negative beginning can escalate into mutually unrewarding responses within seconds. A discussion about the need for a haircut can shift to feisty and confrontational blowups about a kid's general appearance, messy room, bad manners, and undesirable friends.

The Laundry Mother and Her Child

Two of Constance Hammen's subjects, a fourteen-year-old girl and her mother, set themselves the task of discussing chores. The mother started by posing a question: "So, you think you do enough chores?" "I think I do," replied the child, "I do as much as you do." The mother then listed all the chores *she* handles, such as picking up the dog's messes and changing lightbulbs. The daughter pointed out that she, too, cleans up after the dog sometimes, that she recently changed the bulbs in her room ("But not everywhere," snapped back the mother), and that she often does the laundry. Her mom interrupted to say that the daughter thinks it's a big deal when she picks up a couple of piles of laundry while she, the mother, is out there doing it all week long. After further off-track haggling about laundry, the mother concluded with the statement, "I'm sick and tired of doing all those terrible and yucky things. They're not easier for me just because I'm older."

Not only did they fail to settle the problem of chores; the mother neglected to give her daughter either credit or praise for those she does accomplish. Just reading this dialogue sparks distaste for the parent and sympathy for her daughter. Similar exchanges between them are surely a daily occurrence. Over time they not only will shape the child's self-image but also may lead her to construct a dysfunctional model for dealing with confrontation that she will use in social interactions with others. When she does, she surely won't win either arguments or friends.

It bears repeating that the laundry mother, despite the dreadful dialogue, probably cares deeply for her child, but her illness infuses every aspect of their relationship, as well as their respective view of themselves and their lives. Low self-esteem, feelings of helplessness and hopelessness, and the resulting demoralization are symptoms of both depression and its fallout.

While psychosocial problems created by maternal depression put pressure on the pedal, genetic vulnerability provides the fuel. A side-by-side comparison of the Hammen UCLA study and one conducted by Myrna Weissman, professor of epidemiology and psychiatry at Columbia University, is an arresting reminder that the nature-nurture issue should never be posed as a simplistic either-or question; both bear on depression. An estimated 10 million American kids suffer from some variety of this illness or from the anxiety disorders that often precede or accompany it; younger children can and do develop depression, but adolescence is the period of greatest risk. Informed parental awareness of this is crucial to avoidance or amelioration of the problem.

How Depression Travels from One Generation to Another: The Yale Study

Depression is a family affair, not only in the present but in the past and future, too. Professor Weissman's study of parents and their children amply demonstrates this truism. Launched over twenty years ago as an exploration of depression prevalence rates, it is known as the Yale Study because the original group of 260 parents was drawn from patients at the university's Depression Research Unit and from the surrounding New Haven community. Many of the parents' children, aged six to twenty at its start, now have kids of their own; indeed, the original ninety-one couples have already been blessed with a total of 175 grandchildren, a few now as old as eighteen.

The Yale Study is all about risk, and bookies wouldn't like

the odds. It has found that kids with a depressed parent are three times more likely to develop depression than those without a depressed parent, and that if the parent's illness began before age twenty, the children's risk rises as high as eight or even nine times that of the control group. Offspring are at equally high risk for a range of related disorders from overanxiousness to agoraphobia.

The study confirms that depression, once sown, takes root and grows exponentially in families, putting out early shoots of anxiety and a cluster of related disorders that often precede or accompany it. The data yielded by the study are a rich source of information about their genetic travels from one generation to another and invites a closer look at anxiety disorders, which usually appear during adolescence and are heralds of depression.

The Role of Anxiety Disorders

Most of us think of anxiety not as a psychiatric problem but as the staple of a busy life. We intermittently worry about everything from getting the kids to school before our next commitment to the fear that bills will outrun the bank account, or that the next mammogram will come up positive. That's normal, but always having to spend an hour on back roads because a ten-minute trip on the freeway fills you with dread is not. That brand of excessive concern probably qualifies you as suffering from a mild panic disorder, one of the most common disturbances under the overall heading of anxiety disorders. Like depression, they appear to be genetically transmitted, although, like depression, they sometimes spontaneously spring out of nowhere.

When researchers first began studying depression in women, they discovered that anxiety was often its precursor as well as its companion. That posed the question, still unanswered, of what causes anxiety and the phobias that are manifestations of it. Jack Nicholson, in the film *As Good As It Gets,* accurately portrayed one of them, obsessive compulsive disorder (OCD), when he had to arrange knife, fork, spoon, salt, glass, and napkin in exactly the same pattern before eating the same meal served by the same waitress at the same table in the same coffee shop, day after day. He knew he didn't *need* to do that, but he couldn't stop any more than the time-pressed driver can suppress panic at the thought of being on a freeway. OCD, panic, and other anxiety disorders respond well to some of the medications used for depression, suggesting that they are linked in some mysterious way.

When the Yale Study uncovered such a high incidence of anxiety disorders in the second and third generations, it revealed more problems for parents to worry about, but also more opportunities to recognize and treat them early before they become disabling. Dr. Weissman, a nifty-looking blonde with four grown children of her own, calls the lack of ongoing monitoring of children's mental health a national scandal. "If such monitoring had been in place at the time, we might have known that something was going on with those kids out in Colorado and other communities where violence has erupted so tragically," she told me. Indeed, newspaper reports on all the school killings are peppered with references to depression. "Of course it's important to know about arthritis and high cholesterol and heart disease," she added, her voice rising with indignation, "but monitoring only children's physical health isn't enough. We should be on top of their psychiatric problems at the same time."

Bolstering her point is confirmation from the Yale Study that offspring and grandkids of parents with a history of depression are generally in poorer health than those from depression-free families. Of a list of fifteen medical problems, ranging from cancer to cardiovascular disorders, prevalence rates among the depressed-parent offspring were higher than in the control group, particularly in genitourinary diseases, headaches, hospitalizations, and unconsciousness. Unconsciousness in this context means being knocked out, possibly, the researchers opine, because of accidents resulting from inadequate attention on the part of a depressed parent.

The co-occurrence of both general medical and psychological problems amplifies the burden depression places on the individual, the family, and society. Awareness of this could result in earlier identification of mental health problems and a more sophisticated approach to treating them together rather than separately as well as contributing to lower medical costs and improved long-term outcomes.

Depression in young people often manifests itself some time between puberty and the mid-twenties, with the teens a prime appearance time. Nobody knows for sure why the illness crops up, but genetic loading (that family tree again) cannot wholly account for it, as is known from twin and adoption studies. The parenting deficits imposed by depression, the environment they create for the child, and the mutually negative interactions they produce all combine with genes to push some children from being demoralized—that is to say, having the attitudes of this illness—into being measurably depressed.

All depressed moms, and fathers, too, need to be aware of this possibility for obvious reasons, and also because the earlier the onset of depression, the more likely it is to become a life-long illness. Catching it at the beginning, rather than allowing it to dig in and cause lasting problems, can make the difference between a productive and an unproductive life.

Behind the statistics and academic nomenclature are millions of kids who suffer their consequences. Offspring from families with a depressed parent in the Yale Study reported more feelings of worthlessness and had poorer overall functioning in work, family, and marriage. They were less likely to go for treatment when they felt they needed it, and were five times more apt to be dependent on drugs and alcohol. By the third generation, a whopping 49 percent of those who had both a depressed parent and grandparent already displayed some form of psychopathology, even though most of them are only twelve years old or younger.

When Adolescent Behavior Is Misread

One big stumbling block to picking up on adolescent psychiatric disorders is that many parents today have a distorted view of what represents normal behavior in teenagers. When they see their kids suddenly flipping back and forth from sullen gloom to fits of temper, they attribute it to hormones. Taking drugs and drinking, they think, are national problems, so my kid is just one of the bunch. Boys who get in frequent physical fights may earn the tag of "manly" rather than troubled, while girls obsessively concerned with their bodies are thought of as just subject to the postpuberty transformation from girl to young woman. But none of this is normal in the sense that it automatically goes with the territory. True, all adolescents do go through a period when their view of themselves and their place in society changes, and their behavior reflects that. But excessive behavior is a warning sign that something is seriously wrong; quite often it is related in some way to depressive illness.

All parents, whether or not they are depressed, need to cast an educated eye on the way their kids are acting; a mother who suspects that she or another close family relative has depression needs to be constantly alert to its possible appearance in offspring. Dismissing aggression as teenage rambunctiousness, withdrawal as adolescent sulkiness, and obsessive concern with physical traits as the postpubertal norm is both shortsighted and dangerous. Kids heading for depression leave a trail of clues that are relatively easy to pick up on once a parent knows what to look for.

I recently received a long e-mail from a teenager who purposefully surfed the Web for sites concerning depression and came across my own: depressionfallout.com. I have no way of knowing if her mom is depressed, but Melinda, as I will call her, is a perfect textbook example of a depressed fourteen-year-old girl. Her message is headed "Please help."

A Depressed Teenager's Cry for Help

"Hi," it opens, "Ummmm, let me get right to the point im 14 years old and im suffering from depression and I really dont know what to do ive tried everything I could to overcome this depression, I hate everything I dont care about anything and im always moody and always fight with my family. I just cant take it."

Many of her complaints are familiar to any parent of a teenager: A recalcitrant boyfriend who hardly speaks, endless unsuccessful efforts to stick to a diet—she says sadness always sends her back to eating again—what to do with her hair, and what clothes to wear. Everyone judges her on everything, she wails, and "it bugs." More telling is her description of last year as a "disaster," with grades way down, "friendship messed up everything was going wrong and its still continuing and I dont wanna go back to school cause I hate it."

Compounding Melinda's distress is her failure, despite all efforts, to persuade her mother that problems and feelings like these deserve parental attention and discussion. "your the only one i can talk to no one else listens," she explains.

But it is Melinda's reference to suicide that provides conclusive proof of her depression: "plzzz help me I really don't know that to do and im still young im even thinking suicidal." Unfortunately, comments such as these are not always taken seriously by parents, who chalk them up to teenage melodrama. Indeed, I recently received several e-mails from a seventeen-year-old whose closest friend, she reported, has attempted suicide three times. With only my correspondent's information to rely on, I undoubtedly lack many important details, but the e-mails clearly state that her young friend is not on antidepressant medication.

An alarming number of adolescents share Melinda's dilemma, summed up in her final sentence: "We depressed people need someone like you to listen to us." In my reply to her, I explained how common depression is, especially in her age group, and urged her to share both her e-mail and my answer to it with her mother. I also noted that for many years my own depression had often left me feeling just as she does now, suicidal thoughts and all, and that my mother's and my ignorance about this illness had caused both of us years of unhappiness. Melinda never responded.

Depression is high among girls in this age category, but boys get it, too. One eighteen-year-old, looking back on his prediagnosis days, says that his parents were concerned about his lack of interest in and inability to complete schoolwork, but his view was that "the work was neither too difficult nor too easy, it was just too uninteresting and seemed as pointless as everything else in my life." Benson remembers thinking that nothing good could possibly come of school, and that his future was bleak and held nothing positive. "I thought," he added, "that I was more trouble than I was worth. My presence was creating more disturbance than I thought my absence would."

Many children of both sexes display symptoms of depression and of the anxiety disorders and phobias that so often precede full-fledged illness. These kids aren't always teenage copies of depressed adults. They tend to sleep and eat more rather than much less then usual. Although they do lose interest in things they have previously enjoyed such as sports, friends, dating, hobbies, and school, they are also irritable, moody, hostile, and reactive. And they are wildly sensitive to rejection, whether real or perceived. Unlike Melinda, when asked why they usually say they don't know.

Suicide Among Adolescents

Kay Redfield Jamison, best-selling author and professor of psychiatry at Johns Hopkins, devotes her latest book, *Night Falls Fast,* to suicide. In it she describes her almost successful attempt, at age seventeen, to end her life when it "fell fast into a dark night." In the midst of her first depression, she writes, "I became knowledgeable about suicide in something other than an existential, adolescent way. For much of each day during several months of my senior year in high school, I thought about when, whether, where, and how to kill myself. I learned to present to others a face at variance with my mind; ferreted out the location of two or three nearby tall buildings with unprotected stairwells; discovered the fastest flows of morning traffic, and learned how to load my father's gun."

The harrowing statistics cited by Professor Jamison serve as a launching pad for her wake-up call. Nothing short of a national program to reverse the growing numbers of young suicides and suicide attempts will do, and the country is lucky in at last having a surgeon-general, David Satcher, who agrees and is taking on the task. In the United States, between 1980 and 1992, the rates of suicide among children aged ten to fourteen increased by 120 percent. In 1995, more teenagers and young adults died from suicide than died from cancer, heart disease, AIDS, influenza, birth defects, and stroke combined. The 1997 Youth Risk Behavior Surveillance Survey, Professor Jamison reports, canvassed more than sixteen thousand ninth- through twelfth-grade students (fifteen- to eighteen-year-olds) across the country. Fully 20 percent, or one in five, said they had "seriously considered" attempting suicide in the preceding twelve months; 16 percent said they had drawn up a plan.

Melinda, in her e-mail, is up front about her thoughts of suicide. Benson makes more roundabout references to his suspicion that his presence was causing more trouble than his absence would. To a tuned-in, informed parent, both are signaling adolescent depression's most tragic outcome. Many people cling to the fallacious idea that someone who articulates thoughts of suicide will not attempt it. This is a dangerous myth. In truth, it is a reliable indicator of something gone terribly wrong.

Today's teenagers are far more apt to take their lives than were their parents, who in turn have suicide rates higher than those of the preceding generation. The rates of both completed and attempted suicides are variously attributed to breakdown of the family unit and all its related ills, easy availability of guns, increased substance abuse, and stressful economic and social conditions among many segments of the population. While all of these are important, according to Professor Jamison the closest association is with the apparent rise in psychiatric disturbances, particularly depression, among the young. To that can be added a lack of appreciation for the power of this illness to distort the thoughts and feelings of its sufferers.

So what specifically can a parent, especially a depressed one, do about all this? An overwhelming majority of researchers who study the effects of maternal depression on children have concentrated solely on the negatives rather than how to prevent them. A notable exception is Dr. William R. Beardslee, professor of psychiatry at Harvard Medical School and chairman of psychiatry at both Children's Hospital and the Judge Baker Children's Center. Dr. Beardslee is an optimist, and with good reason: His studies indicate that preventive steps can be taken to avoid the negative effects and to increase resilience in children of affectively ill parents. The key, he says, is to approach the problem as a family by learning the medical facts about the illness and discussing depressive behavior and symptoms together—not as vague generalizations, but specifically, within the context of each individual family and its members. What that adds up to is demystification of depression, modulation of shame and guilt (remember, children often see themselves as responsible in some way for their parent's illness), increased capacity for putting things in a more hopeful perspective, and development of a sense of mastery over the situation rather than a feeling of being trapped and helpless.

Dr. Beardslee's prevention strategy stresses the need for an ongoing dialogue. One family conference isn't going to solve the problem, which may fluctuate as the depression waxes or wanes. "Keep talking," he urges, and make sure that the concerns of all members are addressed. If one child is six and another eleven, each will need an age-appropriate explanation. If the parent's depression sticks around for several years, the six-year-old will be eight, and his or her needs and capacity for understanding will have changed considerably.

Dr. Beardslee has written a manual—titled *Cognitive Psychosocial Intervention*—that is addressed to the wide range of health professionals who work with children of a depressed parent, but it is nonetheless easy to understand and remarkably free of jargon. He told me that my readers can request a copy from his office. You will find the title and address under Suggested Reading in the appendix of this book. Some commonsense suggestions of my own are provided below, first for avoiding or mitigating the effects of one's own depression, followed by advice on how to recognize and help kids who have or are at risk for developing this illness.

Prescriptive Advice for Depressed Moms

Begin by checking how you feel and are behaving against what you have learned so far. If you have any reason to believe that you meet the diagnostic criteria, the first step is to go see the family doctor. At the risk of sounding grandiose, unless he or she is exceptionally well informed, you and I probably know more about depression than the doctor does, so be precise and insistent about your symptoms. Given the pressure under which most HMO physicians operate to take the least time-consuming route to a solution, you will probably receive a prescription for one of the most commonly used antidepressants. If nothing changes for the better within four to six weeks, go back with a request that you be switched to another brand, or ask for a referral to a psychiatrist. If your insurance permits, enter into a course of short-term psychotherapy, often an excellent adjunct to medication. (Chapter 8, All About Treatment, gives more details on this subject.)

In the meantime, listen to what your children are saying and observe their behavior carefully. If it has changed for the worse in recent months, something is going on that you should know about. Try to give your offspring's concerns and miseries equal billing with your own since they are probably related. Explain—not in an offhand manner but explicitly—that you love, respect, and admire them, and that however you may have been acting has nothing to do with them. Teenagers are old and wise enough to understand this and your assurances will do much to ease their guilt and hurt.

Help them do whatever they enjoy and are good at, despite your own lack of pleasure. Encourage the singer to join the glee club, the wannabe Gretzky to play more hockey, and the budding botanist to start a garden in the backyard. Buy the artist a book on drawing, take the bowler bowling, help the cook make brownies, and let the racing car driver wash your Bentley.

Go to a movie or watch the Discovery Channel together, and talk about it afterward. Spend at least five or ten minutes each day talking about the lead story in the newspaper.

If they are doing poorly in school, ask them if they have any ideas about why. Pay attention to what they say; if they answer that they don't know, ask them if it's because things have been difficult at home lately. Explain that you recognize your moods as a source of upset and stress, and that you will try to do better from now on. Choose a warning signal word, maybe "Whoops," and invite them to use it if they catch you slipping into old habits. In sum, make your child feel cherished by and important to you.

A Parental Prescription for Kids at High Risk

As always, the number-one prescriptive need is for information about depression in young people and the anxiety disorders associated with them and for greater awareness of your offspring's behavior. A child's natural mood is one of exuberance; when it switches to chronic boredom, apathy, extreme moodiness, or overaggression, it is quite possible you have a Melinda or a Benson on your hands.

Look for other telling signs: no luck in making or keeping friends, constant expressions of self-doubt and self-criticism, dwelling on trivial defeats, and, particularly in the case of girls, laments about their face and figure. Watch for clues that they feel unloved, unwanted, an outsider who doesn't fit in anywhere.

Anxiety disorders are clustered around specific types of behavior. Panic disorder, which starts in adolescence and picks up speed in the twenties, is one of the most common. Attacks come out of nowhere, overwhelming the child with feelings of fear and dread; the heart pounds wildly; it is hard to breathe and easy to think, "I'm going to die," especially the first few times it happens. If attacks keep coming, the child understandably takes self-protective steps. He or she will want to hole up at home where it is relatively safe, resist school, and avoid sports and other group activities. This can lead to agoraphobia, which so incapacitates some adults that they rarely leave the house and lead narrow, constricted lives.

Social anxiety disorder, alternatively called social phobia, is also common. The dilemma anxiety disorder experts face is drawing a line between the real thing and the apprehension many of us experience in certain situations. Lots of people get damp palms and turn pink when they have to speak in public, but for my friend Mary, just responding to a toast at the family dinner table is an act of great courage. Before my depression was treated, I had a glass of wine or two before going to a party in the hope it would subdue the feelings of inadequacy the other guests elicited in me; all that did was ensure I got drunk. Now I go without the wine and my natural shyness usually wanes. Mary has a social phobia, I no longer do; it's a question of degree.

Normal adolescents are anxious about their identity, sexuality, and social acceptance and competence, and disgusted with their parents' failure to move with the times. The initial assessment of whether they have shifted from normalcy to aberrance is up to parents, since they see their kids in action from infancy on. Be on the lookout as well for the physical signs of anxiety: sweating, trembling, and palpitations. If either parent suffers from depression, they should seriously consider taking their child to a specialist with the knowledge and tools to assess accurately the behavior displayed.

Much the same advice pertains to younger kids. Their best-known disorder is separation anxiety. This drives them to cling, terrified, to their mother's skirts while other children shed a few tears and then skip blithely in to school or their friend's birthday party. They are also inclined to simple phobias, as, for instance, an unreasonable terror of animals or subways. Youngsters often grow out of such fears, just as they grow out of shyness and dependency. But when problems like these persist beyond a reasonable time, or if new ones pop up, they may need professional help.

Always bear in mind that anxiety disorders are serious illnesses. Anxiety in the first grade, one study showed, significantly predicts anxiety later on. By the time the anxious first-graders were fifth-graders, they scored lower in math and reading than their anxiety-free peers.

Myrna Weissman points out in a recent update on the Yale Study that anxiety in young children is frequently discounted as inconsequential, a part of normal development and something the child will outgrow. "Our work with [depressed] parents," she writes, "has shown that in high-risk families early anxiety symptoms are a risk factor for the later development of Major Mood Disorder [MMD]," the most disabling form of depression.

Discuss what is going on with your husband or partner, involve him in solutions, and make sure he reads this book from cover to cover, especially Chapter 9, A Father's Role in a Mother's Depression. Should you be finding life with him one long unresolved argument, the next chapter will explain why.

7

Enter Depression, Exit Marital Harmony

A family is a lot more than a collection of individuals who live under one roof. To become a functioning unit that endures, each member must value not only him- or herself but also the others, and must feel valued in return. This sense of interconnection and interdependence is what makes a family pull together instead of apart. Coherence engenders harmony and mutual trust because everyone pretty much knows the behavior expected of them and can rely on the others to act accordingly. When it works, all feel safe and life seems predictable; all share the sense that everything is going to work out okay.

The depression of one parent does away with family coherence as surely as any of the other hard knocks that can unsettle wedded bliss. In fact, keeping a marriage solidly intact and mutually rewarding is virtually impossible when a partner of either sex suffers from this illness. Not only do they no longer behave as expected; they appear to have undergone a personality change for the worse. All their good qualities—patience, reasonableness, affectionate cheerfulness, and responsiveness—have flown out the window, to be replaced by an array of bad spirits. When this happens, both the non-depressed spouse and the children start a journey into the troubled territory I call depression fallout.

Depression Fallout in a Marriage

Depression fallout, provoked by prolonged proximity to someone depressed, is the unhappy progression from initial confusion to self-blame, then to demoralization, then to resentment and anger, and finally to the desire to escape the source of so much stress and unhappiness. Nowhere are the five interlocking stages of this syndrome so evident as in an endangered marriage or relationship. "She" and "he" are interchangeable in the explanation that follows.

Stage one, confusion, leads directly to stage two, self-blame. When a previously "good" wife and mother suddenly starts acting like a bundle of nastiness, everyone, particularly her spouse or partner, wonders what is going on. Unsuspecting of the illness, he is confused and bewildered. Searching for explanations, he comes up with all kinds of possibilities. Perhaps his wife is worried about losing her job, or the family finances, or a child's druggie friends. Maybe she's sulking about the vacation that had to be put off, or suspects a medical problem and doesn't want to worry the family. Then comes the default explanation: She's having an affair. Attempts to find out what's the matter are thwarted by her refusal, or perhaps inability, to talk and to explain what's the matter.

In the face of what looks like silent reproach, the stage-two sufferer assumes blame for the change: He's done or said something that has been misinterpreted, left uncelebrated an important anniversary, or spent too much time in the office and been grumpy at home. He tries making peace overtures, but neither affectionate concern, nor flowers, nor the suggestion of a romantic weekend make a dent in the demeanor of the depressed spouse, who continues to be critical, cross, and dissatisfied.

Soon the confused self-blamer is deep in the heart of depression fallout's third stage, demoralization. As defined by the dictionary, the verb demoralize means to deprive a person of spirit, courage, and discipline; to destroy their morale; and to throw them into disorder and confusion. Demoralization is a lot like a mirror image of depression, minus the somatic symptoms such as poor sleep and a failing appetite. Like the children of overly critical depressed moms, everyone with depression fallout eventually comes to suspect they really may be as flawed as the picture drawn by the depressed person. With self-pity seeping from every pore, they sing the depression fallout mantra: As far as she is concerned, nothing I do is right, nothing I do is enough, and everything wrong is my fault.

Dragging their demoralized state with them, they trudge on to stage four: resentment plus anger. Under such circumstances, who wouldn't feel put-upon, surly, and hot-tempered? Indeed, who wouldn't feel justified in displaying righteous anger? As one husband who had asked his long-depressed wife to please keep the dogs out of the room where he was laying tile explained, "She literally nearly had a breakdown over it. I said I'd rope the room off and the dogs could go in and out the front door, but she said that was stupid. Since her reaction made no sense and I didn't understand, I did the only rational thing a person could do, I got mad. I told her she was acting like a child and that I was sick and tired of this kind of bullshit. What else could I do when I'm in yet another catch-22 situation but get mad?"

Feeling trapped by so many externally induced negative feelings, most depression fallout sufferers proceed to stage five:

a longing to escape from that once lovable and dependable person, the wellspring of their marital dreams and desires. Stage five sufferers try to go on loving their spouse, the pre-depression one, but demoralization and anger are memory eradicators. One wife, only very recently put on medication, acknowledged with gratitude the efforts her husband had made over the years to be supportive of her through "all those horrible feelings depression brings." Nonetheless, he wants them to separate indefinitely. "He keeps saying that he is no longer in love with me, that he cares for me but the feelings of being in love with one another are no longer there. That all that's left is numbness."

Once it digs in, depression fallout is hard to kick. Things do not go automatically back to how they were before the depression began; sometimes family life never returns to its former comfortable state. As another depression fallout husband says, "My wife's not the only person to change. I'm not the same either. I used to be a very high-energy person, very athletic, but now it's very difficult to do anything for myself. I feel like I'm putting my life on hold, waiting for my wife to come back, which happens for a few hours once in a while. Loving her and trying to reason with her isn't working," he said, "and I'm left feeling rejected again. How do you get a person you love to see what's going on?"

In *Should You Leave?*, psychiatrist Peter Kramer provides an answer of sorts. "Many studies," he writes, "indicate that divorce results in depression. My belief is that, at least as often, undiagnosed depression antedates and causes divorce." I agree, but it doesn't really matter which is the chicken and which is the egg. Either way, this illness fills the divorce courts, usually without the awareness of either protagonist that the real villains are depression and depression fallout. Because of that, any percentage of depression as a mediating cause has to be pure guesswork, but surely it is very high.

What makes depression within a relationship so insidious is that it kills the possibility of good communication. All the negative adjectives hitched to both depression and depression fallout are "hot." They stir up tempers and spark unrelated flash fires, just as they led the laundry mother to make her peevish points. Anything and everything leads to contention, but no one can get a firm handle on constructive solutions.

There is always a plethora of words for complaints and criticism, but the ones that accurately describe the feelings underneath them are usually beyond reach. Depression sufferers resort to tears, anger, or the misleading claim that they would be just fine if everybody would shut up and leave them alone. Even Martha Manning, a practicing psychologist with superb verbal skills, could not find a way to express to her daughter Keara how her crippling depression made her feel, how remote and disconnected. For the vast majority, words won't come.

To research my first book, *How You Can Survive When They're Depressed: Living and Coping with Depression Fallout*, I attended during two years a support group for family members of someone suffering from depression or manic depression. As the only person there with depression, I once volunteered to explain what it was like and so help them fathom their depressed person's state of mind. I started out cockily and must have sounded like an amateur shrink. "Depression has nothing to do with just feeling unhappy or sad," I announced, "it's more like existing in a gray, colorless void, like you're floating and drowning in it at the same time. It's, it's . . ." I never reached the end of my perky lecture. Choked up and battling tears, I stopped in midsentence, surveying the sea of expectant faces waiting for wisdom and insight yet unable to proceed.

In truth, my performance probably provided the group with a better indication of the horrible angst of this illness than the explanation of an informed, never-depressed professional. While the members caught on to what was happening, unaware spouses have no inkling that crying jags and unresponsiveness are accurate nonverbal answers to questions like, "What on earth is the matter with you?" Instead, they interpret them as making scenes or stonewalling.

Sex and Depression Don't Mix

Sex is a wonderful method of communication and mutual pleasuring. Innumerable couples head for bed as a way of erasing the aftereffects of an unpleasant exchange. While it is true that sex is sometimes employed as a Band-Aid, satisfying desire while postponing settlement of underlying problems, more often it is a genuine expression of mutual love and affection. Part of sex is nonverbal, but hand in hand with the physicality go all those sweet mutterings and murmurings. Taken together, they're good medicine for marriage. Most couples in which one member is depressed don't get to have good sex; in fact, they often have no sex at all. Under that overall heading "Loss of interest in activities previously enjoyed" is sex, because depression suppresses both desire and performance.

Rejection in the bedroom can be devastating, especially if no one knows the real reason for it. A natural reaction is to find other, more belittling reasons, the two standard being, "He can't make love with me because he no longer desires me" and "She doesn't want to make love with me because she's fooling around with someone else." Both will heighten an already charged atmosphere. Sexual problems are never easy to talk about, and so give free rein to the imagination of troubled partners.

Even more damaging is the cruelty and viciousness that can

characterize depression-speak by both sexes. One long-married spouse of a depressed man observed that she didn't have much to say about sex because there wasn't any anymore, but she added that was only part of her problem. "At one point I gained a lot of weight. I was so miserable. Eating was one of the few pleasures I could count on and I blew up like a blimp. Ben said to me one day, "You're so fat I'm never going to sleep with you again." I don't think I've ever felt so awful, so low and hopeless and ugly. What made it even worse was that he already wasn't sleeping with me, hadn't been for several years, but of course by saying that, he made feel that it was my fault." Although less inclined to express their feelings so openly, plenty of men with a depressed partner must have similar complaints.

An Exercise in Couple Despair

James C. Coyne, professor of psychology at the University Pennsylvania, began looking at the effects of depression on others long before most researchers. Early on he discovered that even strangers will draw away from a depressed person in their midst. In 1985 he published, with his collaborators Jana Kahn and Gayle Margolin, a paper aptly titled "Depression and Marital Disagreement: The Social Construction of Despair." The centerpiece of their study, which involved seven couples with a depressed husband, seven with a depressed wife, and fourteen in which neither couple was depressed, was a ten-minute discussion on what the two considered a relevant marital issue. Before the discussion started, all participants filled out questionnaires about their marital satisfaction and typical approaches to conflict. How would you describe your own and your partner's behavior when tackling a problem together? Who listens well to whom? Who flings insults and engages in name-calling? Who sulks or pouts?

Immediately following the discussion, all rated their own and their spouse's performance, and noted also how they personally had felt during and after the exercise. Were they angry, hurt, frustrated? Had they had thoughts like "Get out of my life" or "It's hopeless"? And what adjectives would they apply to their partner's performance? Had they been dominant, agreeable, mistrusting, remote, inhibited, aggressive, sociable, exhibitionistic? Plenty of choice there, and unsurprisingly the couples that included a depressed spouse chose all the negative ones. Furthermore, within such pairings both partners were equally dissatisfied with their marriage, and the non-depressed spouses admitted that they, too, had been unhelpful.

Perhaps most telling of all, the depressed spouses thought poorly of their mate's performance but found no fault with their own. Both members of these couples did agree, however, that the other was hostile, unsupportive, mistrusting, and competitive or detached. All were sad and angry, and, I assume, relieved when the discussion came to an end.

All the way along the line, the depressed-member couples fared worse than the control couples. Like Constance Hammen's mother-child pairs, they struggled intensely with their topic but couldn't resolve it. They kept running down blind alleys and reiterating how hurt and frustrated they were. One depressed participant put it this way: "We are not very good at communicating. We hide and deny our feelings, and when they do come out, we don't even get to what is bothering us." Couples like these feel helpless; their attempts to change things for the better are so misdirected that they actually serve to maintain the tension between them. Coyne points out the paradox: They are hostile and aggressive at the same time that they are withdrawn. "Withdrawal," he writes with a researcher's restraint, "allows problems and resentments to accumulate so that when discussions do occur they are more intense and hurtful, with little opportunity for resolution."

Many depressed spouses hold a mirror to their own self-hating misery and project that image onto their mate. "My wife tells me that I have no capacity for love," one depression fallout husband observed to me. "She says I have no ability to provide support, that I have a black view of the world, that I am a liar, that I am domineering, that I am manipulative, that I am deceitful, that I conceive and operate remarkably wicked schemes, that I am irrationally suspicious and resentful, and that I suffer from depression." This is a litany I have heard from many spouses of either sex. Like many other storytellers, this husband goes on to say that his wife "has just about convinced me she is right about my having this illness. But how do you know," he plaintively queries, "whether you're suffering from depression or depression fallout?"

That's a good question. It is not uncommon for depression fallout to transmute into real depression. While the typically toxic family environment and the stress and anxiety it generates are surely contributing factors, genes may also be a cause, thanks to what the experts call assortative mating.

Assortative Mating

Life would be beautiful if we all naturally selected a partner who was a perfect match, someone who shared our values and faith, and who miraculously compensated for our deficits and helped us overcome our weaknesses. There are plenty of poor marriages and poor parents to testify that we don't, but in the case of depression, unfortunate pre-altar decisions are often the result of assortative mating. People with the same problems, such as a vulnerability to a depressive illness, anxiety, or a predilection for alcohol and drug abuse, seek each other out like bloodhounds.

According to Professor Coyne and researcher Geraldine Downey of Columbia University, other studies have shown that more than 50 percent of the depressed women surveyed were married to men with a history of psychiatric problems, often including depression, that predated their union, and that an equal percentage experienced spousal abuse. In one community sample of depressed wives, about 25 percent had husbands with a history of depression while a fifth chose substance abusers.

As do other researchers, Coyne and Downey suspect that what may attract such men and women to each other in the first place are commonalities in their respective earlier life experiences. One can easily imagine them comparing notes on a first or second date. "Oh, my gosh, me too! No matter how hard I tried, nothing I did was ever good enough to please my mom," or, "That sounds just like mine. They'd start hitting the bottle as soon as Dad came home and it was fight, fight, fight all the time." Perhaps each had stood, guilty and fearful, outside their parents' bedroom door, listening to the anger erupting within. Shared memories like these are strong mating glue, but they are also indicators that depression may be present in both family trees. When like chooses like in this respect, the odds in favor of marital bliss will worsen.

A Missing Sense of Partnership

The communication difficulties created by such matings pose yet another barrier to harmony. Depression fallout spouses fail to express overtly the love and support that are as necessary to a depressed person as good medical attention. Even among those who are knowledgeable about this illness and its needs, I never hear unequivocal expressions of them. They are uttered only in the form of a complaint: "I love my partner, but," and then come the negatives.

The backbone of every good marriage, regardless of the role sex may play in it, is shared intimacy. All those extraneous details like who got fired in the office and what your friend said about her husband are actually interesting to happy partners. Half the fun of going to a party is coming home and gossiping about the evening. Most important of all is being able to confide private hopes and fears, secure in the knowledge that they fall on empathetic ears. Exchanging views, meeting challenges, and solving problems together make for security and marital harmony. When this sense of partnership is missing, a relationship is in trouble. Combined with the depressed partner's inability to articulate despair other than through withdrawal, criticism, and anger, it becomes a can't-miss recipe for discord.

The high-voltage anger and the absence of affection and companionship easily isolate such couples from their social environment. Washing dirty linen in public leads to few invitations to socialize unless you are Elizabeth Taylor or Richard Burton. When relatives and friends attempt to intervene as mediators, they are drawn into the fray and find themselves branded as meddlers, not peacemakers. Even when the depression has been diagnosed and treated, the persistent stigma attached to it leads to white lies. "I'm so sorry we can't have dinner tonight but my wife has a migraine," or is overtired, or has to work late at the office. The "liar" finds the role distasteful and resents the spouse who made it necessary, who will in turn become more aggressive, withdrawn, or both when blamed.

Lacking other outlets, the increasing negativism has no place to go beyond the confines of the family's most intimate core: mother, father, and children.

What Happens to the Children

The profound unease that living with warring parents induces is like living in a minefield; uncertainty and unpredictability are everywhere. There is no order, no rules and regulations that can be counted on, no secure boundaries. Parental efforts to hide their discord are well-meaning but fruitless if the child's antennae are fully sensitized to what is going on. Offspring, anticipating the inevitable blowup, live in a state of abiding unease. There are other unsettling concerns. Inward-facing couples trying to cope with their own problems can appear to their kids as parents who no longer love them. There are issues of loyalty as well as loss, and of guilt and self-blame when children mistakenly assume responsibility for the discord.

All kids suffer when parents don't get along, but the wild card of depression ups the ante in ways already indicated. Indeed, Dr. Gabor Keitner of Brown University, who has campaigned for recognition of depression as a family's problem rather than just one person's illness, blames much of the school behavior described in the previous chapter not on the depressed mother but on the marital discord her illness generates. School and home are not easily separated. As debts pile up, offspring handle them as best they can. The babies of depressed mothers, for instance, develop coping styles appropriate to their infantile needs and apply them to strangers. Older kids find more complex methods of dealing with their distress, as illustrated by the two following stories told to me.

Cordelia Brown: "I Was the Source of All Their Problems"

Cordelia was an unwanted child even before she emerged, tense and screaming, from her mother's womb. Both parents blamed her for problems of their own making. Her father was four months behind in the rent when he learned of her impending arrival and held his wife accountable for the unexpected and expensive addition to the family; her mother identified her daughter as the source of her husband's critical attitude. The arrival some years later of a planned and wanted son did little to improve Cordelia's standing in the family, and the tense and screaming infant grew up to be a tense and miserable schoolgirl, handicapped by not one but two depressed parents. Her mother, when it was discovered she had for years been recklessly self-treating her lethargy with multiple prescriptions for thyroid wheedled from unsuspecting doctors, turned the full force of her resulting depression on Cordelia, then ten years old. While her father's depression rendered him a silent, self-effacing man who sleepwalked numbly through the motions of life, her mother's was of the intrusive, critical, and manipulative variety.

Neither parent lost the resentment for the firstborn who had weakened an already compromised marriage. Constant oblique references to the timing of her arrival, to the precarious family economics back then and the marital dissatisfactions and disputes they spawned were part of the family dialogue. Even a less sensitive child would have picked up on the hints and innuendo. Cordelia knew she was unwelcome.

Mrs. Brown worked hard to transform her disappointing daughter into a person who more closely resembled herself. "You don't want to be like poor so-and-so," she would say, naming a shy, inept, and joyless classmate. "School offered me no shelter from my unhappiness at home," Cordelia told me, "because it was just the wrong kind of school for me. It would have been far more suitable for my mother's temperament, which was of course the main reason she chose it. I studied hard because it was the one thing I knew I was good at. But it's not good for one's well-being to be miserable at any school for years and years!"

Making friends was difficult. She was constantly afraid of being exposed as vulnerable, a fear, she says today, that grew rather than receded as the years passed. She hides it well. A slim, brisk woman who speaks in perfectly parsed sentences, she is gifted with a Proustian memory that allows her to retain and revisit memories that appear free of layers of invention. Although her recollections are unpleasant ones, she relates them with style and not a trace of self-pity.

One such memory is of standing in the school cafeteria lunch line and announcing that she had no intention of giving up anything for Lent. When another child chorused that she wasn't going to either, Cordelia tried for a friendly connection. Sticking out a hand she said, "Put it there, pardner," but the girl withdrew hers and refused to shake. Unaware that her classmate was Jewish, Cordelia was crushed by the rejection and wondered, as she always did, what she had done wrong. She says her mother announced on her fourth birthday that she was now too old to be punished, too grown up to behave badly enough to warrant it. Yet even the normal transgressions of a four-year-old, knocking over a glass of milk or dirtying a clean dress, were punished. Self-fault and tentativeness became ingrained in Cordelia's nature. The sense of being at fault and inadequate took root early in her life and has endured. "I have always," she admits, "felt undeserving and lesser than other people."

She describes her father as being "at bottom a kind man, but with no instinct for self-preservation." It is easy from her description to picture him listless and helpless either to overcome his depression or to comfort his child. In his mind, Cordelia's unplanned birth, his disappointing marriage, and his own suffocating illness must have been irrevocably intertwined. Indeed, his daughter always had the guilty feeling that his illness, like so much else wrong in the family, was her fault. "He had no skill for handling the manipulations, vaporings, and anxieties of my mother. She was very unhappy with him and remained so through the day he died. There was no shelter to be had from him."

Her stepfather, a recently retired doctor whose social standing appealed to her mother, had no difficulty in dealing with those manipulating vapors. He didn't hesitate to talk back and to tell his wife what was wrong with her. Cordelia's mother complained to her that he was a sadist "just like all surgeons." Departing the family, he left a Mrs. Brown who, her friends opined, had been poorly treated by two husbands and had the added drag of an ungrateful daughter. "Below the surface of the bubbling personality she presented to the world," says Cordelia, "there was a humorlessness, a lack of relish for life. She was entirely a product of her invention and a consummate actress, but underneath it an ungenerous person. My father and her friends never saw her shadow as clearly as I."

Cordelia, like so many other children who grow up with a depressed mother, admits to a lifelong problem with intimacy, although her own failed marriage blessed her with four children to whom she is close. "Not having a role model when one is young makes intimacy very difficult," she said. "There are endless fears that you are both unlovable and unable to love. Behind the curtain we feel ourselves so imperfect that I think it makes it difficult for people to stay around us." Years of therapy, she says, have helped her to better understand both herself and the family dynamic. Although she staunchly believes she has never suffered from depression, she does admit that there was a time some years ago when suicide tempted her.

Cordelia's story is only one version of how depression-driven marital discord can impact on offspring. Other interviewees have shared accounts that added alcoholism and spousal violence to an already toxic mix. Sam's mother was neither violent nor alcoholic, but her eternal lack of energy and self-absorption set her poles apart from an insensitive husband and two rambunctious boys. Wrapped in wretched loneliness, she pulled Sam, the last to arrive, into her web and kept him there for seventeen years.

Sam the Nobody

"I was like a live-in therapist," explained Sam, with whom I fell into conversation during a friend's birthday party for her son. His mother's undiagnosed chronic depression had come to her via Sam's grandmother, whom he describes as "practically living in the cellar"; his grandfather was kind but often drunk. Depression-related traits were to be found in both branches of the family, so perhaps it was assortative mating that led his mother to marry a selfish, abusive man.

Strikingly handsome at thirty-one, Sam must have been the sort of baby that passersby ogle and want to hug. His elder brothers were permitted a normal childhood, full of jubilant rowdiness, sports, and dating. They were close to their father, unlike Sam, who early on was co-opted as his mother's constant companion. When the others took off for the beach, Sam accompanied her to museums and concerts, for which he was derided as a momma's boy. Along with the taunts and disdain went occasional beatings. "When Mom stood up for me, I got whomped by Dad."

Even as a very young child, Sam listened attentively as his mother filled his ears with complaints about her husband and the lack of love and beauty in her world. What she didn't get from the other family members, she sought from her son so it was important, he said, that he knew precisely how she felt. "I saw it as my job to comfort and love her." Whatever she thought, Sam tried to think too. "I understood her Doomsday approach to life. We were so close," he told me, "that when together it seemed to me the same emotions flowed back and forth between us. I tried to explain and interpret things for her. When she cried I held her." Although he was unaware of it at the time, the underlying message communicated by his mother ✓ was, "Thou shalt not grow up and leave me." During her rare absences from home, hospitalized for appendicitis and for pneumonia, Sam felt abandoned. "I didn't seem to matter much to anyone except when taking care of Mother," he recollects.

As he grew older, living in the cocoon of her depression became unbearably suffocating. At seventeen, in a last-ditch effort at liberty, Sam won a scholarship to a college at the other end of the state and used the money saved from summer jobs to see a therapist. The light, he says, came pouring in. "I learned that everything was always about Mother. That she addressed her issues through me. When you're always expected to take care of others, you come to believe you have no right to care about yourself. Self-esteem was not a word in my vocabulary." To this day, even passing contemplation of his own needs conjures up in Sam a sense of impending danger, an amorphous fear of being shut out, abandoned, and punished.

After leaving home but before the therapy that enabled him to face and deal with those seventeen years of self-effacement, Sam went into the bathroom one day with a knife, prepared to slit his wrists and die. Fortunately, he called his parents to tell them of his intention. His mother wept and said he couldn't do that to her; his father said to go ahead, he had two normal sons and that was enough for him. Their reactions caused Sam to reconsider; on reflection he decided his life was important to him. Thirteen years later, he still hasn't figured out what to do with it or whom to share it with, but snuffing it out is no longer an option.

While it would be easy to label Sam's mother as selfish and destructive, that simplistic judgment is unfair. Living in a rural community decades before Prozac became a household word, she knew nothing about depression or its dominance of her life. Devoutly Christian, she turned to her faith and her son for strength and endurance. Neither could cure her illness, and Sam became an innocent victim of it, just as Cordelia became an innocent victim of her mother's depression.

Everyone pays a toll for depression's entry into a household. Each member tries to dodge it but most choose a losing strategy. The depressed spouse rejects any possibility of being "mentally ill" and opts instead in favor of stress or some similarly benign cause for their negativism. The non-depressed partner languishes in depression fallout, resentful and waiting for a chance to escape without guilt. Children are swept up in the turmoil and cope as best they can. Much of this marital and childhood unhappiness depression would abate if treatment were sought. How to go about getting it is the subject of the next chapter, but first, some interim advice for couples threatened by this illness. The following section, although addressed to depressed wives and mothers, applies as well to families in which the husband/father is the depression sufferer. I advise members of both sexes to read it together.

A Prescription for Depression-Driven Marital Discord

The standard prescriptive advice given to bickering, antagonistic couples—Sit down together and talk about what's bothering you—is hard to apply when the discord is caused by depression, because, as one of the participants in Coyne's study admitted, such couples hide and deny their feelings, and when they do come out, they don't even get to what is bothering them. But there are ways to leaven the atmosphere until the nirvana of post-treatment is a reality.

- First, *learn the real facts about depression.* Neophytes are convinced they already know everything about it yet even informed, intelligent people hold simplistic and misleading views. For example, they confuse depression and manic depression, two distinctly different varieties of depressive disorder. When they hear the word phobia, they think only of spiders and heights. One friend of mine, smart enough to be partner in a law firm, thought that "clinical" depression meant it was severe enough to require a stay in a clinic or hospital; actually the term means that it meets the diagnostic criteria laid out in Chapter 3. Faulty beliefs like these explain why there are so many walking wounded who think they haven't got the real thing.

  The bibliography of this book lists titles that cover the subject from varying viewpoints. The Internet has more than two thousand sites dealing with it that can be reached through all the search engines; some Web addresses are included in the appendix. Start a clipping file compiled from the steady stream of articles in local and national newspapers and magazines. Check radio and TV schedules; excellent programs about depression are frequent reruns.

Several national organizations, including the National Alliance for the Mentally Ill (NAMI) and the National Depressive and Manic Depressive Association (NDMDA), are consumer-oriented and offer both materials and advice. Both have state and local chapters throughout the country; most of them have support groups both for those who suffer from depression and for their friends and family members. A nominal membership fee will get you a monthly newsletter with updates on research advances, articles on insurance coverage, federal and state mental health policies, and other relevant topics. The National Foundation for Depressive Illness (NAFDI) has a hotline, responds to requests for information, and maintains a list of psychiatrists around the country. Their 800 numbers are given in the appendix of this book.

• Treatment is the ultimate solution, but it takes preparation. Usually, persuading someone you love to seek help is *an exercise in artful persuasion.* Depressed people fall into two broad categories: those who welcome the news that they suffer from a common medical illness and rush to do something about it, and those who equate depression with a weak character, lack of fortitude, and shame. "Mentally ill" is an accurate but unfortunate term, conjuring up in most people visions of loony bins and deadbeats. Unfortunate terminology aside, depression is a mental illness; its source is in the brain and is expressed by the brain's organ, the mind. Nonetheless, using the term is a poor method of shifting your mate from category two into category one. The best words to use are "common" and "treatable."

Asking your depressive to read a book is akin to asking a toddler to tackle an encyclopedia. Given the lethargy and poor concentration hitched to depression, short pithy pieces plucked from newspapers and magazines are preferable. Choose the right moment to hand them over, which is not in the middle of a heated argument. Alternatively, leave one lying about opened to a meaty page, as though you had been interrupted in the middle.

Be on the lookout for a friend, someone your depressed partner knows and trusts, who has been through a bout of depression and sought treatment for it; ask that person to have a chat with your mate. It won't be very difficult to find one. Sooner or later everybody who lives with a depressed person drops a clue: "John never wants to do anything these days," or, "Ellen's constant negativity is really getting me down." In them you will discover both an old hand at depression fallout with whom you can compare notes and a fellow sufferer who can talk to your spouse with empathy beyond your reach. Mike Wallace of *60 Minutes* fame says he came to recognize his own depression through conversations with two of his closest friends, Art Buchwald and William Styron, both similarly afflicted.

- Suggesting the possibility of depression is touchy. Because of the persistent stigma it carries, your spouse or partner (or parent) may take anything you say as a character assault, the equivalent of an accusation of weakness and laziness. Ease into the subject by citing the one-in-five prevalence rate and follow up by listing some of the distinguished depressives who have made headlines in their chosen professions.

Mike Wallace and his two friends qualify, as do the outstanding women listed in Chapter 3. So do Abraham Lincoln, J. P. Morgan, Michelangelo, former Mets pitcher Pete Harnisch, Sir Walter Scott, the current prime minister of Norway, Winston Churchill, poets Robert Frost, Keats, Shelley, Wordsworth, and T. S. Eliot, billionaire Ted Turner, writers Mark Twain, Charles Dickens, William Faulkner, and F. Scott Fitzgerald, jazz great Ronnie Scott, Handel, Schumann, Irving Berlin, Noel Coward, and ex-linebacker now turned actor Brian the "Boz" Bosworth. *The New York Times* quoted the last not long ago as saying, "Even compared to the height of the Boz, this is the happiest I've ever been," referring, of course, to his post-treatment self.

- Until treatment is sought, the fallout husband needs a vast reservoir of patience and fortitude. One way to muster it is to *cast depression, not your wife, as the villain.* Even though masked, the person with whom you fell in love is still there, waiting to return through treatment. This is admittedly a Herculean task, demanding suppression of one's natural instinct to take personally the behavior displayed. Leaving a room with quiet dignity when you have just been called a liar who has no capacity for love is tough, but it beats shooting off your own volley of insults. Nothing is gained from arguing with someone's depression—that's what you are really doing—except more hurt, frustration, and anger. Engaging in scenes is loss by default, since depressives always win the fight.

Remember, I know what I'm talking about because I am one; without my trusty antidepressants I would resemble your spouse. Think of the nasty words and door-slamming as blowholes through which the depression lets off steam. We don't enjoy the miserable ruckus but in a sense it's confirmation of our view that Doomsday is at hand.

- *Beware of manipulation.* If an argument doesn't ignite spontaneously, we deliberately manufacture one by maneuvering somebody into a corner and then waiting for a negative reaction, which is just another Doomsday strategy. Our black belt in manipulation enables us to turn someone's well-meant offering into offensive and unwelcome behavior. "What's the point of going out to dinner," we'll say, "when you know we can't afford it," as though the invitation was a wicked scheme to bring on bankruptcy.

- *Don't take the standard list of depression's symptoms too literally.* Some sufferers are loud, critical, and resentful; others are of the no-less-maddening sticky-flypaper variety. Sticky-flypapers truly see themselves at the bottom of the totem pole, and they keep pointing it out with (manipulative) pathos: "I know you would be better off without me," "I must be such a drag on you," "How can you stand to live with me?" Initial sympathy in the face of self-eradication eventually turns to an impatient desire to shake them and tell them to snap out of it. If they could they would, but their illness stands in their way.

    Extending the dinner party metaphor, sticky-flypapers will tell their spouses to go without them because "it will be more fun for you anyway." This, too, requires lies from the non-depressed partner who additionally feels guilty of abandonment. The best solution is to order your sad mate's favorite meal from the local takeout joint, tell her you love her and are sorry she feels so terrible, and go to the party alone. On your return, say you had a good time but missed her.

- *Try to appear affectionate no matter how you really feel.* Signs of caring and sympathy are balm on the wounds of depression. I know from my own and others' experience that affectionate tenderness and patient support make us feel better even though we may not show it. For us they are evidence that we're still worthy of love and won't be abandoned. Ben's wife displayed a trying-to-hang-in-there reaction typical of either sex when he asked her, "Why are you still here? Why don't you just get up and leave?" When she replied that she was still there because she loved him, his response—"I don't love anyone anymore, least of all myself"—seemed unanswerable. It is extremely difficult to love someone who refuses to be loved, but if the cause is depression, the effort pays off.

- Self-hatred generates the sudden announcements by many depressed spouses that they want to end the relationship. *Leave the separation/divorce gauntlet lying on the ground* until she has been in treatment for at least three months. Many husbands (and wives, too) have told me tales of depressed mates who casually stated their intention to see a divorce lawyer, usually not during a torrid argument but in moments of relative calm. My guess is that this is a preemptive strike designed to forestall the anticipated answer: "That suits me just fine." When you believe you are unlovable, you hope for disagreement yet at the same time seek confirmation of your worst fear.

    When the gauntlet is thrown, refrain from replying that at last you both agree on something. Instead, reiterate your feelings of love and, using your persuasive arts, bring up the possibility of his or her depression as the source of your mutual distress. Should this provoke the accusation that you are the sick one, say you've read up on the subject and don't have enough of the somatic symptoms to qualify; laying claim to a healthy appetite and untroubled sleep is safer than discussing the psychologically manifested signs of depression. If the person is already on medication but it isn't working well, remind him or her that it's the depression speaking and watch a good movie together.

- Whether waiting for treatment to work or hoping it will be sought, try to *preserve a life of your own.* The metaphor of depression as black hole is apropos. Putting some physical and psychological distance between yourself and the depressed person will lessen the likelihood of being sucked into the vortex of his or her black mood.

  In addition to naming the "it" as villain and resisting a stormy interpersonal style, you can achieve this by injecting order and stability in each day. That means maintaining a schedule dictated by your needs and wants, not just his or hers. It's perfectly okay to think about yourself as long as you refrain from hurtful or rejecting behavior. If your partner is too tired and miserable to join you, then do what you enjoy alone or with friends. Patience flows from respites.

- *Setting boundaries is essential.* Clearly indicate exactly what behavior you will tolerate and what is unacceptable. Sulking solves nothing. Depressed people are not dodos; to the contrary, they are usually conscious of their behavior and will soon cotton to your reactions to it. Verbal abuse calls for a boundary: Leave the room each time you are its target.

Physical abuse, such as slapping and shoving, merits a day or if possible a weekend away from home, but explain why you are leaving. If that doesn't do the trick, make it clear that the next time it happens you will move out for an indeterminate period. Violence, unless directed at inanimate objects, mandates an immediate call to the police, unpleasant though that may be. Once boundaries have been clearly drawn, act on them consistently: Crying wolf is pointless.

Good News About Sex

The numbing mantle that both depression and antidepressants cast over desire and performance can be put aside. Some of the newer medications, among them Serzone and Wellbutrin, are reported by users and their manufacturers as less inhibiting in this respect. So are the first-generation drugs, called tricyclics. While the latter cause such side effects as constipation and dry mouth, many people find them preferable to no sex.

Everyone's physiology is different; simply switching from one brand to another in the same category works for some. Some users, for instance, report that Zoloft is the best choice among the SSRIs (selective serotonin reuptake inhibitors) because it is possible to skip Friday's dose and have a celebratory Saturday night. You can't do that with Prozac because it hangs about in the system longer, and leaving Paxil in the cupboard for a day or two produces unpleasant withdrawal symptoms in some users.

Another category of antidepressants called MAOIs (monoamine oxidase inhibitors) is far less sexually deadening but requires dietary restrictions that will, if transgressed, cause potentially dangerous spikes in blood pressure (more information about them is given in the next chapter).

The foregoing paragraphs assume that ignorance, reluctance, and stigma have been overcome and a decision to start treatment has been made. The following chapter will untangle the choices available and help you decide which approach may be the best for you.

8

All About Treatment

Women everywhere should offer up thanks they were not suffering from depression back in 1867. In that year an English physician addressing the all-male Obstetrical Society said, "Gentlemen, we are the stronger, they are the weaker. They are obliged to believe all that we tell them. They are not in a position to dispute anything we say to them, and we, therefore, may be said to have them at our mercy."

Contrary to appearances, he was one of the good guys and went on to add, "I think that if we should cheat them and victimise them in any shape or way, we should be unworthy of the profession of which we are members." His speech protested the treatment of female insanity—referred to then as "deplorable mental failings" that gave rise to "biological degenerates"—by removal of the clitoris, a practice supported at the time by such eminences as the archbishops of Canterbury and York and the Princess of Wales.

Both women and the medical profession have come a long way since then, but the majority of mental health practitioners still treat the sexes as though only genitalia distinguished one from the other. Women, for instance, were long excluded by the Food and Drug Administration (FDA) from clinical trials of antidepressant medications in the fear that they might prove harmful to a present or future fetus. While the sentiment behind the exclusion sounds positively gallant, it has resulted in ignorance about very real questions. No knowledge has been gained, for instance, concerning such issues as whether women have specific side effect sensitivities and dosage requirements.

Gender aside, you will probably encounter in your search for treatment another version of the nature/nurture, genes/environment, brain/mind dichotomy that crops up in depression research. Should it be medication, psychotherapy, or a combination of both? Practitioners and patients, too, are usually biased in this respect, the former by their training, the latter by their satisfaction with results.

Only those with a degree in medicine may write prescriptions; nurse practitioners (you are not likely to encounter one in your quest for an antidepressant) are the sole exception to this rule. A doctorate in psychology does not count in this respect. Thus, the list of those from whom men and women may seek depression medication is limited to general and family practitioners, psychiatrists, and psychopharmacologists, the super experts of drug therapy. Today, most psychiatrists have reverted to their medically oriented training, focusing on the brain's biology as the locus of depressive illness. They prefer to treat it with pharmacology, and usually refer patients they think would benefit from the addition of talk therapy to a psychotherapist. The rest practice talk therapy and must refer their patients elsewhere if they believe medication is warranted.

This bias has created a fractious fissure between psychiatrists and psychologists that puts the burden of choice on patients. The informed consumer of mental health treatment is far more likely to receive what he or she needs than the one who blindly accepts what is offered. Just what you are offered often depends on whom you go to rather than on the nature of your problem.

Titles do not automatically confer excellence upon their holders. There are excellent, average, and poor practitioners in all these disciplines. Helping you to distinguish between them is a task of this chapter. Another is to lead readers to a better understanding of how both medications and talk therapies do their tasks, when one or a combination of both might be the better choice for you, and what the integrated treatment wave of the future may be. For the historically minded reader, these are prefaced by a brief history of the either/or treatment debate.

The Either/Or Dilemma

The origins of the psychiatrist/psychologist fissure are twofold: the stranglehold maintained by Freud and his followers on the practice of psychiatry, and the absence until recently of knowledge about or tools to explore the nexus between brain and mind. Freud, writes Edward Dolnick in *Madness on the Couch*, damned psychiatry as he found it—an established profession centering on state hospitals since roughly 1800—for its "purely descriptive" approach. He judged medical doctors just as harshly, noting that neurotic patients of all sorts go to doctors, "by whom [they] expect nervous disorders to be removed. The doctors, too, lay down the categories into which these complaints are divided. They diagnose them, each according to his own standpoint, under different names—neurasthenia, psychasthenia, phobias, obsessional neurosis, hysteria. They examine the organs which produce the symptoms, the heart, the stomach, the bowels, the genitals, and find them healthy. They recommend interruptions in the patient's accustomed mode of life, holidays, strengthening exercises, tonics, and by all these means bring about temporary improvements—or no result at all."

Freud, originally trained as a neurologist, invented psycho-analysis as the avenue to an understanding of the mind's inner workings. Through what he claimed was insightful interpreta-tion of his patients' dreams, he led them to "cures." If and when his patients did improve, it's likely that the cure resulted from remission of their particular psychiatric disturbance rather than dream interpretation, particularly since so many of his insights centered on sex. He insisted, however, that psychoanalysis was a science and that his discoveries were laws of nature. His own and his followers' faith in them was unshakable. From the mid-1940s through the 1970s, medical school graduates who opted for psychiatry as their specialty aspired to become psychoana-lysts, too. If they were interested in the brain, that was really the only game in town; it was also where the big reputations were made and the most money earned.

The chance discovery in the early 1950s that Iproniazad—a drug prescribed at the time for tuberculosis—caused patients to stop moping around the sanatorium and become upbeat caught the attention of a few astute analysts who found it help-ful to their patients, too. The rest continued to place them on the couch up to five times weekly, encouraged them to free as-sociate back to their childhood, resolve the sexual conflicts there, and restructure their ego and id.

In its American heyday being analyzed was hot stuff pro-vided you could afford it. My cousin Jeffrey paid a fortune to one of the best-known. At the end of twenty-two years, when he ran out of money, patience, or both, he was, in the eyes of his friends, as charmingly screwed up as when he began. Although some male couch potatoes may have fared better than Jeffrey, few females did unless possessed of a healthy ego before beginning the trek. Psychoanalysts blamed women for a range of illnesses in their children from schizophrenia to autism and manic depression even though by the 1960s lithium had been recognized as an effective treatment for the latter.

The anti-pharmacology stance analysts took was grounded in their theory that behind every fear lies "the wish." All human beings are pleasure seekers at heart, goes the argument, so being in a state of pain is really an expression of a pleasure-seeking goal. A phobic fear of being in public, for instance, is actually a desire to drop one's pants, blocked by an overly severe superego. Fix up the id and you will be dancing naked on the tabletop. But then along came Prozac, the first antidepressant largely free of the uncomfortable side effects of earlier ones. Suddenly, many previously shy and inhibited people were growing self-esteem in a matter of weeks, discarding their negative affect and enjoying the attentions of others. Psychoanalysis, its power already on the wane, slipped further into decline and the handful of pill-oriented psychiatrists rapidly expanded.

But old ways die hard and university-trained psychologists still emerge cloaked in Freudianism. Many of the most able among them willingly acknowledge that their first task on embarking in clinical practice is to discard much of what they have learned in favor of approaches more suited to reality and their patients' needs. Dolnick quotes Harvard's Jerome Kagan, a major leader in the field of developmental child psychology, as writing, "I blush to admit that I repeated to my first class in child psychology what I had been taught as a graduate student. I said with certainty that some children found it difficult to learn to read because they interpreted the act of reading as aggressive behavior toward their parents."

My own encounter with talk therapy—which predated my

use of medication—was less traditional but still way off the mark in figuring out what was wrong with me. The therapist I selected had come late to her new career and assured me on starting out that her brand of therapy was quick and dirty, by which she meant that it would deal more with the present and recent past than with my early years. She saw my problems with the men in my life as chained to my father's early departure from the family nest. When I attempted to discuss the exit of yet another boyfriend, the therapist transmuted him into absent Dad. She instructed me to paste my father's face on every male figure floating through my dreams. I eventually did so unasked in order not to waste any of my precious, and expensive, fifty minutes in fruitless argument. My mother, the sharpest thorn in my psychological crown, remained invisible in this Freudian briar patch, or so my therapist led me to believe.

This encounter with psychotherapy, which lasted a year and a half, has left me ambivalent about its value as a treatment for most depressions. While it was a welcome relief to unburden myself to someone who seemed to like me despite my short-comings and fears, we did not, I realized a few years later, resolve much of anything. Further, during this period my depression upgraded itself from local to express train. In fairness to the therapist, she did once mention the possibility of medication, but twenty years ago psychiatric drugs seemed to me only a step away from padded cells and restraints; she never spoke of it again.

Even today such experiences are not uncommon. A referral for medication, even when clearly indicated, often comes only after months or longer of talk, and sometimes never. As one former analytic psychiatrist turned psychopharmacologist puts it, practitioners of talk therapy "seem to have difficulty distinguishing between their patients and an annuity." But plenty of pill-prescribing psychiatrists, he added, also think in terms of money. Instead of referring their patients elsewhere for therapy, they administer it along with the medication. As in other professions, greed often takes precedence over sound practice when it comes to sharing the riches.

Few general medicine practitioners are skilled at diagnosing or treating depression. Of the less than 50 percent of people in the grip of depression who seek their help, only one third receive what they need. Some physicians prescribe tranquilizers that temporarily mask symptoms of anxiety and despair. Others bestow a condescending pat on the head and advice about playing more tennis and taking a holiday from problems, just like the doctors of whom Freud complained. Many commonly prescribe antidepressants but in dosages too low to have any effect, switch patients from one brand of pills to another before they have a chance to work, or stick with the first drug even if it has no effect. Worse still, they send their patients off with a prescription but unarmed with information about how long medications take to work, what their side effects are, for what period they should be used, or what may happen if they are abruptly discontinued. Should these doctors mention psychotherapy at all, they do as a casual aside: "Oh, yes, and you might find it useful to talk to someone."

Psychiatrists can be fallible, too. Luckily for me I fell early into the hands of an empathetic master who guided me through the byways of a hard-case depression. To this day he still tinkers with my medication, as well as answering crisis calls when its effects are temporarily overwhelmed by events or my neurotransmitters go out of whack and get the sulks. My initial ninety-minute diagnostic interview was preceded by a request to complete a long questionnaire and get a medical checkup before our appointment. Most patients are denied such a blessing.

The time and expertise he placed at my disposal was unusual even for a three-star psychopharmacologist, and well worth the hefty fee and monthly followup visits.

A lot of the blame for assembly line treatment lies with the HMOs, but plenty of psychiatrists and even psychopharmacologists aren't as knowledgeable as they should be. A few are rightfully labeled pill pushers. They don't listen carefully to patient's complaints about side effects and other relevant concerns and show little or no interest in the home and work environments of their patients.

Mercifully, that's pretty much the extent of the bad news. The good news is that there are excellent practitioners in all these professions. The initial antidepressant, Iproniazad, that elevated the mood of tubercular patients in the 1950s has expanded to about twenty, with new versions coming out every year and more in the pipeline. Psychotherapy no longer means the open-ended, Freudian-flavored variety I and countless others underwent fifteen and more years ago. Best of all, there is hope for an integrated approach to treating women's depression. One example of it, described below, is so commensensical that it may be replicated despite the bifurcated either/or view of the hidebound mental health establishment.

Fault Lines, Tremors, and Earthquakes

The practice of Deborah Sichel and Jeanne Driscoll is an oasis in the dry and rocky turf of women's mental health care. A psychiatrist and a psychiatric nurse respectively, they met back in 1981 in a hospital when Jeanne entered a patient's room and found Deborah sitting on the bed chatting with one of her charges. "I had always had this mind-set of psychiatrists as crusty old men who blamed everything on the woman," says Jeanne, "all that ego and id stuff. But here was one chatting with her patient as though she was a friend that she wanted to know better."

Getting to know their patients is the keystone of the Sichel-Driscoll psychobiological approach to care, described in *Women's Moods: What Every Women Must Know About Hormones, the Brain, and Emotional Health.* They call it the Earthquake Assessment Model. The metaphor is apt: The fault lines laid down by genes are located in the biochemical brain; the tremors are the sub–full blown symptoms of depressive illness; the earthquakes are the major psychiatric episodes. Diagnosis and treatment depend on an assessment of their patients—who range from adolescents to postmenopausal women—similar to the one I received.

All psychiatrists assess their patients, but often they pose their questions in a manner, and within a time frame, that fails to extract the nuanced information about a woman's, or indeed anyone's, mental and physical health that Sichel and Driscoll consider essential. "Ask someone if they have a psychiatric history and they'll immediately think 'crazy' and 'institutionalized,' so of course they tell you, 'no.' We ask, 'Have you ever seen a therapist or had pastoral counseling, maybe couples therapy, or thought about it? Are you lonely? Have you family and friends you can count on?'"

That's just for starters. They also want to know about general health and a wide range of development issues and life situations. Their queries include, When did you start to menstruate? What about PMS? Anything like date rape or unwanted touching when you were young? Are you seeing someone? Married? How's it going—is the sex satisfying? Ever had an abortion? A miscarriage? Are you working, do you enjoy your job? Any financial problems troubling you? How were things in school and college? Are your parents alive and well, and how do you get on with them? Has anyone in your immediate family abused alcohol or drugs, or had mood problems?

"Women are born talkers," says Jeanne, herself a motor-mouth with a compassionate sense of humor as ample as the body that houses it. "They'll willingly tell everything about themselves to someone genuinely interested in them as a human being." Relevant information not revealed by the typical if-yes-check-this-box format provides Sichel and Driscoll with a detailed personal portrait full of fault lines, tremors, and often previous earthquakes, all induced by the ever-changing lava that lies below the deceptively smooth surface of a life. Many substantive clues to depressive illness emerge through this nontechnical conversational style. Patients answering no to a question about OCD will say yes to compulsively cleaning the house at two o'clock in the morning and the need to straighten all the pictures and magazines before feeding the baby. An indication of generalized anxiety may come from comments like, "I feel just totally wired all the time, like I'm too big for my skin. It's like, you know, really yucky."

Perhaps the most important product of a detailed assessment is evidence that the depressive episode for which the patient has sought help is not a discrete one-time event but part of a pattern long in the making. Sichel and Driscoll portray this in graph form with the impact of biological and psychosocial events noted vertically and their chronology horizontally. The graph on page 171 tracks the course of forty-eight-year-old Helen's psychobiological history, revealing her genetic vulnerability, how and when it has been stressed, a previous undiagnosed episode lasting almost six months, and evidence of co-morbid (often present with, in medical parlance) disorders, all part and parcel of the circumstances leading up to her present dismal, tearful state.

Firmly disclaiming any "real depression" in her past, Helen acknowledges herself as moody, "But this is different," she says, "I've always managed to keep my life together but lately I can't. I can function more or less okay in the office, but when I'm alone everything falls apart. Life seems so pointless. I just don't care anymore." Despite displaying all the classic symptoms, she insists that life events are getting her down, blaming disagreements with her boss and a painful and costly series of root canals for her current distress. The graph Sichel and Driscoll made of Helen's history is shown here; when they explained their interpretation of it, she dropped her protestations.

Earthquake damage like Helen's needs immediate repair. For this treatment team that means medication first and then, when it has taken hold, psychotherapy. Tossing in another metaphor, Sichel likens the brain to a master computer that orchestrates each breath we take and movement we make, our menstrual cycle, our sleep and appetite, our heartbeat rate and the state of our immune system, to name only a few of its responsibilities. Forever in search of stability, it constantly adjusts as best it can in response to stress and change as it goes about organizing our moods, actions, thoughts, planning, memory, and even problem-solving.

Although brain tissue itself is insensitive to pain—surgeons can rummage around in it without using anesthesia—diagnosticians look for signs of its distress in symptoms both somatic (such as changed eating and sleep patterns) and psychological. Each of those tremor-producing stressful events noted in a patient's assessment history have taken their toll somewhere in the brain. "The brain you were born with," Sichel reminds her patients, "is not the brain you have today."

Pile up enough tremors and eventually the repeated shaking will open up vulnerable fault lines and produce the earthquake.

HELEN'S CHART: FAULTS, TREMORS, AND EARTHQUAKES

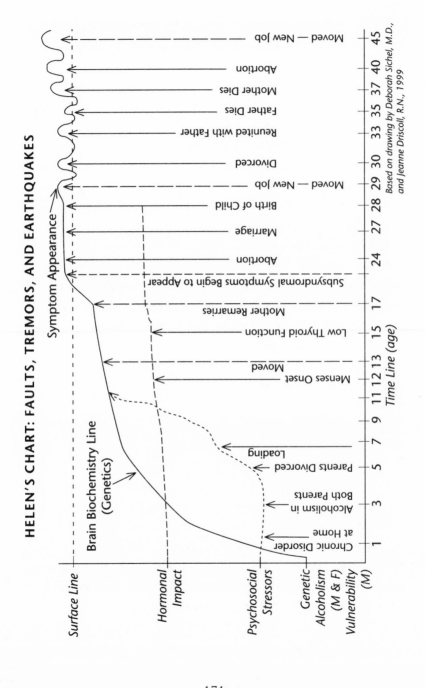

Based on drawing by Deborah Sichel, M.D., and Jeanne Driscoll, R.N., 1999

The longer the brain remains in a dysregulated state, the more apt it is to learn how to operate dysfunctionally. Because it is governed by biology, Sichel and Driscoll side with those who prefer to take care of that aspect first and then, when neurotransmitters and the rest of the brain's chemistry are back in working form, move on to a therapy that addresses psychological issues like the habit of negative thinking.

Unfortunately, there aren't many practitioners like this team, which includes several psychotherapists. Most treatment seekers are offered medication or talk therapy depending on which type of professional they initially see. Many are influenced by the experience of friends but often such advice is irrelevant: They may have a milder or more severe depression than yours, may by chance have consulted the right doctor or therapist for them, or indeed may have a physical or psychological makeup quite different from your own. This illness is too complex to permit facile predictions. As in buying a car, consumers need to know what the market offers. That calls for two quick cram courses, one in psychopharmacology and one in psychotherapy.

Psychopharmacology 101

Even patients in the care of a competent psychiatrist need information about the current range of antidepressants. The best results will come from teamwork; if only one member knows what is going on, effectiveness can be elusive or delayed. This section lays out the basic facts about the most commonly prescribed medications and provides insider tips on specific drugs and doctors.

There are four classifications of antidepressants: the tricyclics (TCAs), the selective serotonin reuptake inhibitors (SS-RIs), the monoamine oxidase inhibitors (MAOIs), and a less cohesive category called the "atypicals."

TCAs were among the earliest antidepressants. They are very efficient drugs but they cause unpleasant side effects including dry mouth, constipation, blurred vision, difficulty in urinating, weight gain, and either drowsiness or trouble sleeping. Although most of these side effects disappear or abate over time, they are unpleasant enough to make many people go off their medication. The most frequently prescribed are marketed under the brand names Tofranil, Elavil, Norpramin, and Pamelor.

SSRIs appeared in the mid-1980s and made an instant hit because they have fewer side effects, many of which also lessen or go away in a month or two. They are widely prescribed under the brand names Prozac, Zoloft, and Paxil. All of them specifically target the neurotransmitter serotonin.

MAOIs, sold under the brand names Nardil and Parnate, are the most effective medications for atypical depression, a form of depression that is consistently underdiagnosed. Atypical depressives sleep and eat more rather than less, have a great time at a party if someone manages to drag them there, and are supersensitive to rejection. Although about 45 percent of all depression sufferers are atypicals, the MAOIs are infrequently prescribed because they require dietary restrictions that if ignored can cause dangerous spikes in blood pressure. However, feeling great instead of so-so may be worth giving up cold cuts, most cheese, overripe bananas, red wine, and certain over-the-counter and prescription drugs. If any of these are carelessly ingested and the telltale pounding, back-of-the-head headache and racing pulse ensue, patients can immediately take a blocker pill that stops them cold. This potential risk frightens many doctors and patients away from the use of MAOIs; they are never prescribed for anyone considered at high risk for suicide, or for those who might be careless or forgetful.

Reversible MAOIs, known as RIMAs, are free of side effects, including sexual ones, and are in common use throughout Europe and elsewhere. Unfortunately, their manufacturer, hoping for a better share of the U.S. market by touting them for social phobia rather than for atypical depression, spent millions of dollars on the clinical trials for efficacy required by the FDA—all to no avail, since they proved of little use for the socially phobic. Since the years remaining on their patent did not justify a repeat performance for atypical depression, RIMAs remain unavailable here unless you have a patient-friendly doctor. He or she, if willing to go the extra mile, can fill out a form and receive from the FDA a so-called Compassionate IND number; the drug can then be ordered from a pharmacy in Canada and will pass through U.S. Customs without problems. If you have been on a couple of SSRIs without success, and you fit the atypical symptomatology, it's worth discussing this with your physician.

Confusingly, drugs in the category called "atypical" have nothing to do with atypical depression. Their name derives from the fact that they differ in structure from the other categories but share no unifying factor. Their brand names are Wellbutrin, Effexor, Serzone, Remeron, and Deseryl. Like all antidepressants, they have pluses and minuses that are covered in the section titled insider tips.

Some people resist the idea of drugs despite consuming alcohol, using marijuana or cocaine, and popping pills for insomnia, nerves, and weight reduction. Others do so because their religious faith or Alcoholics Anonymous counsels against them, or because of a fear born of ignorance about how antidepressants work to restore the brain's chemistry to normal. Instead, they seek help in "natural" remedies that are sold over the counter and so do not require a visit to a doctor.

Of these, St. John's Wort is the only one that can help some mild, nonchronic depressions. This herbal remedy is extremely popular in Germany where it has been used for some time. The NIMH is now conducting efficacy and safety trials that should clarify what dosage works the best under what circumstances. In the meantime, for those whose symptoms are not too impairing, and whose insurance doesn't cover prescription drugs, St. John's Wort is certainly worth a try. If you do decide to take it, keep the diary suggested below and be honest in your entries.

A nonprescription supplement called SAM-e hit the headlines in mid-1999. Beware of the unfounded claims made in its behalf. The FDA prohibits manufacturers of supplements, herbs, and vitamins from making medical claims for their products—for instance, "Vitamin C reduces the risk of cancer," or, "St. John's Wort cures depression"—but no curbs are placed on the media or on advertisements for books that make heroes of these products. In July a full-page ad in the *New York Times* for one such book, entitled *Stop Depression Now,* trumpeted SAM-e as "a supplement that can conquer depression safely and naturally in a matter of days," and quoted a *Newsweek* article as saying, "There is little question that [it] can help fight depression." The latter statement is far closer to the truth. The psychiatrist coauthor, Dr. Richard Brown, clarified his position a few days later on a Sunday morning TV news interview show. He explained that he rarely took his patients off the antidepressant medications he routinely prescribed for them and used SAM-e only as an adjunct to their use.

I have since spoken at some length with Dr. Brown, who is indeed an enthusiastic booster of SAM-e, but not as a first choice, stand-alone treatment for this illness, especially if it is chronic, severe, or hard to treat. Many of SAM-e's adjunctive benefits that he mentioned, among them strengthening the immune system and lessening arthritic conditions, are not directly related to depression, although he has indeed found it helpful in ameliorating the usual antidepressant side effects, including sexual dysfunction.

Insider Tips

- About 75 percent to 80 percent of all patients respond positively to the right medication for them, so your mood ought to improve dramatically within three, four, or at the most, six weeks. Often improvement can come from one minute to the next. I remember feeling a sudden shift or click in my brain, as though a tiny geological fault had been repaired. I was visiting friends and had been pleading the demands of work as an explanation for spending hours in my room instead of hiking and going to parties. That evening I put on makeup and joined the human race again. If you experience no significant mood change within a reasonable time, or if it stagnates at the halfway mark, your doctor should suggest another medication in the same category, or Effexor or Wellbutrin. Prozac may work for one person but cause disagreeable side effects or no improvement in another. Switching to Zoloft, Paxil, or Luvox, many patients claim, can be the answer.

- A phenomenon known as Prozac poop-out has been reported in several magazine articles, although it would be fairer to call it SSRI slide. Between 10 percent and 30 percent of all who start off on any one of them experience vast improvement, only to have it slip away months or even several years later. SSRIs specifically target serotonin but other neurotransmitters are also implicated in depression. Some psychopharmacologists treat this by switching patients to or adding antidepressants like Effexor or Wellbutrin, which stimulate the release of dopamine. Alternatively, they add a stimulant, usually either Ritalin or Dexadrine, which also help activate that chemical.

The likeliest explanation for the poop-out is that the patient suffers from atypical depression and would respond far better to an MAOI. Despite its prevalence, remarkably few doctors accurately diagnose it. Others are leery of the dietary restrictions; the more knowledgeable among them combine the SSRI with a small daily dose of Dexadrine. Good psychiatrists admit that treating depression is still as much an art as a science. The best have tricks up their sleeve that would dazzle a less expert doctor and solve cases others have given up on. Should you experience a poop-out or slide, do not despair. Instead, find yourself a superstar.

- If your doctor persists in keeping you on "average" dosage, does not suggest switching to a new medication if the first doesn't help within a reasonable period, or dismisses specific complaints without explanation, ask him or her why. None welcome a know-it-all patient, but all owe you an informed answer. If you don't get one, change your treatment provider or seek out an expert for a consultation.

- You can locate an expert by consulting such reference guides as *The Best Doctors in America* or by calling the National Foundation for Depressive Illness (NAFDI). Alternatively, find a support group by contacting the nearest local affiliate of the National Alliance for the Mentally Ill (NAMI) or of the National Depressive and Manic Depressive Association (ND-MDA); their 800 numbers and national headquarters addresses are in the appendix. The support groups they run always include members with hard-to-treat depressions who know the expert doctors in their area.

Select someone with professional heft, preferably a doctor associated with a different hospital than the one you have been seeing. Ask Doctor Number One for your treatment record, which will include the dosage of the medication(s) you have been on and for how long. If for some reason this is not possible, write down in detail everything you can remember that may be relevant. This will ensure that the consultant doesn't revisit treatment territory already explored.

After completing the assessment and discussing it with you, the consultant will then telephone your current doctor and suggest a revised treatment plan. If the latter's nose goes out of joint at being upstaged and the recommended changes are not made, you definitely need a new provider. Either stick with the expert or ask him to recommend a less pricey substitute. A top-notch consultant who plays by the rules will remain available to your original doctor at no charge if the expected progress is not made. Unfortunately, not all do.

- Nobody, least of all a depressed mother trying to juggle child care, job, and home life, can retrospectively provide accurate information about how she felt a month, a week, or even twenty-four hours ago, so keep a diary from day one. A couple of daily sentences will do: "Bad night. Dreadful awakening. Somewhat better in afternoon but no energy," or, "Still exhausted and dizzy when I got out of bed but managed to do some errands later. Went to movies with Jean." Entries like "Horrible fight with Bob," "Felt like hitting the kids," and "Don't know how long I can hold on like this" are important clues to what's going on in your brain.

The record does more than give your doctor a serial picture of your mental state; it will also help you recognize gradual changes for the better that are imperceptible on a day-to-day basis. Note any dosage or drug changes, days you may have forgotten to take your pills, your menstrual periods, aches and pains, and anything you did or felt that might be relevant. More is better than less but you don't have to be Proust.

• Every antidepressant choice should take into consideration the presence of any co-morbid anxiety disorders. Zoloft, for example, also addresses symptoms of OCD, and Paxil does the same for both panic disorder and OCD. Prozac has recently been approved for bulimia. Depression sufferers are prone to smoking because nicotine is a stimulant, and have far more difficulty giving it up than do non-depressed tobacco addicts. Wellbutrin, also marketed as an aid to quitting smoking under the brand name Zyban, could be a choice for them.

• Celexa, approved by the FDA about a year ago, is a highly selective SSRI that has been used to treat depression in over 8 million people in Europe. It has been shown to have very few interactions with other non-depression-related drugs and also appears low in side effects. Some studies indicate that it may be effective in preventing relapses.

• As already noted, Serzone and the TCAs appear less likely than SSRIs to suppress sexual desire and performance. RIMAs leave them totally intact. However, Serzone, according to one leading psychopharmacologist, doesn't do much for depression unless the maximum dose of six hundred milligrams a day is taken, at which point it has such a soporific effect that many of its users behave like sleepwalkers.

- The antidepressant Deseryl, with the generic name trazadone, is quite often co-prescribed with other antidepressants because it helps eliminate the sleep-impeding effects they have on some users. By the way, the Melatonin Miracle didn't stand up to investigation. Travelers may find it helpful for jet lag, but it is useless as an aid to sleeping difficulties in medicated or unmedicated depressed people.

- Many go off their antidepressant because of such side effects as dizziness, dry mouth, nausea, nerviness, or somnolence. Most side effects taper off in a month or two, with the exception of sexual problems and sleeplessness, which is why doctors seem rather unsympathetic when you complain of them. A side effect of major importance to many is the associated increased appetite and weight gain they often induce. One of the worst culprits here is Remeron. For those who must struggle with diets under the best of circumstances, Wellbutrin is reportedly the best choice. Bear in mind that not everyone suffers the same side effects from the same antidepressant.

Beyond Medication: ECT and Hospitalization

Some patients go through years of failed medication before turning to electro-convulsive treatment (ECT), yet in at least half the cases where medication fails, ECT works. It can often be done on an outpatient basis and, as currently administered, is quick and painless. Memory loss, which used to be common, is now minimal and short-term. It is fast-acting, and patients usually feel better immediately. Between nine and twelve sessions is the standard course of treatment. Although some patients experience a total remission of their depression, most need refresher sessions.

Most depression sufferers and their families view hospitalization as the equivalent of being institutionalized, but they are rarely right. If your doctor puts you in a hospital, it is because you are in danger of hurting yourself. Fifteen percent of all people suffering from depression complete suicide and many more make the attempt. This is a first-class reason for being in a protected environment until medication takes hold and it is safe to be on your own. Your stay there will not be long; it is harder today to remain in a hospital than to get out of one, thanks to economy-minded HMOs.

The Value of a Support Group

Do yourself a big favor by joining a depression support group if there is one in your area (you can check with NAMI and ND-MDA to find out). You will find extraordinary solace in realizing that your thoughts, feelings, and problems are all common to depression and shared by others. Only fellow sufferers can persuade you of that. Women, perhaps because they are more ready than men to admit and give voice to their emotions, gain insight, perspective, and courage in the company of their peers. Attendance at a well-run group, which costs pennies or nothing at all, is second only to the psychotherapist of your dreams.

If none exist within reach, try the Internet, but be warned:

Depression chat rooms are often peopled with sufferers so demoralized and negative that they could push even the depression-free over the precipice. Billboards, where participants can post messages and questions about specific situations, are more useful. Some Web addresses are given in the appendix.

Exercise Helps Depression

When energy levels are at minus zero and life appears pointless, suggestions about exercising have the sound of one hand clapping. Yet any physical activity, even a quick walk around the block, will raise the spirits, however briefly. Choose your exercise wisely. This is an inauspicious time to enroll in an expensive health club only to find it insupportable after one hour on a bunch of machines under the direction of some perky, skinny instructor.

Instead, make yourself a promise to spend a minimum of thirty minutes a day on an exercise you enjoy, be it biking, swimming, roller-skating, lifting weights, playing tennis, or whatever. Anything that elevates your heart rate and gets oxygen to the brain will do. Walking a brisk mile every day, which takes only twenty minutes, is a good choice since you can do it solo and need no equipment other than determination. Immediately following each successful attempt at exercise, add a few words to your depression diary so as to remember that it helped. This will encourage you to try again for longer and with more enthusiasm.

My personal favorite is yoga, which is not just sitting around cross-legged trying to think about the infinite. When done correctly under the supervision of a good teacher, it calls for deep, controlled breathing synchronized with slow movements from one posture to another. The concentration demanded wipes the mind clean and floods the body with energy. Afterward, you feel calm, focused, and in control. I often go off to class depleted and negative, sure that this time I am far too down for it to work its magic. But it always does.

Of all its benefits, the feeling of mastery that yoga generates is its most valuable asset for the helplessness and pessimism associated with depression. This transcends the usual sense of accomplishment that comes from all exercise; yoga makes you feel as though you have control over your life. Just moving through a set of the classic poses, even when not preceded or followed by a short period of meditation, is calming and centering.

Kudos for Meditation

Meditation, which originated in India, had an almost twenty-five-hundred-year run as a physical and mental health booster and then was stopped dead by modern medicine. Until, that is, about thirty years ago when Dr. Herbert Benson coined the term "relaxation response." Since then it has been gaining ground. In 1998 Congress gave the NIMH $10 million to expand a network of mind-body research centers and provide training for health workers in a variety of meditative approaches.

The purpose of meditation, one popular version of which is called "mindfulness," is to open the mind to sensations and thoughts and temporarily tune out everyday life. Not only does this induce calm, it also can bring about specific, quantifiable changes in the body. Most who consistently practice meditation feel different and better afterward, but at least five people now have provided specific proof that something beneficial has indeed happened.

In a 1999 study conducted by a Harvard team of researchers,

five accomplished meditators spent about forty minutes in an MRI (magnetic resonance imaging) machine, stared at a dot on a computer screen, thought up random lists of animals, and meditated. The resulting pictures of their brains showed that the regions that process positive emotions and influence cardiorespiratory function were most active during the meditation.

A Brief Reminder About Diet

Along with exercise goes eating right. As a former secret binger, I can testify to the worthlessness of cake, ice cream, and bologna and mayo sandwiches as mood enhancers. After a sugar- and fat-laden feast I would curl up and zonk out, only to awaken feeling even worse and guilty to boot. Excess alcohol has an equally dreadful effect on depression, although many engage in heavy self-medication. One beer or a glass of wine is okay, but not Chianti if you are taking an MAOI. If you cheat you will regret it.

What to Do If You Are Hoping to Become or Are Pregnant

Every mother knows she should neither drink nor smoke during pregnancy because alcohol and nicotine can adversely affect the fetus, and that many drugs are contraindicated because they may be harmful, especially during the first trimester. Even aspirin comes with a warning to consult a physician before taking it if pregnant or nursing. Small wonder that mothers and ob-gyns are reluctant to mix pregnancy and antidepressants, even though the available evidence points to their safety. What is new is the growing recognition by experts that maternal depression and anxiety may pose a greater risk to the fetus than the very antidepressants they worry about. This section reviews the findings on both sides of the equation and provides you with enough information to have a rational discussion on the pros and cons with your physician.

First, the safety issue. Taking an antidepressant during pregnancy has been problematic, not because any ill effects on the fetus have been observed in the millions of women taking them, but because establishing indisputable proof of their safety is a formidable task. To know for sure would entail assembling at least twenty thousand nondrinking, nonsmoking, drug-free, just-pregnant women, all of them healthy and relatively stress-free, half on a specific antidepressant and half not, then following them through delivery and charting the early developmental growth of their infants. The overall rate of fetal abnormalities in all deliveries from any cause is 5 percent. If researchers studying this hypothetical research population were to find a 6 percent rate in the pill-taking group and the usual 5 percent rate in the other, they would then attempt to pin the increase on the antidepressant by statistically adjusting their findings to eliminate other possible reasons for it.

Thalidomide was identified as harmful, but retrospectively, not prospectively. When the fetal abnormality rate spiked, statisticians went to work and found that a significant number of mothers whose fetuses were abnormal had taken the drug, the only risk factor common to all of them. What makes that tragedy so shattering is that thalidomide had already undergone FDA trials (less stringent and demanding than they are today) without yielding evidence that it might cause birth defects. That may have been because an insufficient number of women participated in the trials (it takes ten thousand people on the same drug to establish accuracy within 1 percent or 2 percent), or because the drug did not cause birth defects in the babies of every mother who took it, or that the vulnerable were by happenstance left out of the trials.

One recent study of 267 women on SSRIs and an equal number unmedicated revealed neither more malformations nor higher rates of miscarriage, stillbirth, or premature birth than the statistical average. However, warns Dr. Zachary Stowe of Emory University's School of Medicine, in lab studies of pregnant rats the researchers did find higher-than-expected concentrations of antidepressants in the brains of the fetal rats, but no problems when they were born. Although rats and mice serve as remarkably reliable surrogates for humans in many research programs on drug development, we are not interchangeable.

The Stressed-Out Fetus

The decision for or against antidepressants should be stacked against the severity of the depression and the possible effects of maternal anxiety and depression upon the fetus. A mother's emotions during pregnancy may play a role in setting the preliminary wiring of the fetal brain, a process continued after birth by the baby's environment. Doctors Catherine Monk and William Fifer at Columbia University's College of Physicians and Surgeons have devised a way to test their hypothesis that a pregnant woman's emotions, such as anxiety and stress, influence fetal development. The physiological changes associated with them, they suspect, are transmitted to the unborn child. To investigate this they monitored the maternal and fetal heartbeats, as well as the mother's blood pressure and respiration, while concurrently submitting her to a fiendish five-minute arithmetic stress test. Although even the mere description of the test left me sweaty-palmed and anxious, perhaps one day it will be routinely administered as a diagnostic aid.

The mothers-to-be lie supine, clutching to their swelling bodies a sort of pocket calculator device with ten unmarked buttons representing the numbers zero to nine, distinguished only by a bump on the central number five button. A nearby computer then flashes a number on a screen, say 1,189, and a researcher directs the mother to tap out a downward count by sevens—1,182, 1,175, 1,168, and so forth—all the while urging her to hurry up and go faster. Worst of all, no peeking at the calculator is allowed; sums must be registered by touch alone, and a mistake necessitates starting from scratch.

Before the test begins, the women are asked to complete a self-rating form with boxes to check like "I am calm" or "I am tense." Monk and her team have found that the heart rate of the fetuses of those women who rated themselves as more anxious than average increased during the test, while the heart rate of the fetuses of low-anxiety mothers did not. Newborns of mothers suffering from anxiety and depression have been found to be overactive or less attentive and harder to soothe than those of other moms. This leads scientists to suspect that the characteristics of risk for anxiety or depression may be identifiable in utero or in infants.

Jerome Kagan has observed that a distressed infant's behavior can translate into a more inhibited temperament, with infants as young as four months old showing an elevated heart rate and more arousal on the right side of the brain, the one that houses many negative emotions. Anxiety-ridden women are subject to hormonal "flooding," and that may alter fetal development. Once the fetus has become sensitized to aberrations, it may continue to function abnormally, even when maternal stress is no longer present.

A new 3-D sonogram technology soon will allow researchers a perfect fetal image in the round that can be rotated on the screen so as to actually observe any changes in movements or facial expression. Although eerily futuristic and alarming to the uninitiated, this will once and for all cast anxiety, and the depression closely associated with it, as far more likely to place the fetus at risk than the possible, although unobserved, adverse effects of antidepressants.

The rate of antenatal depression, once thought to be nonexistent, is now estimated at 10 percent or, according to Catherine Monk and others, even higher. This one-in-ten statistic reveals a serious threat to the health of women and their unborn children. Mothers-to-be who suffer through endless sleepless nights and are so impaired by their illness that they neglect to take care of themselves—eating little and skipping prenatal visits—are usually prescribed an antidepressant. But most depressed pregnant women attempt to tough it out on their own because they are ashamed to admit, even to close family members, that their feelings about the impending birth are ambivalent. The evidence Fifer, Monk, and others are accumulating may lead doctors to more routinely recommend antidepressants during pregnancy.

What to Do About Antidepressants If You Are Nursing

There is no evidence to support fears that taking an antidepressant while nursing is harmful to the infant. Dr. Cynthia Neill Epperson of Yale University is one of many researchers who have put this to the test. She recruited infants of depressed mothers, some breast-fed and others not, and then measured the level of antidepressant (in her work, Zoloft, which targets serotonin) and of serotonin in the infants' blood. Reporting on her work, Epperson states that she detected no Zoloft in their bloodstreams and that there was no change in the level of serotonin in most of the infants. She concluded, with the scientist's reserve, that "it does not appear that the administration of Zoloft in breast-feeding women is likely to have a physiologic effect on their children."

Many depressed women derive much-needed joy from breast-feeding and become even more upset when deprived of the opportunity. Physicians who still caution against combining antidepressants with feeding except when the illness is severe recommend substituting a bottle once or twice a day to further reduce any possible risk. As always with depression, each sufferer should take into consideration all the known facts and with the help of her doctor make an informed decision. What is right for one person may be wrong for another.

Psychotherapy 101

The headlined arrival of Prozac in 1988 applied a spur to the practice of psychotherapy. The profession responded admirably to the challenge posed by the stream of new antidepressants that followed with innovations of their own. Instead of taking their patients on long, expensive odysseys to excavate the ego and the id, psychotherapists began to offer them shorter, special-interest trips that focused on their current mood, life view, and relationships with others. Two of these newer approaches, called Interpersonal Therapy (IPT) and Cognitive Behavioral Therapy (CBT), are helping many cope with depression and its habit of coloring the world and everyone in it black and blue. While their introduction hasn't healed the rift between psychiatrists and psychologists, it has narrowed the gap. Those who believe wholeheartedly in the power of the pill are far more receptive to short-term therapies, usually completed in eight to sixteen sessions, than to traditional psychoanalytic or psychodynamic ones, and many recommend it as a useful adjunct. And although it's only an unsubstantiated guess, short-term therapists may be more likely to recommend medication than dedicated Freudians.

Although diehards remain on both sides, the dust kicked up by an attempt to compare the effectiveness of IPT and CBT with medication has settled. In 1989, the National Institute of Mental Health announced the conclusions drawn from a four-month study in which 250 people were prescribed an antidepressant, received a placebo, or underwent a course of IPT or CBT. Pills, claimed the study, were only marginally more effective than psychotherapy in treating depression. That conclusion stirred up a ruckus. For several years, the pages of scientific journals were clogged with ardent, often extremely angry responses criticizing the methodology of the study, the people who conducted it, and the claims they made. These were followed by criticism of the criticizers.

Dissenters had some excellent reasons for complaining. Prime among them was the choice of Imipramine, a TCA antidepressant with side effects so unpleasant that many users can't or won't tolerate them. They further pointed out that the statistical analysis did not sufficiently take into account the fact that some participants had mild depression and others were severely incapacitated, thus skewing the results and weakening the study's conclusions. Since then other studies have looked at how depressed patients fare on therapy and, using various rating scales, have demonstrated that they can indeed reduce the symptoms of many who suffer from relatively mild depression.

Exiting the meds-therapy-or-both dilemma calls for a quick course in Psychotherapy 101 but first, a caveat. If your depression is severe enough to be causing serious problems in your family, in your relationships, or at work, you need medication and then, when it has taken hold, you can add psychotherapy. That is my personal bias, but many experienced experts agree on this point. Having this illness is punishment enough; allowing it to continue wreaking havoc in your life is folly. Even a short-term therapy course of three or four months is too long to wait for the wisdom it may bring you.

But medication, remarkable as its ability is to rapidly alter one's outlook, cannot always complete the job alone, nor does it meet everyone's needs. Depression is isolating. Sufferers feel like outcasts and misfits, that others neither reach out to nor understand them, and that there is little hope of a turnaround. Having a good and knowledgeable therapist is like falling off the high wire into a welcoming safety net, one with a ladder down to terra firma. Be aware, however, that starting therapy while still walking the wire can blunt its good effects. A negative, pessimistic outlook warps reality; trying to concentrate and sort things out while it is still in full force can lead to more discouragement and wastes precious HMO-paid sessions.

Choosing a Therapy

Whether you decide to start therapy immediately or later, you and your therapist's choice of IPT or CBT (the two types covered here) should be guided by the way your depression has altered your outlook. Are you subject to defeatist thoughts about yourself and the world? Do you automatically expect everything to turn out for the worst? Do you rate yourself ineffective, inadequate, and of little value? If so, CBT, developed by psychiatrist Aaron T. Beck of the Beck Center for Cognitive Therapy in Philadelphia, can help. Or are you constantly embroiled in conflicts with your significant other, your coworkers, and the people with whom you deal on a regular basis? Are all your relationships going sourly up blind alleys, leaving you and everyone else antagonistic, frustrated, and angry? If so, IPT, designed by psychiatrist Gerald Klerman, will help you understand that your attitudes and behavior affect others, and that you need to grasp the dynamic at work and adjust your ways.

Attempts to justify one or the other of these two therapies as the best ring hollow because different people have wildly varying psyches and lives. A study that assembles a small group of depressed people, treats some with CBT or IPT, and then proclaims that either is better fails to take this diversity into account. While some generalizations are true—"Depression leads to negative thinking" and "Talk therapy helps many"—it overstates the case to argue that people fall neatly into this or that category of human being. Some who have severe interpersonal problems and so appear to be prime candidates for IPT, one psychiatrist told me, gain insights but not solutions to their problems and end up in an even worse bind than before. The same is true of CBTers with dysfunctional attitudes. The mind resists pigeonholing, and so do experienced therapists.

These short-term therapies share certain rules. They are time-limited (eight to sixteen weekly sessions); their emphasis is on changing current behavior and thinking; they require self-monitoring of change and progress and often involve "homework" between sessions; and the therapist is active and directive. The last is of particular importance. Traditional, open-ended psychotherapy puts the burden of self-discovery on the patient, who is expected to talk and talk while a therapist listens, occasionally interjecting a question like, "What does that bring to mind?" but without making helpful suggestions.

Practitioners of the newer therapies get involved. They help their patients recognize the connection between their illness and the problems it is causing and work jointly with them to discover alternative modes of thinking and behaving. Short-term therapists will not interpret your dreams, delve into your early childhood, encourage you to free associate, take a look at your fantasy life, or explore past origins of your current actions. Another important distinction is that they discourage "transference" and dependency on the therapist, concentrating instead on providing patients with insights and tools to function well on their own.

If an undiagnosed depression has been around long enough to cast negative thinking in concrete, the therapist may suggest that short-term therapy be followed by some of the more traditional sort, termed "expressive." If you decide this may be helpful and the allotment of therapy sessions reimbursed by your HMO has been used up, you can always wait until the following January. What you have learned from your short-term work should serve you well in the meantime and you may even turn up some insights of your own. Even if you believe further therapy isn't necessary, an occasional booster session or two will keep you on track.

Psychotherapy for Postpartum Depression

I admit to a lingering skepticism about the benefits of talk versus pills but had I been forced to endure postpartum depression, I would surely have banged on a therapist's door. A 1999 conference held by Postpartum Services International (PSI) provided an opportunity to talk to many practicing psychotherapists who have suffered through this illness, among them the two mothers, Jill and Hanna, whose experiences with postpartum depression and psychosis are related in Chapter 5. The combination of personal experience and clinical training makes for an excellent choice of therapist for a PPD mother.

Jill never volunteers to patients her own decision to forgo antidepressants because, she explained, "I'm aware that maybe they'll think, 'If she can do it, so can I.'" She believes there are many situations that mandate their use, including sleep deprivation and postpartum psychosis, and she warns mothers who decide against them that they will have to work much harder. Luckily, her own depression eventually receded and did not return when she gave birth to a second child two years ago. Living through the illness has changed her treatment strategy. "Psychologists are taught never to show their feelings. I threw that training out the window, stopped splitting the strength of my depressed feelings from my psychotherapeutic persona." Many of the other psychotherapists with whom I spoke during the conference have done the same.

"I'm a Bad Mother"

The psychotherapists interviewed for this section of the book tell me that approximately 90 percent of all PPD moms are convinced, as Jill was, that they have made a huge, irreversible mistake. Mothers often believe that their depression comes from not loving their baby, rather than the reverse. And while they may not be aware of the specifics, they strongly suspect their illness of being harmful to their child. "Every single one of them," said one therapist, "is exquisitely sensitive to the tape constantly running in her head, telling her that she is hurting her baby."

Apprehensive that a professional will agree and thus validate their fears, depressed mothers often fail to seek the help they need. The therapist's job is to turn off the tape and get rid of guilt and shame. Mothering instincts tend to go underground when depression is present. "She needs to know she is perfectly capable of love," said another therapist. "Once she understands that all-important truth, it's time to talk about some better coping strategies." The earlier talk therapy begins, the less time there is for reinforcement of distorted thinking.

Experienced therapists know how to open the door to secret guilt and misgivings. Many encourage mothers to bring the baby to therapy sessions because interactions with the infant are revealing. Anxieties show up in moms who refuse to go to the bathroom without taking their child along, or who pay little heed to a tearful infant. Whether or not the child is present, the therapist will pose nonthreatening questions that reveal the presence of depression: "How much weight has the baby gained?" (Is he failing to thrive on schedule?) "Has teething begun?" (Is she fretful and hard to handle?) "How's the new father doing?" (Are you subject to irritability and anger?) "Have you any problems balancing motherhood with the rest of life?" (Are you exhausted and overwhelmed?) Nonaccusatory questions like these uncover depression without provoking guilt and shame. Therapists are nonjudgmental and can reassure self-denigrating and "unloving" moms that their feelings, or lack of them, are a normal symptom of postpartum depression that will disappear with treatment.

While therapists are interested in feelings, they seek information about the home scene. Answers to such questions as, "Do you have to make breakfast for a husband and another child or two?" and "Are you worn to a frazzle during the day?" are followed by suggestions: "Ask him to take on that job until you feel better," and, "Consider hiring the teenager down the street to babysit for an hour or two each day." Perhaps the best advice of all comes from Jill: If you think you don't love your baby, pretend you do. He'll never know you're faking it and soon it will be true.

From Marital to Massage Therapy

The transition from spouse to parent is a major role shift in even the most harmonious relationship. Given depression's propensity for prying apart what love has joined together, marital or couples therapy is often helpful, either alone or in conjunction with individual therapy. The Sichel and Driscoll team includes several psychotherapists trained to tackle a range of options. For instance, a woman may receive short-term therapy and during or after its conclusion realize that she and her husband are still brimming with resentment and distrust. (Sometimes bewildered dads call the therapist's office to voice their concerns, a subject covered in the next chapter.) As with IPT and CBT, couples therapy should be problem-oriented and seek solutions, not just permit reiteration of the same dreary complaints and accusations.

Family therapy is another option. As explained by one of its leading practitioners, Dr. Gabor Keitner, it entails the involvement of "significant others." Significant others may be elderly live-in parents or siblings old enough to articulate their distressed feelings. Marital and family therapy have both been tested for effectiveness and received respectable marks. One consistent finding is that both can speed the depressed person's recovery and act as a bulwark against relapse.

Anyone who has been given a good shampoo knows that a good pair of hands can relieve stress. Babies are no different: Like puppies and kittens, they, too, respond with evident enjoyment to a gentle head or body rub and mothers reap the benefits. A fussy, irritable infant transformed, however briefly, into a cuddly bundle is the equivalent of a rewarding talk therapy session.

Tiffany Field of the Touch Institute, housed in Miami University's School of Medicine, has devoted her career to investigating the benefits of touch, massage, and music therapy on depressed mothers and their infants. One of several researchers who have observed aberrant patterns of brain activity in depressed mothers and their babies through the use of EEG (short for electroencephalogram), she has investigated nonverbal methods of reducing stress. In one of her studies, depressed adolescent mothers received ten thirty-minute sessions of massage therapy over a five-week period. At the close they reported having less anxiety, and Field found hormonal and other biological changes for the better. Pampering can pay off for mother and child.

Insider Tips for Getting the Most Out of Therapy

Psychotherapy is an investment requiring time and money, so make sure before starting that you get some answers from your HMO or other insurance provider, and also from the therapist you are considering.

- First, check out the HMO's reimbursement policy. A belated discovery that you will be stuck with the bill won't help your depression. In the event that your HMO does not cover your therapy, you may want to dip into savings or give up movies, smoking, and manicures to pay for it. For many people it can be a lifesaver.

- Ask the therapist ahead of time, when you are setting up your first appointment, if he or she practices expressive or supportive therapy. If the therapist sounds as though intent on going for insights into the childhood origin of your feelings and problems, say, "Thanks a lot, maybe some other time."

- There are some four hundred varieties of therapy out there. Anyone can hang up a shingle that says Welcome. When you locate a likely therapist, ask if he or she specializes in IPT, CBT, or some other version, how long they have been in business, and if they received any special training and are licensed to practice. Also ask if the therapist has experience in treating depression. A negative reply does not necessarily disqualify him or her from helping you, but a practitioner who knows the ins and outs of this illness is, I personally believe, preferable to someone who doesn't.

- A question about the therapist's view on medication is also wise. Most will respond by saying, "That depends," but you may pick up on a strong disinclination to make a referral to a psychiatrist. If so, proceed with caution. You are not always the best judge of whether you need an antidepressant; a therapist who is not prepared to suggest one when indicated does you a great disservice. One approach is to ask if he or she has a referral list so that you can check to see if it includes any doctors approved by your insurance provider. If they haven't got one, keep looking.

If you are already on medication, ask if the therapist is willing to talk to your psychiatrist or psychopharmacologist so that both know all the facts about your depression's course and treatment.

- Many talk therapists are adamant about confidentiality. This is appropriate if they mean that they won't repeat to your partner, parent, or child what you have said during sessions. However, situations do arise that call for a joint visit with a family member; some practitioners are less apt to accommodate this need than others. Requesting that your husband, for instance, attend a session for a particular need is not a violation of confidentiality, and a therapist who answers with a flat "no" is a poor choice.

The information provided here should ensure that your choice of both therapy and therapist pays off handsomely. If six sessions of a short-term, or indeed any, therapy have yielded no progress after twelve weeks, or if progress is only partial, don't plod on, grim and frustrated. A reputable, experienced therapist will probably agree that not much is being accomplished and may even suggest someone else who might better meet your needs. Or perhaps you and your therapist are just a mismatch and will never work well as a team. It is best to air your doubts early rather than later on. Don't waste time worrying you'll hurt your therapist's feelings, because they are not at issue; yours are.

The decision to select medication, psychotherapy, or both in combination ultimately lies with the depressed person. Do not unquestioningly allocate all responsibility for it to either physician or psychotherapist. As already noted, there are inadequate practitioners in both areas. Your choice should be informed by the psychiatry/psychology dichotomy. All cats may look black in the dark but depressions are not so uniform, nor are the lives and personalities of those who suffer from them. Think carefully about what is best for you.

9

A Father's Role in a Mother's Depression

Fathers who assume that a book on maternal depression relegates them to a minor role in the affair are mistaken. Any story of a mother's depression defies staging as a one-woman show. While it is true that the research literature places mothers at stage center, fathers are prominent members of the cast. How they respond to their partner's depression, how they address the parenting deficits it may have caused, and how they interpret the changed role thrust upon them will influence all the characters in this family drama.

The knowledge and skill you bring to your performance may well dictate the script of the closing act. While this drama will never play as comedy, it should and can have a happy ending. To ensure it does, fathers need to be patient and supportive, preserve a clear memory of the pre-depression partner who with their help will return, and take on some of the parenting responsibilities previously delegated to her. Some of the information in this chapter has already been covered in previous chapters; acting on the suspicion that many fathers won't choose to tackle the entire book, I have summarized it here from a father's rather than a mother's perspective.

The Do's and Don'ts of Husband-Wife Communication

Given the combustible nature of depression-speak, none of the above is easy, but your response to your wife's depression can affect the severity and the course of her illness, not to mention the future of your marriage. On the assumption that you want the former to end and the latter to continue, you must avoid the perils of depression fallout. Collapsing into a state of demoralization and angry resentment results from seeing her, rather than her illness, as the villain.

Shifting that focus isn't easy, but the effort will spawn a welcome side benefit: respite from spats and shouting matches. No rational person engages in an argument with an illness. Casting depression as an "it" rather than a "she" will remind you to retreat from arguments both large and small. When they loom, disengage and get out of range, avoiding such exit lines as, "I can't take any more of this." Rationing the ready supply of disputes minimizes the stress upon both of you, and your children as well.

Two more pieces of advice, equally difficult to put into action: Suppress the urge to criticize and instead offer support. Drs. Gabor Keitner and Ivan Miller, in an overview of depression's impact on family functioning, nail these as critical factors in depression's course and relapse rates. One of the many studies cited in their paper points to criticism as the single best predictor of relapse from tolerable to intolerable depression, or from remission to its return. "You are always negative," "You never want to do anything," and "You really turn me off" may seem at the moment unexaggerated statements of fact, but to a wife and mother trying to stay vertical, they are uppercuts followed by a knockout punch.

Your wife is all too ready to believe what you are saying. The depressed think very poorly of themselves, and although they may behave as though they consider they are the rational one and you the thick-headed, fault-ridden lout, this attitude is adopted as one of the few self-protective mechanisms at their disposal. The husband in Chapter 6, whose wife reproaches him for having no capacity for love, for being manipulative, deceitful, irrationally suspicious, and resentful, is actually listening to her describe herself. When you buy into it as a tirade directed at you and add it to the long list you are compiling as evidence that she is a vindictive loony, you do her and yourself a disservice.

Many depressed spouses employ this technique without conscious awareness. When I was hopelessly depressed and didn't know it, I saw my partner as a hotbed of meanness waiting for a chance to hurt me. I thought a well-aimed character attack would let him know how in control I was. Instead of proving a clever first (and second and third) strike, it encouraged him to leave me.

In those days, a walk on the street was a contact sport. Plowing angrily ahead, I gave no quarter to passersby and indeed relished the jarring bumps I deliberately staged; yet I blamed them. Audibly muttering "son of a bitch" and "God, you're ugly," I looked forward to each such encounter as proof that the world was full of people out to get me. When a depressed wife accuses her husband of being incapable of love, she is going through the litany of qualities and abilities lost to her depression. You won't help her get them back if you make the reply that springs to mind. What's needed is sympathetic support.

Support Leads to Treatment

No matter what their sex, depressed persons need support from the very person they seem working hard to alienate. Disaffected husbands are advised to try to perceive the pre-depression spouse behind her disguise. Those convinced they no longer love their wife have much to gain from holding thoughts of separation and divorce in abeyance. Returning her to normal entails persuading her that she is depressed and that seeing a doctor is the quickest road to recovery.

Some suggestions for doing this have already been given in the chapter on marital conflict, but they won't be successful if unaccompanied by constant support and expressions of your love. One study cited by Dr. Keitner found that depressed men were better able to tolerate—in the sense of resisting relapse—"high levels of expressed emotion" than were the depressed women studied. That's the academic's way of saying you should avoid yelling at her and hurling insults. If that implies we women are the weaker sex, so be it, but it also implies that the male must rise to the challenge of being the stronger.

So handle the topic of treatment with care, wrapping it in assurances that you know there must be something way out of the ordinary to cause her to be so unhappy and unlike her usual self. Bill Parcells may be able to motivate the Jets by goading and shouting, but your wife is not Keyshawn Johnson. If you want her to do what is best for both of you, use a less exasperating model. You might try this approach: "By the way, a guy in the office was telling me that his wife had been feeling so edgy and irritable that she thought she had hypertension, but the doctor said it was only depression. Do you think maybe that could explain why you've been upset lately?" Then assure her you love her, and that it's time you looked after her for a change instead of the other way around—whatever suits the relationship you have in good times.

When the husbands of some of Jeanne Driscoll and Deborah Sichel's patients called to voice their distress at what was going on at home, they were invited to come into their office as a group of four. According to their wives, the ones least expected to open their mouths talked their heads off, although at home they had avoided any dialogue at all. These men all felt they had to tiptoe around for fear of upsetting their wives, who in turn took this as proof that their spouse didn't care about them or understand their pain. In truth, these men had yearned to talk and to be helpful, but had no idea what to say or do, so they opted for silence and distance. When they were encouraged to express their concern and desire to be helpful, the home front atmosphere cleared, husband and wife felt closer to each other, and the family as a whole benefited.

It takes on average four to six weeks for antidepressants to kick in, so from persuasion to peace will require at least twenty-eight more days of patience and support, maybe longer. To a depressed person, that's a lifetime. You leave the house in the morning and don't come back until dinnertime, but your wife—whether she is at home with the kids or in the office—has to cope with depression twenty-four hours a day. If you cruise in and start talking about what a hard day you have had compared to hers, it may provoke a recitation of her own miseries and her conviction that the pills aren't doing any good at all. Instead, bring her flowers, ask how she feels, and reassure her about the waiting period, which varies from person to person.

Remember, too, that marriages don't automatically spring back into their former pattern when depression lifts. Once the gloom and doom are gone, make this a subject for conversation. Work out a game plan together that will prevent you both from falling back into habits of communication acquired while the depression was in residence.

Do Fathers Step In to Fill the Parenting Gap?

The research on the effects of maternal depression on kids gives the impression that offspring are the product of immaculate conception. Even though the research consistently identifies spousal conflict due to depression as a dominant contributor to behavioral and other problems, the word "father" rarely turns up. A partial explanation for this lies in the assumption, usually accurate, that the mother is the principal caregiver. But even research on how fathers interact with the children when Mom is depressed is largely absent. What little work has been done in this area casts dads in an unflattering light. Many trapped in the chaos depression creates within a family beat a retreat from the fray, distancing themselves from both wife and children. One researcher, Eugene Dadds, offers some insights into the processes linking conflicted marriages, parental depression, and child difficulties.

Dadds argues that it is likely that as fathers withdraw from parenting the mother's exposure to coercive, emotionally taxing exchanges with the child increases. This increased exposure induces and exacerbates her depressed mood, further undermining her attempts at effective parenting. As the child grows more difficult to handle, the father steps further and further away from both at a time when they are in particular need of his understanding, love, and support.

Another possible scenario is that instead of benching himself, the father focuses excessively on the child, "triangling" him or her and turning the child into a Super Bowl trophy for which both he and the mother compete. The son or daughter is labeled ally by one and turncoat by the other, with appellations shifting from one minute to the next. Not only does this deprive the child of any comfort at all; it also breaks down any effective distance between the child and the parents' distress. This predicament opens the way for conflicted loyalties, and to a great deal of stress as well. Kids don't want to have to choose one parent over another; they need and deserve a mother and a father who work together to serve their child's best interests.

While stressed-out children whose parents seem to hate each other may feel they are somehow responsible for the war, that doesn't keep them from blaming Mom for the disruption in their daily life. She is, after all, the person spending the most time coping, albeit unsuccessfully, with the behavioral problems her illness has invoked in them, while you're only home in the evening. Constant criticism from her child—very often her only source of comfort and pleasure in a world that seems lacking in promise or hope—is unendurable. Already feeling incompetent and dangerously low on self-esteem, she will sink even lower when the child's criticism is added to yours. It is a vicious circle of the nastiest sort, easy to enter and difficult to break. Since her ability to break this vicious circle is undermined by her depression, this responsibility rests with you.

The Father As Hero: What He Can Do for His Child

Whatever parenting role it has been your habit to assume, now is the time to be coach, quarterback, center, and tight end rolled into one. Nobody else is available to play these positions.

If you are not a football fan, think of yourself as both designer of your child's well-being software and power for the hard drive.

First and foremost, spend more time with your child. Start by letting your wife know that you understand she's pushed to the max and that you want to take some of the pressure off. This will help to circumvent suspicion that maybe you're just trying to replace her in your offspring's affections. If your immediate reaction to the more-time suggestion is that your job won't allow it, consider that millions of single and married mothers juggle careers and parenting.

Most employers routinely make allowances for a mother's absence when her child is ill or when babysitters cop out at the last minute, but fathers rarely think of asking if a similar dispensation is available to them. Many men are fearful of taking time for home duties because they think bosses and coworkers will see them as lightweights or wimps. But any employee who asks for time to attend to a spouse's illness is granted it without questions. There's no need to explain exactly what the illness is; hints that it is very worrying will forestall more probing queries.

If your child is acting up in school and the teachers want to talk about why, an hour or two out of the office won't ruin your career prospects. If he or she has a big game and no one to root from the sidelines, or if they seem particularly lonely and in need of comforting, leave the office a little early and take them to McDonald's for a treat. Give your child your office telephone number and encourage calls at times of need. If they come in the middle of an important meeting, tell him or her to stand by the telephone and call back as soon as possible, even if only to say that you'll be home by seven and have nothing more important to do than spend time with them.

What Children of a Depressed Mother Need

Children whose mother becomes seriously depressed grieve for her loss in much the same manner they do for a father who is absent due to separation or divorce. They miss her warmth, her availability, the reassuring discipline she imposes, and the coherence and predictability this brings to their day. Even loving fathers sometimes neglect a child's need for predictable continuity, preferring to spend time playing instead of on their basic needs. Dads are more apt to joust and tumble with their kids, to introduce new ideas, and to encourage them to think big. Children need all this, which is one of the many reasons fathers are so essential to their development, but they need the mothering attention as well. It's the combination of the two that makes for an outward- and upward-bound kid.

The bickering and selfishness typical of a depression-ridden household bring in their trail a lack of order that is extremely upsetting for younger members of the family. One of the reasons children of a depressed parent do poorly in school is that previous rules about homework, dating, and chores are no longer enforced. Kids complain loudly about discipline, but they are lost without it; knowing what their parents expect of them is reassuring. Whether or not they are consciously aware of it, they interpret discipline's sudden absence as an indication that they are less important than before, and that their parents no longer care what they do. An angry retort, such as, "Do what you want and see where it gets you," is contrary to their hopes and expectations, and sounds dangerously like "You don't matter to me."

Mothers suffering from depression are poor discipliners because they cannot handle the hassle and haggle. Fathers need to take up the slack. Facing up to a child bent on watching television or playing with the computer instead of doing homework may not be the ideal way to end a day, but your offspring's school performance will suffer if you don't. The best discipline is fair and based on previously set criteria. In this respect, children do not like surprises. When they know what has always been expected of them, too many sudden allowances make them feel uneasy and insecure. Because most aren't yet equipped to navigate on their own, they may choose negative paths.

Whether or not fathers help their kids with homework and other class assignments, they should make it clear that they have to be completed on time. All assigned chores, as, for instance, bed-making and table-clearing, should be enforced. Set and stick to boundaries about television-watching, bedtime, and phone time. Allowing routines to crumble is dangerous for kids and will also give you and your wife yet another reason for accusations like, "You can't even control the kids," and "What kind of a mother are you anyway?"

Restrain the temptation to commiserate with your child by criticizing your depressed wife. At some point he or she will begin a conversation by saying, "Mom is always so cross," doesn't understand me, stays in her bedroom with the door closed, cries about everything, and so forth. While all children engage in the game of playing one parent off against the other, this is the worst possible time to for you to take the child's side. The child may have good reasons for complaining of a depressed mother, but chiming in with your own concurring views is obviously not the way to handle it. Instead, explain that she's upset because she doesn't feel well, that her behavior doesn't stem from any lack of affection, and that she will be better soon.

Make your message age-appropriate. Little kids need cuddling and more quality time with you. Those in grade school ask more probing questions about just what exactly is making Mom so different from usual, and they deserve a fuller explanation. Many teenagers are aware of depression: Don't dodge their questions and concerns. Instead, emphasize how common this illness is, how many well-known, successful people suffer or have suffered from it, and how easy it is to treat. Your goal is to demystify the mother's behavior and to ensure your son or daughter doesn't connect it to her love for them.

For Fathers Who Are Separated or Divorced

Absent fathers have an even greater challenge than resident dads. Quite possibly, they aren't living at home because the depression caused friction and fighting. Already aggrieved separated or divorced dads sometimes welcome bad news from home because it validates their decision to leave. When kids report that their mother is interfering with their fun and making life impossible, some ex-partners will be tempted to fall into an I-told-you-so mode. There is a homily in the Bible (Jeremiah 31:29) that says, "The fathers have eaten sour grapes, and the children's teeth are set on edge." The obvious course is to keep your sour grapes to yourself and nourish your child with milk and honey instead.

As a divorced parent myself, I am fully aware of how difficult this is. To my credit, I fought against trashing my ex-husband, an undepressed but truly atrocious parent, until my daughter was entering her mid-teens and was well aware of his shortcomings. No matter how poor your opinion of your former mate, your child loves and needs her. Hearing unpleasant things from you about his or her mother is not comforting.

All the suggestions for compensating for temporary maternal parenting deficits apply also to weekend fathers. If you aren't permitted to see your child at other times, step up your phone calls. Lest your wife resent this, make it clear that the purpose of each call is specific: Did your son by any chance catch the Jets game on Monday night? Did your daughter score a goal in the soccer match? How are the measles spots looking, and are the contact lenses easier to put in? When you do see your kids, try to say something positive about your ex-wife and hope your child will deliver the message that you noticed her great new haircut or that the party she threw for her book club sounded terrific. Make sure you maximize the time you are allowed to spend together by diverting your child's attention from problems at home with expeditions to the zoo or a museum.

Trying to bake a cake and playing a new computer game are good activity picks because your child will find your ineptitude hilariously funny. This is not the time to teach a clumsy child how to ride a bike or to take a self-consciously overweight one shopping for a new pair of jeans. Choose activities they are good at and let them shine with self-esteem. Next to love and attention, it's what they need the most.

Fathers Get Depressed Too

Whether the gender gap in depression rates is an artifact or real, many men do become depressed. When they do, they are often even worse than women at detecting what is wrong. Most firmly reject the idea of depression as the culprit because they subscribe to the macho myth that men don't cry, that they should pull themselves up by their masculine bootstraps and take charge of their feelings. Boston psychologist Terrence Real, in his book *I Don't Want to Talk About It: Overcoming the Secret*

Legacy of Male Depression, advances the thesis that the traditional socialization of boys and girls results in differing reactions to their experience of depression. "Girls, and later women," he writes, "tend to internalize pain. They blame themselves and draw distress into themselves." Boys and adult men, on the other hand, tend to "externalize pain; they are more likely to feel victimized by others and to discharge distress through action." Male modes of action cited by Real as "covers" for depression include workaholism, alcoholism, and lashing out at others, sometimes violently enough to be termed abuse. However they express it, depressed men are every bit as miserable and difficult to be with as depressed women.

When Andrew Solomon, a successful young writer, had published his novel, had come to terms with the death of his mother three years earlier, was getting along with the family, and had bought a beautiful new house, "Depression came slinking in and spoiled everything. I'd felt acutely," he writes, "that there was no excuse for it under the circumstances, despite perennial existential crises, the forgotten sorrows of a distant childhood, slight wrongs done to people now dead, the truth that I am not Tolstoy, the absence in this world of perfect love, and those impulses of greed and uncharitableness which lie too close to the heart—that sort of thing."

He read the good reviews of his book with indifference and felt tired all the time. When he returned from a trip to Europe, the phone calls, social events, and conversations he used to relish became intolerable. "I started to feel numb," he continues, "I didn't care about work, family, or friends. My writing slowed, then stopped. My usually headstrong libido evaporated."

When Andrew broke a dinner date with his father and admitted to having no idea why, his parent went round to his apartment and took charge. Through the long battle back to normalcy, one that included enough antidepressants to start a pharmacy before finding one that worked well for Andrew, the senior Solomon remained in charge. He was patient and encouraging and assured his son that he would soon be back to working twelve hours a day and going to four parties every night. "He might as well have told me I would build a helicopter out of cookie dough and fly to Neptune," writes his son. If Andrew, devoid of appetite, was defeated by the challenge of getting a piece of lamb chop onto his fork, his father did it for him, cut the rest into little pieces, and made him promise to do the same for him when his teeth fell out from old age. At last the sky turned blue and stayed that way; to Andrew it seemed nothing short of a miracle. "Recent happiness feels enormous and embracing," he writes, "and beyond anything I have ever imagined. . . . The opposite of depression is not happiness but vitality, and my life, as I write this, is vital, even when it's sad."

Recovered, Andrew spoke with other male sufferers of depressive illness, among them Robert Boorstin, a senior advisor to the secretary of the treasury and an outspoken advocate for the mentally ill. Boorstin, who lives with a lifelong diagnosis of manic depression, told him that during four years on Prozac he did not have an orgasm in intercourse, which he "considered a fairly major drawback." Since the quote is couched in the past tense, he must, like many other men, have figured out with the help of his doctor how to circumvent this extremely distressing side effect of many antidepressants.

Lack of sexual desire and impotence send many men to doctors, who tell them that depression suppresses sexual desire and performance, and also that antidepressants tend to do the same. News of this catch-22 isn't as much of a blow as it may appear. Expert psychiatrists and psychopharmacologists tinker with medications and try various combinations until they find one that suppresses depression without inhibiting sexual desire and performance.

Depressed men aren't wimps. Major sports stars, kings of industry and finance, famous artists, writers, and entertainers suffer from this illness. They go on succeeding despite it because treatment allows them to do so. Mike Wallace admits that when his first bout hit it was his wife, Mary, who recognized it as depression. "I didn't want to acknowledge to my pals at *60 Minutes* what was going on, nor did I tell my children," says Mike. "I was simply ashamed of having to bear the stigma of that shameful word depression." Since then he has positively shouted the word to the wide audience he commands. "There is no way possible," he adds, "to describe the anguish that a depressive can put his family through. Gloom, doom, no love, no real communication, short temper, and leave-me-alone fault-finding. Why more marriages don't break up under those desolate circumstances is a puzzle for you know deep down the damage you're doing to the ones you care about."

These are persuasive reasons for treating depression as soon as it appears; Bob Boorstin and Andrew Solomon make equally telling points. Genes aren't fussy about where they travel; the vulnerability to depression they carry can deliver the same punch to a man as to as woman. So, would you prefer to be in top form like Mike Wallace, or would you rather risk emulating Ernest Hemingway, who lost both his talent and his life to depression?

10

When Older Mothers Are Depressed

I know three sixty-something mothers with depression. Two have been on antidepressants for a dozen years or so; the third should be but isn't. The first now enjoys a glorious relationship with her child after years of friction and hassle that culminated in a two-year boycott by her daughter. She attributes her fortunate outcome to a combination of medication, an exceedingly wise and sensitive child, and sheer determination on the part of both to actualize the love and devotion that they bear for each other.

The second mother avoided the years of heartbreak endured by the first because she realized at a tender age that her own mother, a depressed, tyrannical, and remote woman, was grossly lacking as a parent, and used that knowledge to keep her relationship with her five kids intact through her own pre-medication years. Both these mothers are leading satisfying and productive lives, enhanced by involvement in the lives of their grown children.

The third mother is aimless, often dissatisfied, seems lonely despite a wide acquaintanceship, and is subject to countless minor health problems. She obviously loves her two offspring but complains of them to her friends. Among the eight children these women have collectively borne, five suffer or have at some point suffered either depressive symptomatology or full-fledged depression of their own, plus associated problems of drinking and drug abuse. All five struggle in varying ways with interpersonal relationships.

I am mother number one. An old friend who wishes to remain anonymous is number two; she has chosen for herself the name Abby Smith. The third I will call Diana. Together, our stories map the various routes depression can take through a woman's life, how it can affect relations with her adult children, and how awareness, treatment, and constructive thinking can at any stage of life put an upset family back on track. They also illustrate why some researchers on depression have shifted away from discussion of it as just a biological illness or the product of dysfunctional thinking about the self and the environment and instead look at it as an "interpersonal disorder"—academic shorthand for being unable to engage with others in mutually rewarding fashion.

One such researcher is Constance Hammen, observer of the laundry mother and her child, introduced to you in Chapter 6. The symptoms Professor Hammen associates with an interpersonal disorder are loss of pleasure, usually entailing diminished enjoyment of formerly engaging relationships, often accompanied by social withdrawal; irritability directed toward others; increased dependency as a result of feeling helpless and inadequate; and heightened sensitivity to perceived rejection. As you now know, these are most of the psychological symptoms of depression. "Reduced energy and motivation," Professor Hammen observes, "commonly result in difficultly sustaining effort or participation in activities, including interpersonal contacts. It seems to [such people] easier to give up on effortful interactions, or to avoid them entirely. The characteristics of this sort of depressive thinking undoubtedly lead sufferers to evaluate themselves and those around them in pejorative terms." Although longing for contact and support, they may nonetheless believe that others are insensitive and incapable of providing them. Indeed, she adds, when offered them, they are unlikely to feel comforted.

As you will see, Professor Hammen's words describe my friend Diana to a T, from her state of mind and her personal history to her relations with her kids and former spouses. Depression is always isolating, especially so for older women. Depressed or not, in the second half of life they often find themselves widowed, divorced, and spending less time in the office or in community activities and more on their own. For those suffering from an interpersonal disorder, or from depression, their sense of feeling alone and neglected by their grown children can easily escalate. Suicide, always a possible outcome of serious depression, can become a tragic reality.

This illness is vastly underdiagnosed in the fifty-plus age group because many physicians explain away its symptoms as "normal" reactions to living in a youth-oriented culture and to loss, constricted financial circumstances, a weakening of the traditional family, or to the illnesses that plague many older folk. Doing so endangers a woman's health and concurrently deepens her distress by suggesting that age goes hand-in-hand with loneliness and insoluble problems, that somehow they are an older person's lot. Nothing could be further from the truth. In reality, depression prevalence rates among older women are lower than in younger ones, but afflicted seniors are even less likely to be recognized and to be properly treated for the illness.

As a result, many depressed older women resemble my friend Diana, a poster child for depression as an interpersonal disorder. This chapter starts with her story and ends with my own. In between come Abby's experience and what she has learned from it, and a discussion of depression as a health hazard to the over-fifty age group.

Diana: "I'm Not Depressed, I Just Have Problems"

Diana had three attractive, intelligent husbands, but over the years they must have decided that her many gifts weren't worth the effort that daily life with her required. It's dangerous to assess a marriage from the outside. Perhaps their behavior, variously described by her as insensitive, manipulative, or cruel, took place behind closed doors, but today all three are contentedly married to other women. Can her son really be so wayward and stubborn, and her daughter so selfish and unable to take constructive criticism as Diana suggests? Far more likely, this mother's pervasive gray mood and sporadic sorties into black gloom are largely responsible for the troubles with her ex-husbands and for the stressful relations she has with her kids.

It wasn't always that way. When we first met almost forty years ago, Diana was dynamite—the good kind. Energetic, bright, beautiful, and accomplished, she was the object of admiration and envy of all her friends. Long before the rest of us felt secure in our chosen careers, she was excelling in hers as membership director of a major museum. She hung out with Jackson Pollock and other greats of the times, was invited to international seminars and conferences, and made a real splash in the art world. Her then husband was a likeable but reserved man. When she traded him in after a childless five years, we figured he just couldn't keep up with her, that she needed a more dynamic mate as a challenge.

She soon found one and they had two children who were seventeen and twenty when the couple finally split after two decades of locking horns, sometimes in public and presumably in private, too. Parker was, she told her friends, resentful of her success, even though he made a lot of money on the stock market for his family and clients. She often complained that he didn't pay enough attention to either her or the kids. "He doesn't care about us as people, we're just something he owns and supports," Diana used to say. Nevertheless, he bought a handsome house in the country for the family and taught his children how to ride and swim, knew their teachers well, and turned up at school events.

When Diana was passed over for an expected promotion at the museum, Parker advised her to resign and look for another job, a suggestion she characterized as insensitive. "How can he be so flippant and casual," she asked us, "when he knows how hard I've worked at this one, all the time and effort I've invested in it?" She stayed on for years but never achieved that next level of accomplishment. When she informed us that Parker had gotten involved with another women, we took her side and ostracized him. By the time Parker remarried, Diana was embroiled in an alimony battle with her third husband, whose time in the picture was so short we hardly came to know him.

According to Diana, her children are more of a trial than a source of support. Her journalist daughter is busy with work and family and rarely comes to visit so Diana travels to Michigan to stay with them. "I don't see why they can't ever come home," she says, adding that last year the ritual Christmas phone came on December 26 because they were off skiing somewhere. "I suppose she forgot," she adds, with more than a hint of self-pity. Her son, an actor, has yet to land a leading role. Diana's take is that he isn't aggressive and cunning enough to succeed. "Look at my own experience," she sighs, "Where did naivete get me except under other people's feet?"

I love my old friend Diana. She is an entertaining, informative encyclopedia, full of facts and theories about art, literature, and other mutual interests. When focused on them, she is a delight to be with, but I limit the time I spend with her because I weary of the negativity she dips into when discussing anything personal. I used to think that I could, by holding up my own experience, awaken Diana to the probability that she suffers from depression and that medication would help. "But I'm not depressed," she would tell me with an indignation bordering on outrage. "I just have a lot of problems." Then she would go on, as she often does, about ailments for which doctors can't find medical explanations, such as constant headaches, back pain, rashes, and so forth.

Whenever I mention my own trials and tribulations, Diana offers the kind of advice she would give herself: "Life isn't fair. You really can't do much about it because that's the way things are." And then she interprets whatever is bothering me, whether to do with my daughter or the rest of my life, in terms of her own negative view. "Like it or not, things have changed. Kids nowadays are ungrateful. Half are screwed up and the rest are too busy to care about us."

Even if they haven't had three husbands, many depressed mothers will recognize themselves in the preceding paragraphs. Reading them may spark awareness that some of the problems encountered with your children (and your spouse, too) spring not from their loss of manners or empathy. Rather, your inner compass may be permanently or periodically pointing toward N for negative.

If your daughter is having trouble with her marriage, are you listening to what she has to say and asking questions about how she feels, or are you jumping in with advice based on your own frustrated or failed experiences of married life? When your son moved to Texas for a new job, did you query him on what he will be doing and tell him how proud you are, or did you start off by complaining that now you won't get to see your grandkids? Do you love your children for who and what they are, or do you see only myriad ways they could change for the better, and offer instruction on how? If you turn up on the wrong side of the "or's," perhaps, as happened to depressed Diana, your children love but avoid you because they're put off by your negativity and insistence on molding them to fit your own image. In sum, you may be communicating with them through the filter of depression, just as Abby's mother did.

Abby Smith: "I Am Me, Not My Mother"

Abby, a former classmate of mine, had a parent she describes today as an admirable woman in many respects but "a truly dreadful mother." Every morning she was summoned to her bedside for an interrogation. "Have you done this? Why not?" she would be quizzed, and was then instructed to do it again, this time her mother's way. Item by item, each notation on that day's list would be ticked off neatly with a gold pen. "Nothing I did pleased her. Nothing was ever enough," Abby told me, intoning the depression fallout mantra. "Mother was a total controller and a manipulator, and terribly critical, too," she added. "She wanted my soul and I wasn't about to give it to her. Trying to change her mind was like bouncing off a Teflon shield."

Abby insists that as early as age five she already knew she had a terrible mother. Although Mrs. Smith appeared generous and attentive to her own friends, always remembering their birthdays and sending them checks in hard times (in part, says her daughter, because she enjoyed their indebtedness to her), she never sat Abby on her lap, never read her a book, never gave her a spontaneous hug.

A loveless childhood was rendered even more distressing by a succession of poorly supervised nannies. One veritable ogre of a nurse, hired because she claimed to have a degree in psychology and thus presumably would know how to deal with a difficult child, spanked Abby with a hairbrush and resorted to other disciplinary measures that a good caretaker would never consider, let alone employ. Nevertheless, she stayed with the family for two years. Indeed, Abby's mother later admitted that she hadn't wanted either of her two children to become overly attached to someone else. When, in the fourth grade, Abby acted out her misery by being obstreperous, angry, and hard to control in the classroom, her teachers suspected that something was amiss at home. A call to Mrs. Smith, however, elicited the confident response that, No, of course not, everything was fine.

In truth, nothing was fine in Abby's life. At twelve she was packed off to see a child psychiatrist, who, on the initial visit, asked if she knew why she was there. "Because my mother wanted me to come," replied Abby, "but then why isn't she here, too?" He observed that that was a good question, and then offered some revealing advice: "Let me tell you something about your mother. She is an entirely inflexible woman. Since she's only thirty-three, if you want to enjoy your childhood, you'll have to be the one to change." Abby did try to change, not in order to please her mother but to improve her relationships with peers. When she returned from a year in the country, her old classmates were not pleased to see her again. "Why did you come back?" they asked her. "Don't you know how unpopular you are?" So Abby embarked on changing her façade. She would strive, she decided, to be the nice, flattering person she thought they would like. She overdid it. "It became a habit," she says. "Even today I find it difficult to take a strong stand in opposition to anyone. I can't deal with confrontation."

At nineteen she tried Catholicism, in part to annoy her Jewish mother, but principally in the hope of finding a more benign source of direction than her parent. "I felt I wasn't a good person, that I couldn't possibly be as good as I should be. I was full of guilt and angry at myself. I always felt lesser than others." A few years later Abby abandoned Catholicism, because, she realized, she was looking for a way to be a better person, not for a religion.

Abby had prefaced our conversation by stating that she had no medical proof of her mother's depression, but with so many stories from similarly raised children under my belt, and from my personal experience, I join her in identifying maternal depression as the primary cause of her mother's poor parenting. In addition to Mrs. Smith's remote, critical, and controlling behavior, there is evidence to be found in Abby's giveaway emotional hangups: her fear of confrontation, her insecurity, her dissatisfaction with her achievements, and a demeaning self-image. A slim and elegant woman, Mrs. Smith was furious to learn that she had become pregnant on her honeymoon; in later years she blamed her daughter for ruining her figure. I was not surprised to learn that like myself, Abby became an overweight secret eater, nor that for years she viewed her own body with distaste.

There are inklings of intimacy problems in confidences shared with me about Abby's first, failed marriage, and her comment that she hadn't felt herself deserving of nice, normal men, although the couple had three kids to whom she is very close. She appears to have chosen wisely the second time round and delightedly confirmed my guess that her current husband, the father of her fourth and fifth children, is also her best friend.

The Prozac unavailable to her mother has transformed Abby's life, as she gleefully told me three times. Soon after she began taking it some ten years ago she suddenly realized, "Oh, my God, I really am all the things I've been pretending to be. I'm nice and I'm smart. Now I don't have to pretend anymore!" Her whole world changed as a result.

She now gives herself due credit for an impressive list of accomplishments, including several successful books and the chairmanship of a large and powerful organization. But although Prozac catapulted her out of the negative and toward the positive, she is still not entirely free of a past during which she felt herself to be "an utterly fraudulent person. I was scared silly when they asked me to join the board of directors," she said. "I had never felt confident to do anything other than give money."

About the same time Abby went on Prozac, her mother died at the age of ninety-two. She describes the moment when she and the trained nurse were sitting on either side of her mother's hospital bed, each holding a finger to the pulse. When it stopped, she blurted out, "Now what?" The nurse began sympathetically to explain the various steps that would be taken. "But what I really meant," says Abby, was, "What do I do with all this relief and freedom?"

Growing up, Abby says she always had a strong need to preserve her own personality; wondrously, she has. And unlike the depressed offspring of some depressed moms, she has become a solid source of loving attention, support, and companionship to her five kids. The nightmare of her own upbringing and its ill effects upon her must have been like a primer on good parenting, one she constantly reviewed. Even when her long-unmedicated depression was in the ascendant, she told her children that her behavior had nothing to do with them: "When I'm in a bad mood you mustn't think, as I always did, that it's your fault, because it's not." Fortunately, they believed her. "Given your depression," I asked her, "do you think you could have done that if you hadn't been aware of your own depressed mother's shortcomings?" "No way," she replied. "I would be a very lonely parent right now."

Pressed to give an example of how she acted as a depressed mother, Abby chose the Christmas party for 125 friends and family members she used to insist on throwing every year. Despite financial resources that might have made help possible, her perfectionism and need for control drove her to do all the cooking and preparation herself, right down to the last polished piece of silver and the vases full of flowers. "I was irritable, anxious, and cross. I made my husband and kids miserable and told them to get out of my way, that there was nothing they could do to help. I was an Iron Maiden," she added, "just as driven and puritanical in my way as my mother was."

At the first sign of pressure, whether at Christmas or any other time, the mom who played delirious games of Sardines in the dark was replaced by a copy of her mother. After each blowup, however, she would apologize and hug her family. "It's me, you know, not you," she would reiterate, and that insight is what distinguishes her from so many other depressed moms.

Depression and Loneliness

Unlike Abby, many older depressed mothers are lonely and alienated from children who love them. But love isn't enough to counteract the feelings of inadequacy, guilt, and self-condemnation that such a negative parenting style engenders.

One forty-eight-year-old informs me that her mom used to tell her to be sure to get a job and have fun when she grew up because once she had children she would be trapped and have no life of her own. "I can remember her crying and saying, 'I just want to curl up on a nickel and die.' She would say that if I didn't make life so difficult for her, she wouldn't feel that way. For years I thought I was a horrible person because I didn't live up to her expectations." No one in the family, this still-alienated, middle-aged daughter reports, ascribed to anything other than laziness their mother's lack of initiative to get jobs, make friends, or do much of anything with her life.

Another woman, herself the mother of two, forces herself to visit her depressed mother several times a week, but feels guilty for not doing more. "I just hate spending time with her or even talking on the phone because all she does is moan and complain and criticize. I know I shouldn't feel that way but I have problems, too. Even if I'm fifty-one years old I still need a mother who cares about me," she wistfully added. "Now I haven't got one anymore and sometimes I feel my life would be better without her. That's a dreadful thing to feel, isn't it?" Her mother stubbornly refuses to try medication. Although both need each other, they remain locked in mutual loneliness. I suggested that she be more insistent about treatment, and that she call her mother's doctor, give him the facts, and make an appointment for all of them to talk together.

Although it is relatively rare for depression to make a first-time appearance late in life, it can happen, usually following a traumatic event such as the loss of a husband or retirement. Grieving is a normal reaction: Most people gradually pull out of it and adjust to the loss; some find this impossible and become mired in permanent gloom. Adult children rush to comfort their widowed or listlessly inactive mother and end up suffering from depression fallout. There are no winners in these situations.

One such child said she is lucky because her mother didn't become noticeably depressed until the age of fifty and lives two thousand miles away. "But her emotional withdrawal has hurt me," she says. "I feel that I have lost a friend. I had pretty much become passive in the face of her anger, but now that I have a better understanding of what is driving her, I hope I can interact without being flooded by anger of my own." She plans, she added, to keep up a low-level but constant effort to get her mom to consider treatment, but "she is a tough nut to crack. She says her life is over and that treatment is no use because it cannot change her situation." Helpless dismay was evident in her voice. All the symptoms of depression fallout—confusion, self-blame, demoralization, anger, and avoidance of her parent—were there, inhibiting the affection and attention both presumably miss.

When Depression Is Overlooked in Older People

All the things that older people most prize and work hard to maintain take a beating from depression. The ability to think and to feel, to interact with others, to share a sense of purpose, to work, to love, to express gratification, to care for others, and to live independently are all adversely affected. And so is their health. For this age group, depression is a real killer, not only from suicide but also from its exacerbating effects on many other illnesses. Depression cohabits with cancer, cardiovascular disease, arthritis, and neurological disorders such as stroke and Alzheimer's. In addition, it is strongly suspected of lowering the immune system, increasing the likelihood that a serious illness will get worse. So why is depression even more consistently underdiagnosed in older people than in younger ones? Part of the answer lies with doctors and part with the sufferers themselves.

Depression at any age, and especially in over-fifties, often mimics the symptoms of other illnesses and so gets overlooked. Many doctors and patients buy into the ageist myth that with spouses and friends dying all around you and other serious health problems to worry about, feeling sad and discouraged is a normal reaction. Further muddying the waters, while younger people are more apt to be better educated about depression and accept its biological basis, older folk see it as a stigma, a sign of being weak-kneed and short on gumption. Instead of complaining of despair to a doctor, they talk about their dwindling appetite and uneasy sleep, symptoms not specific enough to make most physicians reach for the prescription pad.

Self-awareness is always elusive but is particularly so for over-fifty women. In their case, it is often the doctors who come up with other explanations for hopelessness and apathy. Some physicians—the ones who advise you to go out and have a little fun, maybe take a cruise—are just plain out-of-date and insulting to boot, with their hints that "mature" women lead dull lives. Those who think you have lost your pleasure in living because you've had a mastectomy or a serious heart attack are closer to the mark, but even they may fail to suggest antidepressants as a good solution because they are unaware that depression and the state of one's health are intimately related.

The cost of medication, which runs from sixty dollars to a hundred dollars a month, can be another formidable obstacle to getting well. Given the existing constraints on reimbursement, when their pharmacist says, "That will be eighty dollars for this month," many sufferers say "No thanks" and walk away. Even if they do reach for their wallet, they often take the pills and then abandon them because their doctor has not told them that these drugs often take longer to work in older than in younger people, sometimes from six to twelve weeks instead of three or four.

A further complication is that many in this age group are more apt to experience side effects, among them agitation, nausea, or dizziness, and there can be adverse reactions when antidepressants are combined with some other medications. Sometimes the poor concentration that accompanies depression teams up with the I-know-you-I-just-can't-remember-your-name forgetfulness of middle age to cause 70 percent of older pill-takers to skip their daily dose frequently enough to reduce its effectiveness.

All these factors add up to alarming statistics: Only about one sixth of all older people with depression seek treatment and only one sixth of that one sixth ever receive it. Of those who do begin a course of treatment, a whopping 75 percent give up before they ever experience its benefits. That postretirement dream of having time to enjoy children and grandchildren, to play golf and laze in the sun, to pursue hobbies and learn new skills, fizzles out in apathy, irritation, and the feeling that it is time for an exit.

Many exit by their own hand. The suicide rate in the general population is 12.4 per one hundred thousand, but in the eighty to eighty-four age group it is 26.5 per one hundred thousand, with younger elders not far behind. Shockingly, the majority of those who choose this way out of despair have seen a doctor within the preceding month, over half of them in the week before their self-inflicted death. But even for those who choose to stay, untreated depression can have serious health consequences.

Unhappy Hearts and Cardiovascular Illness

Which comes first: depression or heart disease? So intimate is the connection between the two that the medical world is hard put to decide which is cause and which is effect. While about 5 percent of the entire population is depressed at any given moment, in patients with heart disease, it is closer to 18 percent. When Dr. Nancy Frasure-Smith of the Montreal Heart Institute followed 222 patients who had suffered heart attacks, she found that the depressed among them were four times as likely to die in the next six months as those who were not depressed. According to her, depression turns out to be as good a predictor of imminent death from heart disease as a poor heart history. Dr. Robert Carney, professor of medical psychology at Washington University in St. Louis, found that depressed people with newly diagnosed heart disease were twice as likely to have a heart attack and to require a bypass in the next year as similar patients free of depression.

Evidence that depression actually leads to heart disease is mounting. In a study of fifteen hundred Baltimoreans, Dr. William W. Eaton of Johns Hopkins discovered that those who were depressed were four times as likely to have a heart attack in the next fourteen years, making depression as grave a risk as elevated levels of cholesterol. The supposition of researchers is that depression brings about certain chemical changes in the body that can injure the heart. Its sufferers have a more rapid heartbeat even when asleep, have higher blood pressure, and have blood that tends to clot more easily, all putting their hearts and blood vessels under increased stress.

Depressed people also secrete too much of the stress hormone, cortisol. Cortisol is responsible for the fight-or-flight response, evolution's tool for alerting the body to possible danger and dealing with it. Normally, the response lasts for a few hours or days, but in depression, says Dr. Philip Gold of the NIMH, it turns on and stays that way for weeks, months, or even years. During that period, all the body has time or attention for is mobilizing the necessary fuel for fighting or fleeing. There is none left over for eating, sleeping, sex, or even tissue repair. Necessary as cortisol is to our survival, it's not a good thing to have too much of it racing through the brain and bloodstream. It speeds up the heart rate and can exacerbate arrhythmia, the erratic beating that often precedes sudden death. Moreover, it decreases the secretion of growth hormone, a change that shifts the body's cholesterol in the wrong direction, diminishing the desirable high-density lipoproteins (HDLs) that protect the blood vessels and upping the bad ones. In addition, cortisol spurs accumulation of abdominal fat, enhancing the risk of heart disease.

Additional Serious Health Hazards of Depression

If the above is an insufficient spur to taking your depression to your doctor's office, consider the following. One study of ten thousand men and women over sixty-five with blood pressure readings higher than 160/95 found that over a three-year period, the ones with symptoms of depression suffered strokes at almost three times the rate of their hypertensive but undepressed peers. Depressed patients recovering from a hip fracture and from pneumonia and other infections had more difficulty regaining functions like walking. Other research suggests that up to one third of Alzheimer's patients become clinically depressed at some point in the course of this illness. Doctors, and families, too, often take a fatalistic approach to Alzheimer's and do nothing about the depression, even though some of the afflicted will make small but significant improvements when treated for it.

Psychiatrists who specialize in treating cancer patients say that much the same problems arise there as well. Doctors fail to prescribe an antidepressant because they think, "If I had that illness, I'd feel dreary, too." Often, cancer-related problems, such as pain, are prominent provokers of depression—another major reason some patients adopt what physicians think of as a "rational" approach to suicide.

Depression and Menopause

Given the suspected (although unproven) relationship between a woman's reproductive cycle and depressive symptomatology, one might expect depression to be closely associated with both perimenopause (the seven years preceding menopause) and menopause. This is not the case as reported by many studies. Although perimenopausal symptoms have been observed in up to 10 percent of women, advancing age may actually be a protective factor against the onset or recurrence of major depression. In general, those women who do seek treatment in their menopausal years appear to suffer from minor rather than major depression, and most have been previously troubled by it at some earlier period in their life.

As is so often the case, many doctors discount hormone-related symptoms of depression as "women's complaints," and so fail to prescribe antidepressants. Since hormone replacement therapy (HRT) can for a fair number of women effectively address their symptoms of depression and so make taking an antidepressant unnecessary, it is important to seek a treatment provider who is knowledgeable and experienced in both areas.

Treatment options, which can include HRT or antidepressants, or a combination of both, depend on a number of factors, among them a women's previous experience of depression, her family history, and any possible contraindications to estrogen replacement.

All in all, this hateful illness lays waste to lives in countless ways. It almost laid waste to mine, both as a human being and as a mother. Fortunately, thanks to a hero, my psychopharmacologist, and a heroine, my daughter Pandora, my own story of depression has a happy ending.

My Own Story As a Depressed Mother

Just as I thought I had a happy childhood, I thought I was a good mother, although I came belatedly to realize otherwise. From the start I was determined to be a better parent, albeit a single one, than my mother had been to me. And I would, I silently pledged, make up to my daughter for the shortcomings of her father, who never sent a Christmas or birthday card or present, and who provided the grand sum of one hundred dollars a month for her support—and no alimony. An old-fashioned English nanny and, when she was older, mother's helpers saw to those parts of her parenting needs my job precluded. For a long time it was easy. Like most parents, I thought my child the most remarkable one ever born: the most beguiling, the smartest, and the most beautiful. So did just about everyone else. Her grandmother, her teachers, my friends and hers, even strangers, all praised Pandora with the same enthusiasm I did. She personified the word "blessing."

A few days before her fifteenth birthday she gave me a present: a bound notebook of poems by D. H. Lawrence, Wallace

Stevens, Robert Graves, and other of her favorites, as well as some by her classmates, interspersed with compositions of her own. All were penned neatly in orange ink and preceded by a title page that read, "Mummy, I love you. Lots. Forever. Pandora." I was overwhelmed and thrilled. Although I read the poems not once but many times, sharing them with anyone who would take a look, it was the title page that swelled my heart with joy and complacent parental pride. Basking in its brilliant beam, I myopically overlooked the cri de coeur emanating from the pages that followed.

Rereading them twenty-five years later moves me beyond tears to my first true understanding of my remarkable child. From the first entry—a quotation from Carlos Castenada explaining that the world is "so-and-so only because we tell ourselves that," and that if we change our tune the world will stop being so-and-so—to the final poem of her own, she made me a gift of her fifteen-year-old view of her world. And, more obliquely, of me. One poem about loving and leaving, written by her, should have warned me that all was not well between us.

> Loving is leaving life.
> Don't you agree?
> It's necessary to leave your sanity
> To love.
> Don't you agree?
> Love seems to be a passing phase
> Into which one drifts on a sea of tears.
> Don't you agree?
> I do.

Ten years later, at age twenty-five, she opted out of my life in favor of a motherless one in which she could become herself.

In those intervening years my periodic dips into unrecognized depression became increasingly frequent and fierce. My resentment for her father's cavalier absence from her life found a friend in my growing anger at my own departed parent. When Pandora made a strong case for going away to boarding school, one that seemingly had nothing to do with me, I found her arguments convincing. Each time she returned for vacation or a weekend, we would have a delighted reunion. But soon we would disagree and fight and exchange sulky looks until she mouthed some dim apology I was all too ready to accept without discussion or thought about why we had fallen into such a pattern.

Halfway through her senior year at Yale, she allowed her marks to slide dramatically. Refusing to return home after graduation, she chose instead first to remain in New Haven and then to move into her own apartment in Washington, where I was living at the time. Having recently quit my job for what I thought were rational reasons, I drifted from dissatisfaction with everything around me to blanket despair and soon moved back to New York in the hope of leaving my troubles behind. For a couple of years we visited each other sporadically, using our shared love as a barrier against the looming rift.

When it came, it came abruptly. Sitting in a crowded Washington restaurant one evening, she pressed all the right buttons to ignite the fuel tank of frustrated anger I had been filling since my own unhappy youth. Terrified of the impending explosion, halfway through the meal I dizzily rose to my feet and stomped out, pausing only long enough to say, "Have it your way. I don't have to listen to this." Had I thought then to revisit her poems I would have read, "People are more likely to accept emotions and gifts if everything is kept alive, / Meaning that no one is depressed. / Stationary people accept no gifts. / So often one must force things upon unwilling people./Life is such as strange thing." But I never looked at them.

A few days later I phoned to make up. She didn't return the call, or the many that followed. I tried contacting her two closest friends whom I knew well. They were noncommittal but kind in their assurances that Pandora was well, and that they were sure that everything would work out okay. Having no other mode of contact, I took to writing her letters, the early ones filled with questions and the later ones with expressions of love and loneliness, but she never wrote back.

Eighteen months later, two things happened almost simultaneously. The first was the entrance of the hero of this story, Dr. Donald F. Klein, master psychopharmacologist. Ignoring my assertions that there was nothing the matter with me except a little moodiness and that I had come only to satisfy the concerned urging of a depressed coworker, he convinced me that a little moodiness was okay, but how about telling him some more about the problem with my daughter? And the job that I had quit. And about my mother, whom I didn't seem to like at all. As he prodded my layers of self-deception, I got the picture and rushed to have the prescription filled. Ironically, this took place in the context of my then job, helping to launch the National Foundation for Depressive Illness.

The second event, a month or two after seeing Klein, was an out-of-the-blue phone call from my story's heroine, Pandora, who after all those months of silence announced that of course she was coming home for Christmas. Perhaps it was ESP on her part, or perhaps my last letter or two had sounded less desperate and grasping. Or perhaps she had accomplished her task of freeing herself emotionally from my intrusive negativity and was ready to try to love me again. A clue to the last reason lay hidden in another of her poems: "Hide and seek,/That's

237

what we're playing. / Yet seeking the same thing. / Who do you think will win our game? / No one: unless it's us." We had a great Christmas, and we've had many more since. To this day we are inordinately fond of each other and tell each other constantly how wonderful and lucky we both are. Although she lives in Florida and I in New York, we bridge the gap with frequent, sometimes daily phone conversations. She is far wiser in many ways than I, but she, too, suffers from depression and we help each other over the rough spots.

If I hadn't had a Dr. Klein and a Pandora, my life would be otherwise. I often contemplated suicide back then, restrained only by the thought that I could not do that to my child. Jumping in and out of relationships with men, all of which left me feeling mistreated and rejected, love and stability seemed eternally out of reach. I had no idea what I wanted to do. Everything seemed temporary. Nothing caught and held my attention, and the projects I took on always concluded in a clash with coworkers. I had no center anymore. With nothing to hold me or to hold on to, I was headed for years of misery.

One other poem of hers, the last in the notebook she gave me, hits at the heart of the problem many depressed mothers and their offspring share. "Unfortunately, life is not what it seems. / It can change as quickly as an artist's work. / People's feelings change as quickly as a painter's stroke. / Life is but a canvas. / You must make the best of it by painting what you can upon it." When Pandora went off to create her own canvas and to cover it with strokes of her own making, it was to erase those of a good mother felled by depression. Standing not long ago in front of paintings executed by Jackson Pollock when depression had enveloped him, I shivered in recognition of what the chaotic, clumsy splashes of black and red meant. It's just not possible to keep that paint from splashing on those you love.

11

Maternal Depression:
Past, Present, and Future

The power maternal depression holds to disturb the mother-child relationship and to poison the family sphere threatens the hopes, health, and promise of millions of American children. Research claims that this illness is heritable are convincing, as is fast-gathering evidence that points to the role of environment in generating depression's symptoms in vulnerable offspring. My own anecdotal evidence strongly suggests that many carry their emotional burden into early adulthood and beyond, that this load colors their view of both themselves and those around them, and that it is reflected in their own parenting style.

Fitting depressed mothers and their children into neat categories is a tidy approach to understanding the problem but it has drawbacks. Depression is a messy and unpredictable illness, moving in for a visit or for good, sometimes sneakily and sometimes shouting raucously. One mother withdraws into her silent pain while another gives angry voice to hers. However it chooses to make itself known, this illness damages every family member. You now know from the copious research presented in earlier chapters that maternal depression's effects on children follow certain well-defined paths. Infants become fussy, anxious, and fail to thrive. Toddlers throw tantrums. School-age kids and adolescents have problems with their social life and perform below their academic potential; many turn to drugs and alcohol, enter into unhappy marriages, and have unrewarding careers.

Drawing exact boundaries between what happens to kids of depressed moms in infancy, in adolescence, and in adulthood is not possible. Few mothers are consistently depressed, month after month, year after year. They are more apt to cycle into and out of negative moods. A depression that erupts during a child's adolescence may well have made covert appearances earlier, as Sichel and Driscoll suggest in their earthquake theory. If so, have those unrecognized mood changes already left their mark on impressionable youngsters? Who is to know if Jill and Hanna, whose postpartum depressions collided with the mothering needs of their respective infants, are free from this illness forever? Perhaps it will crop up again when their kids are in school or college. If it does, will the effects be cumulative, or will the earlier, infantile ones have faded, leaving the field clear to more typically adolescent reactions? In the end, there are no neat and tidy categories, no precisely delineated time periods, no absolute certainly that this happens now and that happens then. Like us humans, depression is a time traveler and has little respect for such conventions.

What is evident is that the components of depression fallout—bewildered confusion, guilty self-blame, demoralization, resentment and anger, and a longing for escape—can be detected in all such offspring, from stammering Earl in Chapter 1 to my own daughter and others like her. Even the nameless infant of the Face-to-Face Still-Face Paradigm, who slumps dispiritedly when his mother pretends to be expressionless and unresponsive, and the listless babies who failed to seduce the clinic nurses into cuddling and playing with them, are already collecting and storing away their growing accumulation of negative feelings. The laundry mother's daughter and Sam the Nobody have backpacks filled with more than books.

Intimacy-shy Christina and my French friend Ginette are laboring under emotional loads that allow them little time for the luxury of love. Marilyn Monroe found hers so heavy that she shucked it with a lethal dose of sleeping pills. Evvie's efforts to lighten her burden by picking and choosing between good and bad memories of her mother have left her unable to distinguish which are real and which the product of an imagination that seeks to provide her with the mother she wishes she had.

Only the most resilient children escape the effects of a mother's untreated depression unscathed and emotionally untouched. The rest of us travel through life with our charged memories. Whether buried or in full view, they jeopardize our psyche. Ralph Waldo Emerson wrote that poetry is emotion recollected in tranquility. Our poems, obdurate reflections of our past, cloud our troubled present. We move to their rhythm because we are unable to resist their power and tenacity.

The Damaging Absence of Love

I believe that what all survivors of every age miss most is the expression of their mother's love for them. So many of us tell our stories in the context of its absence. When Rachel, whose saga is related in Chapter 2, asked me how it was possible that her parent never wanted to hold her as an infant, I gave her a brisk pep talk—"It's not that she didn't love you, it was because she was depressed"—but while I know I am right, I was hard pressed to sound convincing. Some depressed mothers, like Jill and Hanna, continue to express love for their child even through psychosis and despair, but others seem to misplace it forever. Fathers may do their level best to make up for the loss, but often their own sense of sorrow and lack interferes. "I don't feel lovable," Rachel told me when first we talked, brushing aside the father she had spoken of with such gratitude. Many of us survivors feel unlovable because we missed out on maternal love. George, whom you also met in Chapter 2, expresses our darkest suspicion: "Even my own mother didn't love me."

The effects of what experts term "unwantedness" have been studied. Thirty years ago in the country then known as Czechoslovakia, permission for abortion was granted only if a jury of physicians deemed it necessary. Appeals often led to a second denial, with the result that the babies born had already been rejected twice by their mothers-to-be. The government wanted to investigate whether this policy had harmful effects on offspring, so it asked a team of Czech and American researchers to track its impact on them. Since then, these children—matched against an equal number of wanted offspring—have been revisited four times: at ages nine, fourteen, twenty-one, and thirty.

Clearly, being unwanted has made a lasting impact on their development. Poor academic performance, unpopularity, and problematic behavior in school have later transmuted into "less satisfaction with life," less optimism and self-confidence, a higher rate of unemployment, greater alcohol and drug use, and more anxiety and depression than in the wanted offspring. Grown female children in particular were more apt to remain single or to divorce, and showed problematic parenting of their own children. While the study did not include assessment of their parents' psychiatric health, it clearly demonstrates how unwantedness can permanently compromise the development of children. The study's fourth and final phase included a look at the siblings of unwanted kids and found they did not conform to this negative pattern.

Whether wanted or unwanted at birth, somewhere along the line kids of a depressed mother can latch on to the suspicion that they are a disappointment rather than a joy. This probably won't happen to children like Mercurial Megan and Julie the Smiling Buddha, who are bathed in affectionate parental care. Megan's mother spent less than two years feeling helpless, inadequate, and irritable before realizing that her feelings stemmed from depression, not from a mismatch with motherhood; during that time her daughters received the attentions of a father who put aside his own concerns and devoted all his nonoffice hours to their needs. Now they have two fully engaged parents, both knowledgeable about depression and its fondness for family trees, and about the pharmacological and psychotherapeutic treatments available. Should Megan show signs of it as she moves into adolescence, they will know what to do.

But what of Melinda, who broadcast her sadness through the Internet in hope of reaching someone who would listen and understand? She is living in the age of Prozac, but in a faraway country where depression, especially among women, is not well understood or recognized as dangerous. "I hate everything I dont care about anything and im always moody and always fight with my family. I just cant take it. . . . im even thinking suicidal," she e-mails. "your the only one i can talk to no one else listens." Her words echo the frustration of other adolescents whose parents mistake such feelings for normal teenage angst. If Melinda doesn't find a listener closer to home, she will in a few short years become yet another depressed young mother, thus perpetuating the cycle.

Support group members Dawnell and Earl, badly bruised as

they are, have found people to listen and empathize with them. They experience the relief of sitting down with others who share their problem, understand their feelings, and can reassure them that they are good people. But only a handful of support groups exist specifically for young people who are depressed or have a depressed parent. Few pediatricians or general practitioners get to see these kids because it is their mental, not their physical health that is in jeopardy; when they are consulted, they may well miss the root cause of distress and fail to recommend treatment for it. Even when these young people cross the border between depression fallout and depression, they are rarely prescribed the antidepressants and counseling they need.

Depressed Children: A National Problem

The research on maternal depression, other than noting that this illness destroys for its sufferers the possibility of joy, gives little heed to the concomitant sadness and guilt that accompany a troubled mother-child partnership. Whether or not a mother identifies her depression as the source of distress, she is denied the exquisite pleasure of free-flowing love between herself and the child. Like all parents condemned to witness a son's or daughter's wrong turnings, she will wonder what she has done wrong and what steps she could have taken to protect against poor judgment and unwise choices. Today's world, for all its promise, is fraught with dangers; parents can never guarantee that offspring will successfully negotiate all its lures and traps. But every depressed mother who has read this book can now take her own mental health in hand and so remove one major barrier to her own happiness and to her offspring's future hopes.

It is impossible to separate the twin problems of maternal

depression and its impact on children. A televised 1999 White House Conference on children's mental health provided a national forum for the views of doctors like Harold S. Koplewicz, head of New York University's Child Study Center and a leading authority on children's mental health. Parents who tuned in may not have grasped that their own mental health might be responsible for that of their offspring. However, one hopes the discussion did wake them up to the prevalence of unrecognized depression among young people. Timely professional attention for these kids is indispensable, just as it is for depressed mothers. Few understand that the illness is heritable; even fewer that the fallout from their illness can be toxic, and that the resulting demoralization in their offspring can slip from warning symptoms into a full-fledged depression.

According to Dr. Koplewicz, 10 million American children suffer from some form of psychiatric disturbance, ranging from depressive symptomatology to schizophrenia; at least 2 million of them endure severe major depression and many more live with inhibiting anxiety disorders. These alarming statistics have failed to create a matching stir in the general public. Media coverage is growing but most people automatically turn off when they hear the term "mental illness," associating it solely with violent psychotics and deranged homeless people, not with the members of their own family or the one that lives next door. But mental illness is exactly what these kids suffer from, as do the parents of many of them. Children are our future, our most ✓ precious national heritage, and our most pressing problem, but despite the magnitude of the problem, we continue to sweep it under the rug. While every one of these 10 million children deserves our immediate attention and help, the adolescents among them represent our most pressing challenge.

Dr. Koplewicz reminds us that the teenage years are difficult ones. Kids on the threshold of adulthood come face-to-face with tumultuous brain and body changes associated with this period of life. They have to adapt, he points out, to breasts, bleeding, and sudden erections; to come to terms with the fact that they are sexual beings; to learn to make relationships with people outside the immediate family and to establish intimacy with them; to separate from their parents or caretakers; and to establish educational and vocational goals. This is an awesome agenda under the best of circumstances. Those whose mothers are depressed—whether emotionally absent and withdrawn or critical and interfering—will find it even more daunting.

Many adolescents, but by no means all, are able to adjust to such a parent, adopting an attitude of, "She may not be the best mom, but she's mine and I can deal with that." Koplewicz believes that although nurture counts for a lot in the transmission of depression, nature is the principal cause for its transmission from generation to generation. Because, in his opinion, this is a genetically heritable illness, a hefty proportion of kids with a depressed parent will in their turn develop it.

There is increasing evidence, says Dr. Koplewicz, that depressed mothers have more children and bear them earlier than non-depressed ones. Among the probable reasons are their low self-esteem and their view of the future as otherwise friendless and pointless; perhaps they have a particularly strong need for the unquestioning love that a baby offers. If the statistics continue in their upward trend, they will throw light on the reasons for the rising tide of depression among young people. As the number of young depressed moms increases, so does the population of depressed teenagers, who will in their turn go on to bear more children than their non-depressed peers. This problem isn't going to disappear.

There is a lot more at stake here, warns Dr. Koplewicz, than unhappiness. He believes that "the principal cause of moodiness and sadness is life circumstances, like getting divorced, losing a job or friends, and failing exams. The danger point is hopelessness. Hopelessness, a governing symptom of depression, causes people to kill themselves and to kill others." Homicidal, suicidal kids like Eric Harris and Dylan Klebold, the perpetrators of the Columbine killings, may or may not have been clinically depressed, he adds, but they were most certainly hopeless. Adrift and unable to ground themselves through healthy relationships, they opted out of life not with a whimper but a bang.

While the causes of teenage problems extend far beyond maternal depression, it is indisputably a big contributor to them. A depressed mother who hinders rather than helps her child in negotiating the rites of passage from pre- to postpuberty, and in establishing him- or herself as an independent adult, is inviting trouble. Recognizing and seeking treatment for depression, whether in a parent or in a child, is a responsibility that every informed adult can handle. Abdicating that responsibility has far-reaching consequences.

Adolescents are the parents of the coming generation. Those who become depressed are likely to leave upon their own offspring the psychosocial imprint of depression, thus perpetuating the cycle. Although no research agenda presently exists to study the adult offspring of a depressed mother, the tantalizing hints to be gleaned from Constance Hammen's and other longitudinal research projects invite further investigation. The young offspring participating in them are just entering their prime childbearing years. It will be a decade or more before current findings are tested and perhaps organized into a pattern that resembles what I call survivor's syndrome, that cluster of symptoms described by the people who have shared their stories with me: fear of intimacy, the search for perfection and control, dependency on the approval of others, and the conviction that they are flawed and fraudulent.

Each survivor has found his or her own words to describe these feelings of inadequacy and alienation: "I don't feel lovable." "It's hard to be a friend when you're not a whole person." "I feel out of sync with other people." All are locked into past perceptions of their parent as distant, critical, and uncaring. I am sure that they, like me, still search their memories of childhood, expectantly hoping to uncover vignettes of happy togetherness and finding only the same, strongly entrenched negative ones. Perhaps they, too, take sullen satisfaction in fanning the angry glow of such recollections. Memories like these are our explanation for being as we are, our excuse for the negative paths pursued, the friends lost, and the years during which we, like Martha Manning, believed that life was a simple product of will, effort, and design. Even though we may have come to terms with our emotional baggage, it still sits in the attic, waiting to accompany us down dead-end roads.

From Harry Harlow's socially clueless monkeys to Tronick and Weinberg's Model of Mutual Regulation, in which mother and child strive to stay in sync, an attentive, compassionate, supportive, and loving mother remains essential to a positive sense of self and to the belief that one has mastery over one's destiny. The symptoms of survivor's syndrome derive from a diminished self-image and the credo that we are not in control of our fate. Like interlocking gears, they easily enmesh us in false perceptions. Long before adulthood, they set a depressed mother and her child to lockstepping through the years. Even positive achievements do little to disturb a machine set in motion early.

There is just one more adult survivor whom I would like you to meet: Martha Manning's daughter, Keara Manning Depenbrock, to whom you were briefly introduced in Chapter 2. Keara is now entering her twenties and shows no signs of survivor's syndrome, in large measure because she enjoyed parents who were alert to the possible negative effects on her of Martha's depression and conscientiously took steps to avoid them. As a result, she has escaped unscathed and, perhaps most important of all, has no distorted, emotionally laden memories to disturb her in the future.

Keara Manning Depenbrock: A Happy Ending

Keara guesses her mom's depression had been around for some time before it sent Martha to the hospital. Keara was in the seventh grade then, just about the time that, like any normal teenager, she was starting to pull away from her parents, who began to seem embarrassing. "I figured she was about to give me 'the talk' about the changes in your body and all that stuff," she says, "so I'd already created some distance between us. Before she got really ill we'd had a sort of nonrelationship, partly because I don't really think a kid at that age is really aware of relationships in the sense of actively contributing to them, but also because she'd been depressed so long that I had no real memory of relating to her as a person in my own right."

By the time Martha's deepest darkness fell, that seemed to Keara pretty much the way her mother had always been, so she didn't think of her as actually having changed. "Of course she was different because she kind of totally retreated and cried all the time. She stayed in bed all day and often had to leave in the middle of meals because she couldn't deal with how awful she felt," her daughter explained to me. When Keara showed her report cards, Martha wasn't critical. She just dissolved into tears, "like she was just so disappointed by everything. I did feel that I was adding to that disappointment. And she would get angry about even little things."

What might have been a lasting family tragedy became instead a story of hope and of solutions. "My father was awesome," Keara told me. "He had always been a full-time parent and took over when Mom was more or less out of the picture. They told me later that their principal concern was to try and keep my life as normal as possible, and they did a fantastic job." On the publication of Martha's book about her depression, reporters deluged Keara, fishing for stories about how her mother's illness had wrecked her life. Instead, Keara told them: "Mom's illness wasn't my fault. It had absolutely nothing to do with me. And Dad kept everything going." Indeed, she admits to having felt somewhat guilty that she had none of the juicy tidbits she knew they were looking for "about how horrible I felt and how my life was a mess. And I guess I was a little ashamed that I hadn't been more upset at the time."

Keara has practical advice to offer both parents and children. To mothers she says, "Whatever time or energy you have left over from depression, spend it with your child, not your work. Your work won't miss you. Be as open and totally upfront as possible about what's the matter with you and explain it in an age-specific way." And for fathers? I asked. "Tell them to be like mine," by which she means devoted, attentive, understanding, and willing to play the part of two parents until her mother recovered.

She counsels children going through the same experience to try not to overreact to their mother's behavior. "Keep the knowledge that she's suffering from depression as a sort of substratum in your mind, a constant reminder that that's what's making her act as she does." To that I would add my own reminder that kids have built-in radar screens that pick up on things parents think they have managed to hide. Trying to pretend that nothing is wrong when children know that's untrue poses dangers for kids and for the family as a whole. Giving an accurate reason for their mother's behavior and reminding them they are not responsible for it can mean the difference between a safe landing and a crash.

Both Keara and her parents know that the recent depression she herself suffered wasn't her mother's fault: Nobody can control where their genes decide to travel. She says it was like "total pain," that she was very emotional about everything and had trouble with schoolwork and concentrating. "But I was still able to enjoy the things I like, so perhaps it wasn't a very bad episode," she reasons. No longer on antidepressants, Keara says the young people she knows take depression in their stride rather than stuffing it in the closet, although some of her male friends are "by-the-bootstraps guys who can't grasp that it's an illness" and still think determination is enough to overcome it.

Keara's parents did everything right, from the time Martha first went under through their daughter's brief period of depression. The only hint of a misstep is Keara's admonition to other depressed moms: Whatever time or energy is left over from this illness should be spent with your child, not your work. I know from my own experience of depression that some of us cling to our work as the one relatively high-functioning arena left to us, but that doesn't absolve us from all effort in the parenting one. Dispensing hugs, even if we have no words to accompany them, takes little time or energy and reassures kids that we still love them.

I began this book as the result of a suggestion that mothers with depression were an important topic, and that readers would want to know about a subject long studied by researchers yet never communicated to the lay public. Plowing through the voluminous academic research and attempting to parse it for the general reader, I sustained for almost a year a comfortable distance from my personal experience of being a depressed mother, focusing instead on the effects of my mother's depression on me. Somewhere in the writing of the last two chapters, that distance collapsed, leaving me face-to-face with my child and our relationship. My internal kaleidoscope suddenly went haywire. Patterns shifted radically. The new ones cast an intensely uncomfortable light on a part of my legacy I had, I now realize, deliberately ducked and dodged for an excellent reason: I had so very much wanted to spare my child the angry resentment my depressed mother planted in me. Yet despite that conscious goal, I unconsciously forced my legacy on Pandora.

My daughter was and is a joy for me. But from the moment I embarked on this project, I wondered and worried what her response to it would be. Like so many survivors of maternal depression, I know how strong our inclination is to bury the experience and hope for its quietude. We rarely seek or welcome Lazarus-like risings of unpleasantness in our past. Suspecting she might be unwilling to grant me a daughterly interview, I wrote her an explanatory letter I hoped would overcome her reluctance. She sent me an answer in writing that confirmed my hunch.

"Dearest Mummy," she wrote, "I am truly sorry I cannot do an interview for you. You may feel that nothing that comes of it will upset you, but I can't say the same. I really do not want to dredge up a whole lot of stuff that I have resolved. Despite the fact that I have put it in perspective, I don't want to relive it or re-examine it. You know I wish you all the success in the world with your book," she concluded, "and I would be happy to be quoted as saying that I am extremely happy with my relationship with you now and am not interested in looking backwards." The sentiments Pandora expresses are a fitting and helpful conclusion to a book about maternal depression and the price mother and child pay when it is ignored.

No mother can control her genes and the risk they transmit to her offspring, but she can avoid burdening her child with the emotional by-products of her depression. Like many home truths, the solution calls for uncompromising honesty, but it is a surprisingly straightforward one: Absorb and act upon the information in the preceding chapters, be alert to your changing moods and to your child's reaction to them, exercise your parental responsibility, and provide unswerving support and love. The alternative—ignoring depression's symptoms, refusing treatment, and pretending everything will work out okay—may work for the ostrich, but not for us humans. No matter how long you may have been depressed, if you apply this advice diligently you, too, will enjoy a child whose relationship with you is rewarding, happy, and secure.

Resources

Organizations Offering Information, Educational Materials, Newsletters, and Local Support Group Addresses

American Foundation for Suicide Prevention
(888)333-2377
www.afsp.org

Anxiety Disorders Association of America
(301)231-9350
www.adaa.org

Depression After Delivery (DAD)
(800)944-4PPD

Depression and Related Affective Disorders Association
(DRADA)
(410)955-4647
www.med.jhu.edu/drada

National Alliance for Research on Schizophrenia and
Depression (NARSAD)
(516)829-0091
www.mhsource.com/narsad.html

National Alliance for the Mentally Ill (NAMI)
(800)950-6264
www.nami.org

National Depressive and Manic-Depressive Association
(NDMDA)
(800)826-3633
www.ndmda.org

National Foundation for Depressive Illness (NAFDI)
(800)239-1295
www.depression.org

National Institute of Mental Health (NIMH)
(800)421-4211
www.nimh.nih.gov

National Mental Health Association (NMHA)
(800)969-6642
www.nmha.org

National Mental Illness Screening Project
(800)573-4433 (Depression Screening)
www.nmisp.org

Postpartum Services International (PSI)
(805)967-7636

Surgeon General of the United States
www.surgeongeneral.gov

U.S. Public Health Service, Publication Clearing House
(800)358-9295
www.ahcpr.dod

Additional Websites

INFORMATION

www.psycom.net/depression.central.html
(Maintained by psychiatrist Dr. Ivan K. Goldberg)

drkoop.com (Maintained by former Surgeon General
Dr. Everett R. Koop)

NEWSGROUPS (INCLUDES CHAT ROOMS AND BULLETIN BOARDS)

www.alt.support.depression

www.alt.support.manic

www.alt.support.depression recovery

www.depressionfallout.com

PHARMACEUTICAL COMPANY–SPONSORED SITES

www.depression-info.com

Suggested Reading

Beardslee, William R., *Cognitive Psychosocial Intervention* (a manual available on request from Dr. William R. Beardslee, Children's Hospital, Dept. of Psychiatry, 300 Longwood Ave., Boston, MA 02115).

Clayton, A. H., D. L. Dunner, R. M. A. Hirschfeld, M. M. Manning, L. E. Rosen, and T. N. Wise, *Restoring Intimacy: The Patient's Guide to Maintaining Relationships During Depression* (a publication of the National Depressive and Manic-Depressive Association, 1999).

Dalton, Katarina, *Depression After Childbirth,* 3d ed. (Oxford: Oxford University Press, 1996).

Gopfert, Michael, Jeni Webster, and Mary V. Seeman, eds., *Parental Psychiatric Disorder* (Cambridge, England: Cambridge University Press, 1996).

Jamison, Kay Redfield, *An Unquiet Mind: A Memoir of Moods and Madness* (New York: Alfred A. Knopf, 1995).

Kleiman, Karen R., and Valerie D. Raskin, *This Isn't What I Expected: Overcoming Postpartum Depression* (New York: Bantum, 1994).

Kramer, Peter D., *Listening to Prozac* (New York: Viking, 1993).

Manning, Martha, *Undercurrents: A Therapist's Reckoning with Her Own Depression* (San Francisco: HarperSanFrancisco, 1994).

McGrath, Ellen, Gwendolyn Puryear Keita, Bonnie R. Strickland, and Nancy Felipe Russo, eds., *Women and Depression: Risk Factors and Treatment Issues* (Washington, D.C.: American Psychological Association, 1990).

Murray, Lynne, and Peter J. Cooper, *Postpartum Depression and Child Development* (New York: The Guilford Press, 1997).

Papolos, Dimitri F., and Janice Papolos, *Overcoming Depression,* 3d ed. (New York: HarperCollins, 1997).

Real, Terrence, *I Don't Want to Talk About It: Overcoming the Secret Legacy of Male Depression* (New York: Scribner, 1997).

Roan, Sharon L., *Postpartum Depression: Every Woman's Guide to Diagnosis, Treatment, and Prevention* (Holbrook, Mass.: Adams Media Corporation, 1997).

Seligman, Martin E. P., *The Optimistic Child* (New York: HarperPerennial, 1996).

Sheffield, Anne, *How You Can Survive When They're Depressed: Living and Coping with Depression Fallout* (New York: Harmony Books, 1998).

NOTES

1. Shedding New Light on an Old Problem

Page

1 An eminent child psychologist: Urey Bronfenbrenner, "Who Needs Parent Education?" *Teachers College Record,* 79, pp. 773–74.

7 Dr. T. Berry Brazelton, parenting maven: Author interview, March 6, 1999.

10 A number of psychologists: Wendy Davis, Francesca Schwartz, and Margaret Spinelli: Author interviews, June 25, 1999; June 9, 1999; and December 3, 1998.

2. The Legacy of a Mother's Depression: Survivor's Syndrome

Page

16 I wrote that in down times: Anne Sheffield, *How You Can Survive When They're Depressed: Living and Coping with Depression Fallout* (New York: Harmony Books, 1998), p. 12.

17 A magazine article that chronicled: *The Journal of the California Alliance for the Mentally Ill,* No. 3, pp. 31–36.

18 In his autobiography *Timebends*: Ibid., p. 31.

19 Its inventor, psychiatrist Eric Berne: Eric Berne, *Games People Play: The Psychology of Human Relationships* (Harmondsworth, Middlesex, England: Penguin Books, 1964).

20 "I lost a sense of knowing": *The Journal of the California Alliance for the Mentally Ill,* No. 3, p. 4.

31 Psychologist Martin Seligman, in his book: Martin E. P. Seligman, *The Optimistic Child* (New York: HarperPerennial, a division of Harper-Collins, 1996), p. 31.

31 "Self-direction, rather than outside forces": Ibid., p. 35.

32 Parents need to know, he says: Ibid., p. 36.

32 "We [note they have] not only depression": Personal communication to the author.

33 Daniel Goleman writes: Daniel Goleman, *Vital Lies, Simple Truths: The Psychology of Self-Deception* (New York: Touchstone Books, published by Simon & Schuster, 1986), p. 100.

3. What Have I Got? Why Me? Why Women?

Page

34 Martha Manning kept a diary: Martha Manning, *Undercurrents: A Therapist's Reckoning with Her Own Depression* (San Francisco: HarperSanFrancisco, 1994).

34 "In some moment of emptiness": Ibid., p. 93.

35 "A bad mother," she writes: Ibid., p. 110.

35 "Each morning," she wrote: Martha Manning, "The Legacy," *Networker,* January/February 1997, p. 40.

36 But when her depression: Martha Manning, author interview, January 30, 1999.

38 Psychologist Kay Redfield Jamison: Kay Redfield Jamison, *An Unquiet Mind* (New York: Alfred A. Knopf, 1995), pp. 110–11.

38 Novelist William Styron: William Styron, *Darkness Visible* (New York: Vintage Books, 1992), p. 47.

39 "I felt myself": Ibid., p. 75.

40 As Martha Manning laments: Manning, *Undercurrents,* p. 97.

42 Some scientists are investigating: "Virus May Be Linked to Depression," *New York Times,* July 23, 1996.

47 Putting aside the incalculable costs: *NAMI News,* July 1, 1999, p. 2.

48 share a preference for bow ties: Stephen Pinker, *How the Mind Works* (New York: Norton, 1997), p. 20.

48 These children are three times more likely: M. M. Weissman, V. Warner, P. Wickramaratne, D. Moreau, and M. Olfson, "Offspring of

Depressed Parents: 10 Years Later," in *Archives of General Psychiatry,* Vol. 54, October 1997, pp. 932–40.

50 now they know that: Margaret G. Spinelli, *American Journal of Psychiatry,* 154:7, July 1977.

51 When one researcher: J. P. Newman, "Gender, Life Strains, and Depression: Clinical Disorder or Normal Distress?" *Journal of Health and Social Behavior,* 27, pp. 161–78.

51 It postulates that women's willingness: *National Task Force on Women and Depression: Risk Factors and Treatment Issues,* E. McGrath, G. P. Keita, B. R. Strickland, and N. F. Russo, eds. (Washington, D.C.: American Psychological Association, 1990), p. 23.

52 Gender differences also show up: Ibid., p. 53.

52 An unhappy marriage: M. M. Weissman, "Advances in Psychiatric Epidemiology: Rates and Risks for Major Depression," *American Journal of Public Health,* 77, pp. 445–51.

52 The number and age of children: *National Task Force on Women and Depression,* p. xii.

52 Working moms who had difficulty: Ibid., p. 25.

4. The Dyadic Dance of Mother and Child

Page

56 Wray Herbert, writing in: Wray Herbert, "The Politics of Biology," *U.S. News & World Report,* April 21, 1997, p. 79.

59 When a mother holds: E. Z. Tronick and M. Katherine Weinberg, "Depressed Mothers and Infants: Failure to Form Dyadic States of Consciousness," in *Postpartum Depression and Child Development,* Lynne Murray and Peter J. Cooper, eds. (New York: The Guilford Press, 1997), p. 57.

61 Recent studies suggest that infants: "Stress-proof Your Child," *Parents,* December 1998, pp. 97–100.

61 What they seemed most to lack: John Bowlby, *Attachment and Loss,* Vol. 1 (New York: Basic Books, 1982), p. 311.

61 The children who manifest: Margaret Talbot, "Attachment Theory: The Ultimate Experiment," *New York Times Magazine,* May 24, 1998, p. 30.

62 Within a day and a half: Andrew Derrington, "Never Underestimate a Baby," *Financial Times,* July 20, 1997.

62 No one, for instance, has to teach: Hanus Papousek and Mechthild Pa-

pousek, "Fragile Aspects of Early Social Integration," in *Postpartum Depression and Child Development,* p. 38.

62 to favor her left arm: Deborah Blum, *Sex on the Brain* (New York: Penguin Books, 1997) p. 65.

62 Mothers, on the other hand: Pinker, *How the Brain Works,* p. 444.

63 still railing against women who: Talbot, *New York Times Magazine,* p. 28.

64 despite mounting evidence: Susan Chira, *A Mother's Place: Beyond Guilt and Shame* (New York: HarperCollins, 1998), p. 127.

66 In them, he describes three distinct stages: Bowlby, *Attachment and Loss.*

68 such misreadings: Tronick and Weinberg, *Postpartum Depression and Child Development,* p. 64.

70 he'll either abandon the attempt: Ibid., p. 67.

71 Harris agrees with other experts that: Judith Harris, *The Nurture Assumption* (New York: The Free Press, 1998), p. 153.

71 Peers, not parents: Ibid., p. 169.

72 Yes, says Harris: Ibid., p. 153.

72 Many experts have observed: Author interview with Donald F. Klein.

73 Increasingly sophisticated technologies: "Baby Talk," *U.S. News & World Report,* June 15, 1998, p. 48.

74 Infants also come equipped: Ibid., p. 50.

74 babies by ten or twelve months: Ibid.

75 By age three, 90 percent: Ibid., p. 53.

75 One study has demonstrated: Ibid., p. 55.

76 One of the many studies that reveal: "Studies Show Talking with Infants Shapes Basis of Ability to Think," *New York Times,* April 17, 1997.

5. When Depression Cuts In After Childbirth

Page

79 About one of every ten new mothers: Margaret Oates, "Postnatal Mental Illness: Its Importance and Management," *Parental Psychiatric Disorder: Distressed Parents and Their Families,* Michael Gopfert, Jeni Webster, and Mary V. Seeman, eds. (Cambridge, England: Cambridge University Press, 1996), pp. 63–64.

79 singer Marie Osmond revealed: *McCall's,* February 2000, p. 36.

79 Dr. Katarina Dalton has observed: Katarina Dalton, *Depression After Childbirth,* 3d ed. (Oxford: Oxford University Press, 1996), p. 6.

80 the list of possible additional causes: Sharon L. Roan, *Postpartum Depression: Every Woman's Guide to Diagnosis, Treatment, and Prevention* (Holbrook, Mass.: Adams Media Corporation, 1997), p. 7.

82 Harvard researcher E. Z. Tronick demonstrated: J. F. Cohn and E. Z. Tronick, "Three-month-old Infants' Reaction to Simulated Maternal Depression," *Child Development*, February 1983, 54 (1), pp. 185–93.

82 Others are intrusive: M. K. Weinberg and E. Z. Tronick, Abstract, "The Impact of Maternal Psychiatric Development on Infant Development," *Journal of Clinical Psychiatry*, 1998, 59 (suppl. 2), pp. 53–60.

83 as researcher Tiffany Field: Tiffany Field, B. Healy, S. Goldstein, et al., "Infants of Depressed Mothers Show 'Depressed' Behavior Even With Nondepressed Adults," *Child Development*, 1988, 59, pp. 1569–79.

83 act out their anger: Tronick and Weinberg, *Postpartum Depression and Child Development*, p. 69.

83 "red flags" that should alert: Morris Green, "Maternal Depression: Bad for Children's Health," *Contemporary Pediatrics*, Vol. 10, November 1993, pp. 28–36.

84 He recounts a story: Ibid., p. 28.

85 In a similar case study: M. Gopfert, J. Webster, J. Pollard, and J. S. Nelki, "The Assessment and Prediction of Parenting Capacity: A Community-oriented Approach," *Parental Psychiatric Disorder*, p. 281.

94 Current thinking has it that intelligence: Dale F. Hay, "Postpartum Depression and Cognitive Development," *Postpartum Depression and Child Development*, p. 87.

95 In one poignant study: T. Field et al., "Infants of Depressed Mothers Show 'Depressed' Behavior Even With Nondepressed Adults," p. 1573.

95 Professor Dale Hay: *Postpartum Depression and Child Development*, p. 102.

95 This chain of development: Ibid.

96 However, Hay points out: Ibid., p. 100.

96 Experts believe that: Geraldine Dawson, David Hessl, and Karin Frey, "Social Influences on Early Developing Biological and Behavioral Systems Related to Risk for Affective Disorder," *Development and Psychopathology*, 1994, 6, pp. 759–79.

96 It is also a period: Geraldine Dawson et al., "The Role of Frontal Lobe Functioning in the Development of Infant Self-regulatory Behavior," *Brain and Cognition*, 1992, 20, pp. 152–75.

97 In two separate studies: G. Dawson et al., "Frontal Lobe Activity and Affective Behavior of Infants of Mothers With Depressive Symp-

toms," *Child Development,* 1992, 63, pp. 725–37, and T. Field, N. A. Fox, J. Pickens, and T. Nawrocki, "Relative Right Frontal EEG Activation in 3- to 6-month-old Infants of 'Depressed' Mothers," *Developmental Psychology,* 1995, Vol. 31, No. 3, pp. 358–63.

98 when Susan Spieker: S. J. Spieker, "Developmental Trajectories of Disruptive Behavior Problems in Pre-school Children of Adolescent Mothers," *Child Development,* Vol. 70, No. 2, pp. 443–58.

98 A study conducted by Marian Radke-Yarrow: M. Radke-Yarrow, E. Nottelmann, P. Martinez, M. B. Fox, and B. Belmont, "Young Children of Affectively Ill Parents: A Longitudinal Study of Psychosocial Development," *Journal American Acad. Child Adolescent Psychiatry,* 1992, 31,1, pp. 68–77.

98 One funded by the Department of Health and Human Services: NICHD Early Child Care Research Network, "Chronicity of Maternal Depressive Symptoms, Maternal Sensitivity, and Child Functioning at 36 Months," *Developmental Psychology,* 1999, Vol. 35, No. 5, pp. 1297–1310.

98 One final study conducted: J. F. Marchand and Ellen Hock, "The Relation of Problem Behaviors in Preschool Children to Depressive Symptoms in Mothers and Fathers," *Journal of Genetic Psychology,* 1998, Vol. 159, pp. 353–67.

6. *Taking a Mother's Depression to School*

Page

106 a depressed mother described by researchers: J. C. Coyne and Geraldine Downey, "Children of Depressed Parents: An Integrative Review," *Psychological Bulletin,* 1990, Vol. 108, No. 1, p. 61.

106 The school-age kids who stand: A. A. Anderson and C. L. Hammen, "Psychosocial Outcomes of Children of Unipolar Depressed, Bipolar, Medically Ill, and Normal Women: A Longitudinal Study," *Journal of Consulting and Clinical Psychology,* 1993, Vol. 61, No. 3, pp. 448–54.

106 Even when the mother's depression: Ibid., p. 448.

107 Perhaps the single most disturbing assertion: S. R. Cogill, H. L. Caplan, H. Alexandra, K. M. Robson, and R. Kumar, "Impact of Maternal Depression on Cognitive Development of Young Children," *British Medical Journal,* 1986, Vol. 292, pp. 1165–67, and D. Sharp, D. Hay, S. Pawlby, G. Schmuacher, H. Allen, and R. Kumar, "The Impact of Post-

natal Depression on Boys' Intellectual Development," *Journal of Child Psychology and Psychiatry*, 1995, 36, pp. 1315–36.

107　While a depressed mother may: Alyson Hall, "Parental Psychiatric Disorder and the Developing Child," *Parental Psychiatric Disorder*, p. 28.

107　Even Professor Dale Hay: Ibid., p. 85.

108　Commenting on Hay's conclusion: Michael Rutter, "Maternal Depression and Infant Development: Cause and Consequence; Sensitivity and Specificity," *Postpartum Depression and Child Development*, p. 302.

108　Hay builds his conclusion: Geraldine Dawson, David Hessl, and Karin Frey, "Social Influences on Biological and Behavioral Systems Related to Risk for Affective Disorder," *Development and Psychopathology*, 1994, Vol. 6, pp. 759–79.

108　Current mainstream thinking: Dale Hay, in *Postpartum Depression and Child Development*, p. 87.

109　Most of those studying: M. M. Weissman, D. Gammon, and K. John, "Children of Depressed Parents," *Archives of General Psychiatry*, 1987, 44, pp. 847–53.

109　What they do believe: Dale Hay, *Postpartum Depression and Child Development*, p. 91.

110　One of the many manifestations: Constance Hammen, "The Family-Environmental Context of Depression: A Perspective on Children's Risk," *Developmental Perspectives on Depression: Rochester Symposium on Developmental Psychopathology*, Vol. 4, Dante Cicchetti and Sheree L. Toth, eds. (Rochester: University of Rochester Press, 1992), p. 266.

110　When studies report Will or Rebecca: Anderson and Hammen, "Psychosocial Outcomes of Children of Unipolar Depressed, Bipolar, Medically Ill, and Normal Women: A Longitudinal Study," pp. 448–54.

110　Marital discord, which goes hand in hand: Downey and Coyne, "Children of Depressed Parents: An Integrative Review," pp. 50–76.

111　Boys are more apt: Tronick and Weinberg, *Postpartum Depression and Child Development*, p. 69.

111　Girls become more passive: Andrea Pound, "Parental Affective Disorder and Childhood Disturbance," *Parental Psychiatric Disorder*, p. 207.

111　Kids blessed with a loving, insightful, and reliable father: Ibid., p. 210.

114　Hammen suspected that the cognitive problems: Hammen, in *Developmental Perspectives on Depression*, p. 251.

115　To test her thesis: Anderson and Hammen, "Psychosocial Outcomes of Children of Unipolar Depressed, Bipolar, Medically Ill, and Normal Women: A Longitudinal Study," pp. 448–54.

115 The findings of Professor Hammen: Ibid., p. 448.

116 Many experts have noted: Hammen, in *Developmental Perspectives on Depression*, p. 262.

116 "the enormous amount of conflict": Ibid., p. 263.

116 most of them "readily perceived": Ibid., p. 269.

116 Moreover, when their mother: Ibid.

117 Two of Constance Hammen's subjects: Constance Hammen, *Depression Runs in Families: The Social Context of Risk and Resilience in Children of Depressed Mothers* (New York: Springer-Verlag, 1991), pp. 157–59.

118 An estimated 10 million American kids: Dr. Harold L. Koplewicz, director, Child Study Center, NYU, author interview, October 13, 1999.

118 Launched over twenty years ago: M. M. Weissman, V. Warner, P. Wickramaratne, D. Moreau, and M. Olfson, "Offspring of Depressed Parents: 10 Years Later," *Archives of General Psychiatry,* October 1997, Vol. 54, p. 933.

119 It has found that kids: Ibid., p. 935.

120 they discovered that anxiety: N. Breslau, L. Schultz, and E. Peterson, "Sex Differences in Depression: A Role for Preexisting Anxiety," *Psychiatry Research,* 58 (1995), pp. 1–12.

120 When the Yale Study uncovered: V. Warner, M. M. Weissman, L. Mufson, and P. Wickramaratne, "Grandparents, Parents, and Grandchildren at High Risk for Depression: A Three-Generation Study," *Journal of American Acad. Child Adolescent Psychiatry,* 1999, 38, 3, pp. 289–95.

121 Bolstering her point is confirmation: A. K. Kramer, V. Warner, M. Olfson, C. M. Ebanks, F. Chaput, and M. M. Weissman, "General Medical Problems Among the Offspring of Depressed Parents: A 10-Year Follow-up," *Journal American Acad. Child Adolescent Psychiatry,* 1998, 37, 6, pp. 602–610.

121 Depression in young people often manifests itself: Downey and Coyne, "Children of Depressed Parents: An Integrative Review," p. 50.

122 reported more feelings of worthlessness: M. M. Weissman et al., "Offspring of Depressed Parents: 10 Years later," p. 936.

122 By the third generation, a whopping 49 percent: V. Warner et al., "Grandparents, Parents, and Grandchildren at High Risk for Depression: A Three-Generation Study," p. 292.

124 One eighteen-year-old: *The Journal of the California Alliance for the Mentally Ill,* No. 4, p. 41.

125 In it she describes: Kay Redfield Jamison, *Night Falls Fast* (New York: Alfred A. Knopf, 1999), p. 6.

126 the rates of suicide among children: Ibid., p. 48.

127 according to Professor Jamison: Ibid., p. 50.

127 His studies indicate that preventive steps: William R. Beardslee, Susan Swatling, Lizbeth Hoke, Phillis Clarke Rothberg, Polly van de Velde, Lynn Focht, and Donna Prodorefsky, "From Cognitive Information to Shared Meaning: Healing Principles in Prevention Intervention," *Psychiatry,* Summer 1998, Vol. 61, pp. 112–29.

131 Anxiety in the first grade: G. A. Bernstein, C. M. Borchardt, and A. R. Perwein, "Anxiety Disorders in Children and Adolescents: A Review of the Past 10 Years," *Journal of American Acad. Child Adolescent Psychiatry,* 1996, 35,0, p. 295.

7. Enter Depression, Exit Marital Harmony

Page

134 Depression fallout: Anne Sheffield, *How You Can Survive When They're Depressed: Living and Coping with Depression Fallout* (New York: Harmony Books, 1998), pp. 13–26.

136 "Many studies," he writes: Peter D. Kramer, *Should You Leave?* (New York: Scribner, 1997), pp. 160–61.

139 strangers will draw away: J. C. Coyne, "Depression and the Response of Others," *Journal of Abnormal Psychology,* 1976, 85, pp. 186–93.

139 a paper aptly titled: J. Kahn, J. C. Coyne, and G. Margolin, "Depression and Marital Disagreement: The Social Construction of Despair," *Journal of Social and Personal Relationships,* 1985, Vol. 2, pp. 447–61.

141 "Withdrawal," he writes: Ibid., p. 469.

142 result of assortative mating: K. R. Merikangas, "Divorce and Assortative Mating Among Depressed Patients," *American Journal of Psychiatry,* 1984, 141:1, pp. 74–76.

142 other studies have shown: J. C. Coyne, G. Downey, and J. Boergers, "Depression in Families: A Systems Perspective," in *Developmental Perspectives on Depression,* Cicchetti and Toth, eds., pp. 211–45.

144 blames much of the school behavior: Gabor I. Keitner, *Depression and Families: Impact and Treatment* (Washington, D.C.: American Psychiatric Press, 1990), pp. 3–29.

8. All About Treatment

Page

160 "Gentlemen, we are the stronger": *London Times,* March 27, 1999.

160 Women, for instance, were: K. Pajer, "New Strategies in the Treatment of Depression in Women," *Journal of Clinical Psychology,* 1995, 56 (suppl. 2), p. 30.

162 Freud, writes Edward Dolnick: Edward Dolnick, *Madness on the Couch* (New York: Simon and Schuster, 1998), p. 31.

163 From the mid-1940s: Donald F. Klein, author interview.

164 Psychoanalysts blamed women: Dolnick, *Madness on the Couch,* pp. 94–95.

164 The anti-pharmacology stance: Donald F. Klein, author interview.

164 Dolnick quotes Harvard's Jerome Kagan: Dolnick, *Madness on the Couch,* p. 72.

165 As one former analytic psychiatrist: Donald F. Klein, author interview.

166 Of the less than 50 percent: *NewYork Times,* June 22, 1997, p. 11.

167 "I had always had this mind-set": Jeanne Watson Driscoll, author interview, June 25, 1999.

168 the Sichel-Driscoll psychobiological approach: Deborah Sichel and Jeanne Watson Driscoll, *Women's Moods:What Every Woman Must Know About Hormones, the Brain, and Emotional Health* (New York: William Morrow, 1999).

168 "Ask someone if they have": Sichel and Driscoll, author interview, June 25, 1999.

169 "Women are born talkers": Sichel and Driscoll, author interview, June 25, 1999.

170 The graph Sichel and Driscoll made: Prepared by Sichel and Driscoll for the author.

170 Tossing in another metaphor: Sichel and Driscoll, author interview, June 25, 1999.

174 Unfortunately, their manufacturer: Donald F. Klein, author interview.

175 Of these, St. John's Wort: *NewYork CityVoices,* Vol. IV, No. 4, July/August 1999, p. 18.

175 In July a full-page ad: *NewYork Times,* July 7, 1999, p. A15.

175 I have since spoken at some length: Richard Brown, author interview, January 20, 2000.

176 About 75 percent to 80 percent of all patients: *The Harvard Mental Health Newsletter,* December 1994, p. 8.

176 A phenomenon known as: "Mood Swings," *New York Magazine,* October 26, 1998, p. 14.

177 The likeliest explanation for the poop-out: Donald F. Klein, author interview.

179 Zoloft, for example: *MDSG/New York Newsletter,* 1997, No. 2, p. 4.

179 Paxil does the same: Ibid., p.5.

179 Celexa, approved by the FDA: *NAMI/NYS News,* October/November 1998, No. 64, p. 12.

179 Serzone, according to one leading psychopharmacologist: Donald F. Klein, author interview.

180 One of the worst culprits: *MDSG/New York Newsletter,* 1997, No. 2, p. 1.

180 in at least half the cases: Harold A. Sackheim, in a presentation on "Electroconvulsive Therapy: An Update," at Columbia-Presbyterian Hospital conference on Depression: Research and Treatment, October 21, 1995.

181 Fifteen percent of all people: Dimitri F. Papolos and Janice Papolos, *Overcoming Depression* (New York: Harper and Row, 1987), p. 13.

183 about thirty years ago when Dr. Herbert Benson: "Recite Your Mantra and Call Me in the Morning," *New York Magazine,* May 11, 1998, p. 28.

183 In 1998 Congress gave the NIMH: "A Therapy Gains Ground in Hospitals: Meditation," *New York Times,* November 23, 1999, p. F7.

183 In a 1999 study: Ibid.

185 The overall rate of fetal abnormalities: Donald F. Klein, author interview.

186 One recent study of 267 women: *JAMA,* July 21, 1999, Vol. 282, No. 3, p. 222.

186 However, warns Dr. Zachary Stowe: Ibid.

186 have devised a way to test their hypothesis: Catherine Monk and William P. Fifer, author interview, April 23, 1999.

187 Monk and her team have found: C. Monk, W. P. Fifer, R. P. Sloan, M. M. Myers, L. Trien, and A. Hurtado, "Maternal Stress Responses and Anxiety During Pregnancy: Effects of Fetal Heart Rate," *Developmental Psychobiology,* 2000, Vol. 36, Issue 1, pp. 67–77.

187 Jerome Kagan has observed: Jerome Kagan, *Three Seductive Ideas* (Cambridge: Harvard University Press, 1998), p. 73.

188 The rate of antenatal depression: Margaret G. Spinelli, "Interpersonal Psychotherapy for Depressed Antepartum Women: A Pilot Study," *American Journal of Psychiatry,* July 1997, 154:7, pp. 1028–30.

188 She recruited infants: C. N. Epperson, *NARSAD Research Newsletter*, Winter 1998, Vol. 10, Issue 4, p. 16.

190 In 1989, the National Institute of Mental Health: "Fighting Depression," *Washington Post*, November 28, 1989, pp. 7–8.

190 They further pointed out that: D. F. Klein and D. C. Ross, "Reanalysis of the NIMH Treatment of Depression Collaborative Research Program General Effectiveness Report," *Neuropsychopharmacology*, 1993, Vol. 8, No. 3, pp. 241–51.

190 Since then other studies: H. S. Shulberg, M. R. Block, M. J. Madoinia, et al., "Treating Major Depression in Primary Care Practice: Eight Month Clinical Outcomes," *Archives of General Psychiatry*, October 1996, 53, pp. 913–19. See also Michael O'Hara, University of Iowa, presentation of results of a study of interpersonal therapy at Postpartum Services International Conference, Vancouver, June 25, 1999, and "Psychotherapy Found to Produce Changes in Brain Function," *New York Times*, Feburary 15, 1996.

192 If so, CBT: "Changing Thinking to Change Emotions," *New York Times*, August 21, 1996, p. C9.

192 If so, IPT: M. M. Weissman, *Mastering Depression: A Patient's Guide to Interpersonal Therapy* (Albany: Graywind Publications, 1995), p. 7.

192 one psychiatrist told me: Donald F. Klein, author interview.

193 They help their patients recognize: D. J. Hellerstein, H. Pinsker, R. N. Rosenthal, and S. Klee, "Supportive Therapy as the Treatment Model of Choice," *Journal of Psychotherapy Practice and Research*, 1994, Vol. 5, No. 4, pp. 300–306.

194 "Every single one of them": Marjorie Bowles, author interview, June 25, 1999.

195 Many encourage mothers to bring: Francesca Schwartz, author interview, June 3, 1999.

195 they seek information about the home scene: D. Sichel and J. W. Driscoll, author interview, June 25, 1999.

196 marital or couples therapy: G. I. Keitner, I. W. Miller, and C. E. Ryan, "The Role of the Family in Major Depressive Illness," *Psychiatric Annals*, 1993, 23:9, pp. 499–507.

196 the involvement of "significant others": Ibid., p. 499.

196 Marital and family therapy: Ibid., p. 505.

197 In one of her studies: T. Field, N. Grizzle, F. Scafidi, and S. Schanberg, "Massage and Relaxation Therapies' Effects on Depressed Adolescent Mothers," *Adolescence*, Winter 1996, 31(1124), pp. 903–11.

198 There are some four hundred varieties: "Where Does Research on the Effectiveness of Psychotherapy Stand Today?" *Harvard Mental Health Letter,* September 1995, p. 8.

9. A Father's Role in a Mother's Depression

Page

202 an overview of depression's impact: G. I. Keitner and I. W. Miller, "Family Functioning and Major Depression: An Overview," *American Journal of Psychiatry,* September 1990, 147:9, p. 1135.

202 One of the many studies cited: E. C. Vaughn and J. P. Leff, "The Influence of Family and Social Factors on the Course of Psychiatric Illness," *British Journal of Psychiatry,* 1976, 129, pp. 125–37.

204 One study cited: Keitner, *Depression and Families: Impact and Treatment,* p. 16.

205 When the husbands: D. Sichel and J. W. Driscoll, author interview, June 25, 1999.

205 marriages don't automatically spring back: Keitner and Miller, "Family Functioning and Major Depression," p. 1130.

206 Dadds argues that it is likely: J. C. Coyne, G. Downey, and J. Boergers, "Depression in Families: A Systems Perspective," in Keitner, *Depression and Families: Impact and Treatment,* p. 222.

206 Another possible scenario: Ibid.

208 Most employers routinely make: "The Other Working Parent," *New York Times,* March 4, 1999, Op-Ed.

209 Dads are more apt to joust and tumble: Kyle D. Pruett, *Fatherneed: Why Father Care Is as Essential as Mother Care for Your Child* (New York: The Free Press, 2000), p. 27.

209 One of the reasons children: Keitner, *Depression and Families: Impact and Treatment,* p. 18.

213 "Girls, and later women,": Terrence Real, *I Don't Want to Talk About It: Overcoming the Secret Legacy of Male Depression* (New York: Scribner, 1997), p. 24.

213 Male modes of action cited: Ibid., p. 30.

213 "Depression came slinking in": Andrew Solomon, "Anatomy of Melancholy," *The New Yorker,* January 12, 1998, p. 46.

214 "He might as well have told me": Ibid., p. 49.

214 did not have an orgasm: Ibid.

215   Mike Wallace admits: Sheffield, *How You Can Survive When They're Depressed: Living and Coping with Depression Fallout,* pp. vii–viii.

10. When Older Mothers Are Depressed

Page

217   The symptoms Professor Hammen associates: Hammen, *Depression Runs in Families: The Social Context of Risk and Resilience in Children of Depressed Mothers,* p. 140.

217   "Reduced energy and motivation," Professor Hammen observes: Ibid.

218   many physicians explain away: "Diagnosis and Treatment of Depression in Late Life," NIH Consensus Panel on Depression in Late Life, *JAMA,* 1992, Vol. 268, No. 8, p. 1019.

218   Doing so endangers: Ibid., p. 1018.

218   In reality, depression prevalence rates: "Gaps Seen in Treating Depression in Elderly," *New York Times,* September 5, 1999, p. C18.

227   Although it is relatively rare: Donald F. Klein, author interview.

228   For this age group, depression: "Diagnosis and Treatment of Depression in Late Life," p. 1019.

228   Depression cohabits with cancer: Ibid., p. 1020.

229   In addition, it is strongly suspected: Ibid.

229   often mimics the symptoms: "As Fellow Traveler of Other Illnesses, Depression Often Goes in Disguise," *New York Times,* January 17, 1996.

229   older folk see it as a stigma: "Depression in the Old Can Be Deadly, But the Symptoms Are Often Missed," *New York Times,* September 6, 1995.

229   The cost of medication: "Gaps Seen in Treating Depression in Elderly," *New York Times,* September 5, 1999, p. C18.

230   these drugs often take longer to work: "Diagnosis and Treatment of Depression in Late Life," p. 1020.

230   70 percent of older pill-takers: Ibid.

230   Only about one sixth: "Gaps Seen in Treating Depression in Elderly," *New York Times,* September 5, 1999, p. C18.

230   Shockingly, the majority of those who choose: "Diagnosis and Treatment of Depression in Late Life," p. 1020.

231   in patients with heart disease: "Which Comes First: Depression or Heart Disease?" *New York Times,* January 14, 1997.

231   she found that the depressed among them: Ibid.

231 Dr. Robert Carney: Ibid.

231 In a study of fifteen hundred Baltimoreans: Ibid.

231 Its sufferers have a more rapid heartbeat: Ibid.

232 Normally, the response lasts: Ibid.

232 One study of ten thousands men and women: "Depression in the Old Can Be Deadly, But the Symptoms Are Often Missed," *New York Times*.

232 Depressed patients recovering from: Ibid.

232 Other research suggests that: "Depression Hidden in Deadly Disease," *New York Times,* November 10, 1998.

233 even though some of the afflicted: Ibid.

233 Often, cancer-related problems: Ibid.

233 as reported by many studies: P. J. Schmidt, C. A. Roca, M. Bloch, and D. F. Rubinow, "The Perimenopause and Affective Disorders," *Seminars in Reproductive Endocrinology,* 1997, Vol. 15, No. 1, pp. 91–100; T. B. Pearlstein, K. Rosen, and A. B. Stone, "Mood Disorders and Menopause," *Endocrinology and Metabolism Clinics of North America,* 1997, Vol. 26, No. 2, pp. 279–94; and T. B. Pearlstein, "Hormones and Depression: What Are the Facts About Premenstrual Syndrome, Menopause, and Hormone Replacement Therapy?" *American Journal of Obstetrics and Gynecology,* 1995, pp. 646–53.

233 advancing age may actually be: Pearlstein et al., "Mood Disorders and Menopause," p. 293.

234 Treatment options: Ibid.

11. Maternal Depression: Past, Present, and Future

Page

242 Since then, these children: L. Kubicka, Z. Matejcek, H. P. David, Z. Dytrych, W. B. Miller, and Z. Roth, "Children from Unwanted Pregnancies in Prague, Czech Republic Revisited at Age Thirty," *Acta Psychiatr. Scand.,* 1995, O:1–9, pp. 2245–53.

242 Poor academic performance: Ibid., p. 2245.

242 Grown female children: Ibid., p. 2250.

243 The study's fourth and final phase: Ibid., p. 2252.

245 Dr. Koplewicz reminds us: Harold S. Koplewicz, author interview, October 13, 1999.

INDEX

Adolescents, 7, 101, 118, 240
    anxiety disorders in, 131
    cry for help in, 123–25
    depression in, 119, 245–47
    misreading behavior in, 122–23
    peer influence and, 71–72
    suicide in, 124, 125–28
Adoption studies, 121
Adrenal gland, 59
Adult children of depressed parents,
        7, 13–17: see also Older
        mothers
Affect, 70
Agoraphobia, 119, 130
Ainsworth, Mary, 64–67
Alcohol and drug abuse, 3, 15, 48,
        122, 184, 217, 240, 242
Alternative remedies, 175, 197
Alzheimer's disease, 229, 232–33
American Foundation for Suicide
        Prevention, 255
Antenatal depression, 188
Antidepressants, 5, 24, 41–42,
        128–29, 161, 163–67,
        172–80: see also Psychiatry
    atypical, 173, 174

average time for effectiveness,
        205
    cost of, 229–30
    historical overview of, 163–64
    insider tips on, 176–80
    manic depression and, 93
    MAOIs: see Monoamine oxidase
        inhibitors
    men and, 214–15
    menopause and, 234
    nursing and, 188–89
    older people and, 229–30
    pregnancy and, 184–86, 188
    psychotherapy and, 189–91, 198,
        199
    sexual performance and, 158,
        179, 180, 214–15
    side effects of, 173, 180, 190,
        230
    SSRIs: see Selective serotonin
        reuptake inhibitors
    tricyclic, 158, 172–73, 179
Anxiety disorders, 41, 43, 245
    antidepressants and, 179
    in children, 119–22, 130–32
    postpartum depression and, 80

Anxiety Disorders Association of
    America, 255
Approval needs, 13, 21, 27–29, 248
Arthritis, 229
As Good As It Gets (film), 120
Assortative mating, 141–42, 148
Attachment theory, 63–67
    despair, 66
    detachment, 66–67
    protest, 66
Atypical antidepressants, 173, 174
Atypical depression, 173–74, 177

Babies: see Infants
Baby blues, 79
Beardslee, William R., 127–28
Beck, Aaron T., 192
Beck Center for Cognitive Therapy,
    192
Benson, Herbert, 183
Benson (depressed teenager), 125,
    126
Berlin, Irving, 154
Berne, Eric, 19
Best Doctors in America, The, 177
Biological factors in depression,
    49–50
Bipolar depression: see Manic
    depression
Black hole metaphor, 30, 157
Blood pressure elevation, 173, 231,
    232
Bonding, 62, 63–64
Boorstin, Robert, 214, 215
Bosworth, Brian, 154
Boundary setting, 157–58
Bowlby, John, 63–64, 66, 71
Brain, 39, 40, 161, 170–72
    language acquisition and, 73
    left frontal region, 96
    mother's contribution to
        development of, 58–60

postpartum depression effects on,
    96–97
    right frontal region, 96, 187
Brazelton, T. Berry, 7, 95
Brown, Cordelia, 145–48, 150
Brown, Richard, 175–76
Brown University, 144
Buchwald, Art, 153
Bulimia, 179

Cambridge University, 95
Cancer, 228, 233
Cardiovascular disease, 228–29,
    231–32
Carney, Robert, 231
CBT: see Cognitive Behavioral
    Therapy
Celexa, 179
Character, 55–56
Children: see also Adolescents;
    Adult children of depressed
    parents; Grade-schoolers;
    Infants; Mother-child dyad;
    School-age children; Toddlers
depression in, 6–7, 244–49
discipline and, 209–10
effects of marital discord on,
    110–11, 144
"red flag" symptoms of effects of
    postpartum depression on,
    83–84
women's risk of depression and, 52
Children's Hospital, 127
Cholesterol, 232
Christina (survivor's syndrome), 21,
    22–24, 241
Chronic depression, 42
Churchill, Winston, 154
Circadian rhythm patterns, 50
Circumcision, 63
Cognitive Behavioral Therapy
    (CBT), 189–90, 191–92, 198

Cognitive development
    postpartum depression effects on,
        94–96, 107
    in school-age children, 107–10
Cognitive Psychosocial Intervention
    (Beardslee), 128
Columbia University, 118, 142
Columbia University College of
    Physicians and Surgeons, 186
Columbine killings, 247
Communication, 202–3
Co-morbid disorders, 169, 179
Compassionate IND number, 174
Confidentiality, 199
Confusion, ix, 134, 240
Contributing factors, 101–2
Cooper, John, 19
Cortisol, 231–32
Costs
    of antidepressants, 229–30
    of depression, 47
Couples therapy, 196
"Covers" for depression, 213
Coward, Noel, 154
Coyne, James C., 139, 140–41, 142,
    151
Criticism, 114–16
Cuddling, 59
Cuteness, 62
Cyclothymia, 43
Czechoslovakia, 242

DAD: see Depression After Delivery
Dadds, Eugene, 206
Dalton, Katarina, 79–80
Dawnell (support group member),
    15, 243–44
Dawson, Geraldine, 108
Demoralization, ix, 134, 135, 202,
    240
Department of Health and Human
    Services, 98

Depenbrock, Brian, 35–36
Depression After Delivery (DAD),
    255
"Depression and Marital
    Disagreement" (Kahn and
    Margolin), 139
Depression and Related Affective
    Disorders Association
    (DRADA), 255
Depression epidemiology, 51
Depression fallout, ix, 118, 141,
    142–43, 202, 222, 240
    appropriate response to, 154–55
    stages and effects of, 134–38
Depression quiz, 44–45
Deseryl, 174, 180
Dexadrine, 177
Diana (older mother), 217, 218,
    219–22
Diana, Princess, 52
Diary, keeping a, 178–79
Dickens, Charles, 154
Dickinson, Emily, 52
Diet
    MAOIs and, 158, 173, 177,
        184
    in treatment program, 184
Discipline, 209–10
Divorce, 136, 156–57, 211–12
Doctors: see Physicians
Dolnick, Edward, 162, 164
Dopamine, 40, 177
Downey, Geraldine, 142
DRADA: see Depression and
    Related Affective Disorders
    Association
Dream interpretation, 163
Driscoll, Jeanne, 167–72, 196, 205,
    240
Drug and alcohol abuse, 48, 122,
    184, 217, 240, 242
Dysthymia, 42–43

Earl (support group member),
    15–16, 240, 243–44
Earthquake Assessment Model,
    167–72, 240
Eating disturbances: see Weight gain
Eaton, William W., 231
ECT: see Electro-convulsive therapy
EEG: see Electroencephalogram
Effexor, 174, 176, 177
Elavil, 173
Electro-convulsive therapy (ECT),
    180–81
Electroencephalogram (EEG), 73,
    96, 197
Eli (husband of postpartum psychosis
    sufferer), 88–92
Eliot, T. S., 154
Emerson, Ralph Waldo, 241
Emory University School of
    Medicine, 186
Environmental factors, 73: see also
    Nature versus nurture
Epperson, Cynthia Neill, 188–89
Escape, desire for, ix, 134, 136, 240
Estrogen, 50
Evolutionary biology, 54–55, 62, 63,
    67
Evvie (survivor's syndrome), 21,
    24–27, 241
Exercise, 182–83
Expressive therapy, 192, 198
Externalizing behaviors, 98–99, 213
Eye contact, 75–76

Face-to-Face-Still-Face Paradigm,
    81–83, 95, 240–41
Family therapy, 196
Fathers, 201–15, 242
    depression in, 204, 212–15
    filling the parenting gap, 206–7
    focus on mothers versus, 6–11
    as heroes, 207–8

postpartum depression and, 93
providing for children's needs,
    209–11
separated or divorced, 211–12
Faulkner, William, 154
FDA: see Food and Drug
    Administration
Fetal stress, 186–88
Field, Tiffany, 83, 197
Fifer, William, 186, 188
Fitzgerald, F. Scott, 154
Food and Drug Administration
    (FDA), 161, 174, 175, 185
Frasure-Smith, Nancy, 231
Freud, Sigmund, 91, 162–63, 166
Freudianism, 164, 190
Frost, Robert, 154

Gender
    behavioral problems in children
        and, 111
    depression in children and, 124–25
    vulnerability to depression and,
        49–53
Generational depression, 48, 118–19
Genetic factors, 9, 47–49, 55, 73,
    246
    in anxiety disorders, 121
    environmental factors versus: see
        Nature versus nurture
George (survivor's syndrome), 21,
    29–31, 242
Ginette (self-image problems),
    112–13, 241
Gold, Philip, 232
Goleman, Daniel, 33
Gore, Tipper, 52
Grade-schoolers, 97–99
Green, Morris, 83–84, 98
Greenough, William, 56
Grieving, 227
Growth hormone, 59, 73, 232

Haldol, 90, 91, 92
Hammen, Constance, 32–33, 114–16, 117, 118, 140, 217–18, 247
Handel, George, 154
Hanna (postpartum psychosis), 88–93, 194, 240, 242
Hardwiring, 55, 68, 74, 75
Harlow, Harry, 61, 72, 248
Harnisch, Pete, 154
Harris, Eric, 247
Harris, Judith, 71–73
Hart, Betty, 76
Harvard Medical School, 127
Harvard Medical School, Child Development Unit, 68–69
Harvard University, 183–84
Hay, Dale, 95–96, 107–8
Health maintenance organizations (HMOs), 128, 167, 191, 193, 197–98
Health problems: see also specific diseases
    anxiety disorders and, 121
    in older mothers, 228–29, 232–33
Hearing impaired infants, 68, 70
Helen (Earthquake Assessment Model), 169–70, 171
Hemingway, Ernest, 215
Herbert, Wray, 56
Heredity: see Genetic factors
High-density lipoproteins (HDLs), 232
HMOs: see Health maintenance organizations
Hopelessness, 247
Hormonal flooding, 187
Hormone replacement therapy (HRT), 233–34
Hospitalization, 181
How You Can Survive When They're Depressed (Sheffield), ix, 137

Hypersomnia, 50
Hypomania, chronic, 43

I Don't Want to Talk About It (Real), 212–13
Imipramine, 190
Immune system, 229
Indiana University, 83
Infanticide, 63
Infants, 7, 54–77, 240: see also Mother-child dyad
Insecure attachment, 65, 95, 98
Institutionalized children, 61, 72
Intelligence, 107–10
Internalizing behaviors, 99, 213
Internet, 151–52, 181–82, 243: see also Websites
Interpersonal Therapy (IPT), 189–90, 191–92, 198
Intimacy, mistrust of, 12–13, 21, 22–24, 33, 247
Intrusive behavior, 82–83
Iproniazad, 163, 167
IPT: see Interpersonal Therapy
IQ (intelligence quotient), 104, 107–10

Jamison, Kay Redfield, 38, 39, 125–26, 127
Jill (postpartum depression), 86–88, 194, 240, 242
Johns Hopkins University, 125, 231
Judge Baker Children's Center, 127
Julie (temperament differences), 102–5, 106, 243

Kagan, Jerome, 164, 187
Kahn, Jana, 139
Katherine (support group moderator), 14, 15
Keats, John, 154
Keitner, Gabor, 144, 196, 202, 204

Index

Klebold, Dylan, 247
Klein, Donald, 66–67, 237, 238
Klerman, Gerald, 192
Koplewicz, Harold S., 245–47
Kramer, Peter, 136

Language acquisition, 73–77
Laundry mother, 117–18, 217, 241
Left frontal region of brain, 96
Lincoln, Abraham, 154
Lithium, 90, 91, 92, 164
London University, Institute of
     Psychiatry, 108
Loneliness, 226–28
Loss, 20, 22, 64
Love
     damaging absence of, 17, 241–44
     feelings of unworthiness and, 13,
         29–31
Luvox, 176

Madness on the Couch (Dolnick), 162
Magnetic resonance imaging (MRI),
     73, 184
Major depressive disorder (MDD), 43
Manic depression, 14, 43, 49, 115,
     151
     antidepressants and, 93
     postpartum manifestations of,
         88–93
Manipulation, 155
Manning, Martha, 34–37, 39, 40,
     46, 52, 137, 248–51
Manning Depenbrock, Keara,
     36–37, 137, 248–51
MAOIs: see Monoamine oxidase
     inhibitors
Margolin, Gayle, 139
Marital therapy, 196
Marriage, 133–59
     assortative mating and, 141–42,
         148

communication in, 202–3
depression fallout in, 134–38,
     141, 142–43, 202
effects of discord on children,
     110–11, 144
missing sense of partnership in,
     142–44
mutual despair in, 139–41
prescriptive help for discord in,
     151–58
sex and, 138–39, 158
vulnerability to depression and, 52
Massage therapy, 197
"Maternal Depression: Bad for
     Children's Health" (Green), 84
MDD: see Major depressive disorder
Meditation, 183–84
Megan (temperament differences),
     102–5, 243
Melatonin, 180
Melinda (depressed teenager),
     123–25, 126, 243
Memory formation, 59, 74
Men: see Fathers; Gender; Marriage
Menopause, 50, 233–34
Miami University School of
     Medicine, 197
Michelangelo, 154
Miller, Arthur, 18–19
Miller, Ivan, 202
Mindfulness, 183
Model of Mutual Regulation, 69–71,
     97, 248
Monk, Catherine, 186–87, 188
Monkeys, 61, 72, 248
Monoamine oxidase inhibitors
     (MAOIs), 173–74
     dietary restrictions and, 158,
         173, 177, 184
     reversible, 174, 179
Monroe, Marilyn, 17–19, 20, 52, 241
Montreal Heart Institute, 231

Morgan, J. P., 154
Mother-child dyad, 54–77
    attachment theory on, 63–64
    bonding and, 62, 63–64
    brain development and, 58–60
    language acquisition and, 73–77
    Model of Mutual Regulation and, 69–71, 97, 248
    peer influence and, 71–73
Motherese, 76
MRI: see Magnetic resonance imaging
Music therapy, 197

NAFDI: see National Foundation for Depressive Illness
NAMI: see National Alliance for the Mentally Ill
Nardil, 173
NARSAD: see National Alliance for Research on Schizophrenia and Depression
National Alliance for Research on Schizophrenia and Depression (NARSAD), 256
National Alliance for the Mentally Ill (NAMI), 152, 177, 181, 256
National Depressive and Manic Depressive Association (NDMDA), 152, 178, 181, 256
National Foundation for Depressive Illness (NAFDI), 152, 177, 237, 256
National Institute of Maternal and Child Health, 98–99
National Institute of Mental Health (NIMH), 175, 183, 190, 232, 256
National Mental Health Association (NMHA), 256
National Mental Illness Screening Project, 256

Nature versus nurture, 56–58, 73, 118, 246
NDMDA: see National Depressive and Manic Depressive Association
Neuroendocrine system, 59
Neurons, 41, 59
Neurotransmitters, 40, 41–42, 56, 177: see also Dopamine; Norepinephrine; Serotonin
Newsweek, 175
New York University Child Study Center, 245
Nicholson, Jack, 120
Nicotine, 179
Night Falls Fast (Jamison), 125
NIMH: see National Institute of Mental Health
NMHA: see National Mental Health Association
Nonprescription remedies, 175
Nonverbal alternative remedies, 197
Norepinephrine, 40
Norpramin, 173
Nursing and antidepressants, 188–89
Nurture Assumption, The (Harris), 71

Object permanence test, 99
Obsessive compulsive disorder (OCD), 120, 169, 179
OCD: see Obsessive compulsive disorder
O'Keefe, Georgia, 52
Older mothers, 216–38
    cardiovascular disease in, 228–29, 231–32
    depression overlooked in, 228–30
    first-time depression in, 227–28
    health problems in, 228–29, 232–33
    loneliness in, 226–28

Optimistic Child, The (Seligman),
    31–32
Orphanages: see Institutionalized
    children
Osmond, Marie, 52, 79

Pamelor, 173
Pandora (author's daughter), 65–66,
    234–38, 252–53
Panic disorder, 119, 120, 130, 179
Parnate, 173
Paxil, 158, 173, 176, 179
Peer influence, 71–73
Perfectionism and control, 13, 21,
    24–27, 247–48
Perimenopause, 233
Physicians, 46–47
    ignorance of depression in, 166
    older people and, 229
    postpartum depression and,
        85–86, 92–93
Pinker, Stephen, 62
Pituitary gland, 59
PMS: see Premenstrual syndrome
Postpartum depression (PPD),
        27–28, 50, 78–99, 105, 240
    brain development and, 96–97
    cognitive development and,
        94–96, 107
    effects on toddlers and grade-
        schoolers, 97–99
    Face-to-Face-Still-Face Paradigm
        of, 81–83, 95, 240–41
    intrusive or withdrawn behavior
        in, 82–83
    possible causes of, 80
    prevalence of, 93
    psychotherapy for, 93, 193–96
    "red flag" symptoms of effects on
        children, 83–86
    symptoms of, 80
Postpartum psychosis, 88–93

Postpartum Services International
    (PSI), 27, 193–94, 257
PPD: see Postpartum depression
Pregnancy, 7–8, 50: see also
        Postpartum depression
    antidepressants and, 184–86, 188
    fetal stress and, 186–88
Premenstrual syndrome (PMS), 50
Preschoolers, 7
Prescriptive advice
    for depressed mothers, 128–29
    for fathers, 209–12
    for marital discord, 151–58
    for parents of high-risk children,
        130–32
Prevalence
    of depression, 43, 153
    of depression in older people, 218
    of depression in young people,
        118, 245
    of postpartum depression, 93
Progesterone, 50
Proust, Marcel, 18–19
Prozac, 158, 164, 173, 179, 189,
        214, 225
Prozac poop-out, 176–77
PSI: see Postpartum Services
        International
Psychiatry, 129, 161, 198: see also
        Antidepressants
    psychotherapy versus medication,
        162–67, 189–90
Psychoanalysis, 163–64
Psychologists: see Psychotherapy
Psychopaths, 72
Psychotherapy, 129, 161, 189–99:
        see also specific therapies
        listed under Treatment
    confidentiality and, 199
    insider tips for, 197–99
    for postpartum depression, 93,
        193–96

psychiatry versus, 162–67,
189–90
selection of specific type, 191–93

Quality time, 76

Rachel (survivor's syndrome), 21,
27–29, 241, 242
Radke-Yarrow, Marian, 98
Real, Terrence, 212–13
"Red flag" symptoms of effects of
postpartum depression on
children, 83–86
Relaxation response, 183
Remeron, 174, 180
Resentment and anger, ix, 134, 135,
202, 240
Resilience, 20–21, 61
Reuptake, 41
Reversible monoamine oxidase
inhibitors (RIMAs), 174, 179
Ridley, Todd, 76
Right frontal region of brain, 96,
187
RIMAs: see Reversible monoamine
oxidase inhibitors
Risk factors for depression, 47–49
Ritalin, 177
Roosevelt, Eleanor, 52
Rutter, Michael, 108

SAD: see Seasonal affective disorder
Sadness, 20, 22
SAM-e, 175–76
Sam the Nobody, 148–50, 241
Satcher, David, 126
Schizophrenia, 14, 15, 18, 245
School-age children, 7, 100–132,
240: see also Adolescents;
Grade-schoolers
anxiety disorders in, 119–22,
130–32

behavioral problems in, 110–11
cognitive development in,
107–10
contributing factors and, 101–2
criticism and self-esteem in,
114–16
prescriptive advice for parents of
high-risk, 130–32
self-image in, 111–14
temperament and, 102–5
timing and severity of maternal
depression, 105–7
Schumann, Robert, 154
Scott, Ronnie, 154
Scott, Sir Walter, 154
Seasonal affective disorder (SAD), 50
Securely attached infants, 65
Selective serotonin reuptake
inhibitors (SSRIs), 158, 173,
174, 179
decreased effectiveness of,
176–77
pregnancy and, 186
Self-blame, ix, 134–35, 240
Self-esteem, 106, 117
criticism and, 114–16
quintessential role of, 31–32
survivor's syndrome and, 30–33
Self-image, 32–33, 111–14
Seligman, Martin, 31–32
Separation anxiety, 67
Serotonin, 40, 41, 173, 177, 189: see
also Selective serotonin
reuptake inhibitors
cuddling and, 59
women and, 50
Serzone, 158, 174, 179–80
Setting boundaries, 157–58
Sex, depression and, 138–39
antidepressants and, 158, 179,
180, 214–15
Sex hormones, female, 50

Sheffield, Anne
    depression of, 234–38
    mother's depression, 1–6, 12
    psychotherapy experience of,
        164–65
    relationship with daughter: see
        Pandora (author's daughter)
    self-image problems of, 111–12
    suffocation memory of, 19–20
    in support group, 16
    website of, xi, 123
Shelley, Percy Bysshe, 154
Should You Leave? (Kramer), 136
Sichel, Deborah, 167–72, 196, 205,
    240
Sissy (childhood friend of author),
    20–21
Sleep disturbances, 50, 80, 180
Smith, Abby (older mother), 217,
    219, 222–26
Smoking, 179
Social anxiety disorder: see Social
    phobia
Social contagion, 95
Social phobia, 130–31, 174
Solomon, Andrew, 213–14, 215
Solve-a-problem test, 116
Somatic symptoms of depression,
    43
Sonogram, 3-D, 188
Spieker, Susan, 98
Spousal abuse, 142, 158
SSRIs: see Selective serotonin
    reuptake inhibitors
St. John's Wort, 175
Sticky-flypaper depressives, 155–56
Stigma, 18, 43, 153, 229
Stop Depression Now, 175
Stowe, Zachary, 186
Strange Situation, the, 64–67
Stroke, 229, 232
Styron, William, 38–39, 153

Suicide, 47
    in adolescents, 124, 125–28
    author's mother's attempted, 2,
        3, 4, 5–6, 16, 112
    author's thoughts of, 238
    Manning's thoughts of, 34–35, 46
    Marilyn Monroe's, 18
    in older people, 218, 228, 230,
        233
    preoccupation with, 45–46
    serotonin levels and, 41
Support groups, 177–78, 244
    for adult children of depressed
        parents, 13–17
    information on, 255–57
    value of, 181–82
Supportive therapy, 198
Survivor's syndrome, 12–33, 247–48
    self-esteem and, 30–33
    symptoms of: see Approval
        needs; Intimacy, mistrust of;
        Love,   feelings of
        unworthiness and;
        Perfectionism and control
Symptoms
    of depression, 43–44
    of postpartum depression, 80
    "red flag," of postpartum
        depression's effects on
        children, 83–86
    of survivor's syndrome: see
        Approval needs; Intimacy,
        mistrust   of; Love, feelings of
        unworthiness and;
        Perfectionism   and control
Synapses, 41, 59–60, 73

Talk therapy: see Psychotherapy
TCAs: see Tricyclic antidepressants
Teenagers: see Adolescents
Temperament, 55–56, 73, 102–5
Thalidomide, 185–86

Thyroid gland, 59
Thyroid hormones, 50
Timebends (Miller), 18
Timmy (postpartum depression in mother), 85, 109
Toddlers, 97–99, 240
Tofranil, 173
Touch Institute, 197
Touch therapy, 197
Transference, 192
Trazadone: see Deseryl
Treatment, 160–200
    antidepressants: see Antidepressants
    diet and, 184
    electro-convulsive therapy, 180–81
    exercise, 182–83
    family therapy, 196
    hospitalization, 181
    marital or couples therapy, 196
    massage therapy, 197
    meditation, 183–84
    music therapy, 197
    nonprescription remedies, 175
    percentage of people seeking, 43
    psychotherapy: see Psychotherapy
    spousal support for, 152–53, 204–6
    support groups: see Support groups
    touch therapy, 197
"Triangling," 206
Tricyclic antidepressants (TCAs), 158, 172–73, 179
Tronick, E. Z., 69, 82, 83, 248
Turner, Ted, 154
Twain, Mark, 154
Twin studies, 48, 121

Undercurrents (Manning), 34
Unipolar depression, 115–16

University of Alaska, 76
University of Kansas, 76
University of Pennsylvania, 139
University of Southern California (UCLA), 114, 118
University of Washington, 98
Unwantedness, 242–43
U.S. News &World Report, 56
U.S. Public Health Service, Publication Clearing House, 257

Vital Lies, Simple Truths (Goleman), 33
Voice, mother's, 73

Wallace, Mike, 153, 154, 215
Washington University, 231
Websites, xi, 123, 257: see also Internet
Weight gain, 80, 180, 224
Weinberg, Katherine, 69, 83, 248
Weissman, Myrna, 118, 120–21, 132
Wellbutrin, 158, 174, 176, 177, 179, 180
White House Conference on children's mental health, 245
Window of opportunity, 61
Withdrawn behavior, 82–83
Women's Moods (Driscoll and Sichel), 168
Woolf, Virginia, 52
Wordsworth, William, 154

Yale Study, 118–19, 120, 121, 122, 132
Yale University, 188
Yoga, 182–83
Youth Risk Behavior Surveillance Survey, 126

Zoloft, 158, 173, 176, 179, 188–89
Zyban: see Wellbutrin